UNDERSTANDING
WORDS
THAT
WOUND

UNDERSTANDING WORDS THAT WOUND

R ICHARD D ELGADO
AND J EAN S TEFANCIC

Westview
PRESS

A Member of the Perseus Books Group

Published in the United States of America by Westview Press, a Member of the Perseus Books Group, 5500 Central Avenue, Boulder, Colorado 80301–2877, and in the United Kingdom by Westview Press, 12 Hid's Copse Road, Cumnor Hill, Oxford OX2 9JJ.

Find us on the world wide web at www.westviewpress.com

Westview Press books are available at special discounts for bulk purchases in the United States by corporations, institutions, and other organizations. For more information, please contact the Special Markets Department at the Perseus Books Group, 11 Cambridge Center, Cambridge, MA 02142, or call (617) 252–5298, (800) 255–1514 or email specialmarkets@perseusbooks.com.

Library of Congress Cataloging-in-Publication Data
Delgago, Richard
  Understanding words that wound / Richard Delgado and Jean Stefancic.
    p. cm.
Includes bibliographical references and index.
  ISBN 0-8133-4140-X (alk. paper)—ISBN 0-8133-4139-6 (pbk. : alk. paper)
  1. Hate speech—United States. 2. Freedom of speech—United States. 3.
Racism in language. I. Stefancic, Jean. II. Title.
  KF9345.D45 2004
  305.8'00973—dc22
                                                                    200320211

The paper used in this publication meets the requirements of the American National Standard for Permanence of Paper for Printed Library Materials Z39.48–1984.

Text design by Reginald R. Thompson
Set in 10.5 Sabon by the Perseus Books Group

10   9   8   7   6   5   4   3   2   1

I believe any people in the world, when roused to a fury of nationalistic sentiment, and convinced that some individual or group is responsible for their continued and extreme misfortune, can be led to do or countenance the same things the Germans did. I believe that if conditions in the U.S. were ever to become as bad psychologically and economically as they were in Germany in the 1920s and 1930s, systematic racial persecution might break out. It could happen to the Blacks, but it could happen to the Jews, too, or any targeted group.

Sidney Hook

CONTENTS

PART FOUR: HATE IN BROADER FOCUS

ACKNOWLEDGMENTS

We gratefully acknowledge the research assistance of Jillian Lloyd in the preparation of this book. Lung Hung researched and drafted major portions of Chapters 4 and 7; Joey Lubinski, Chapter 5; and Miriam Stohs, Chapters 10 and 11. Linda Spiegler prepared the manuscript with precision and intelligence.

INTRODUCTION

The Bible records the first known discussions of hate speech. In two passages, the Book of Exodus admonishes believers not to curse parents[1] or "the ruler of thy peoples."[2] Later passages warn against cursing the deaf,[3] rebuking neighbors,[4] or scorning others, generally.[5]

Two thousand years later, Anglo-American law handed down some of the first decisions in which a citizen sued another for racial slurs and name-calling. In *Contreras v. Crown Zellerbach, Inc.,*[6] the State of Washington Supreme Court considered the case of a Mexican American whose co-workers had subjected him to a torrent of racial abuse and vituperation on the job. Finding that the "humiliation and embarrassment [that he suffered] by reason of racial jokes, slurs, and comments" stated a valid claim against Contreras's employer, the court declared that "racial epithets that were once part of common usage may not now be looked upon as 'mere insulting language.'"[7]

Less than a year later, the town of Skokie, Illinois, home to many Jews, a number of whom had lived through the Holocaust, was the site of a proposed Nazi march. Arguing that the demonstration and planned display of Nazi uniforms and swastikas would inflict psychological trauma on the town's many Jewish citizens, the town asked a judge to enjoin the march. A court of appeals acknowledged that "many people would find [the] demonstration extremely mentally and emotionally disturbing." Citing the *Contreras* case, the court conceded that tort law was moving in the direction of recognizing the harm of hate speech. Nevertheless, the threat of criminal penalties, the court found, impermissibly interfered with the marchers' First Amendment rights.[8]

This book explores some of the issues hate speech poses for a society like ours. It analyzes the teachings of social science on such matters as: How harmful is racist hate speech to the victim? To the perpetrator? To society at large? It looks at the way our thinking about these issues has changed to accommodate the Internet and virtual pornography, the advent of talk shows, campus hate speech codes, and hate directed against children. It describes how courts and legislators have wrestled with such issues as Confederate flags, words such as *nigger*, *spic*, and *kike*, hate speech against whites, and the experience of other countries in dealing with group-based hate.

Since one of us wrote the first article in the legal literature on hate speech, *Words That Wound: A Tort Action for Racial Insults, Epithets, and Name-Calling*,[9] in the *Harvard Civil Rights Civil Liberties Law Review* (1982), the literature on hate speech has exploded. Authors have deepened our knowledge of how hate speech feels to the victim, and, conversely, how it feels to be charged with a hate speech violation. They have expanded our knowledge of the international dimension of hate speech. Do other nations see hate speech as a problem, and what are they doing about it? Empirical science has sharpened our knowledge of who is victimized by hate speech, how often, and with what words. Courts have upheld penalties for hate crime and—in a bewildering patchwork of circumstances—hate speech, often explaining their reasoning in the form of written opinions. And, of course, many scholars on the right or libertarian/ACLU left have registered their disapproval of any official discouragement of hate speech, putting forward a panoply of objections—to which scholars on the other side have, naturally, put forward answers.

The hate speech controversy has sparked continual interest because it lies at the heart of two of our deepest values—civil rights and equal respect, on the one hand, and freedom of speech on the other. Our society prizes liberty, so that we do not ordinarily tolerate restrictions on what a person can say, without a very good reason. At the same time, our system treasures equality and equal respect. For this reason, we do not lightly tolerate forms of behavior that demean and marginalize on account of race, sex, sexual orientation, or any deeply personal characteristic.

Not only is hate speech said (by those on one side of the fence) to fly in the face of certain intrinsic values important to democracy, scholars have argued that it is linked to actions, such as Indian extermination, Jewish pogroms, and lynching of blacks and Mexican Americans, that humanity has rightly condemned. Hate speech, for these writers, is instrumentally evil, even if it is not such in itself—or even if its regulation poses serious First Amendment problems.

This, then, is a brief overview of some of the main issues that hate speech raises and that are discussed in this book. How should the reader read this book?

How to Read This Book

Suppose that you, the reader, are a dean of students at a medium-size public university that is interested in maintaining an intellectually and culturally cosmopolitan atmosphere. A delegation of minority students calls to your attention a campaign of hate speech, graffiti, and E-mail that makes them feel threatened and unwelcome. You and your staff hold a meeting, at which one of your Euro-American colleagues asks whether this is really a serious problem; why can't the students shrug the insults off? Your colleague's question raises an *empirical* issue. How damaging, in fact, is hate speech of various kinds? You resolve to consult the literature on this question and interview campus experts in the departments of psychology and communication and the school of public health.

At your next staff meeting, you have this information in hand and present it to your colleagues and employees. Now, the same colleague who raised the empirical question asks: Suppose we enact some kind of hate speech code. Would it be constitutional? This is a *legal* question. You assign a student intern to research the legal precedents bearing on this question and have the answers ready at the next meeting.

Just before adjourning, one of your colleagues turns to your intern and asks her to make sure to cover two issues. The colleague wants to know whether hate in cyberspace poses any special issues that the ordinary face-to-face, or written, kind does not. He adds: "I'd also like to know what mechanisms other Western industrialized countries with a healthy respect for free speech are putting in place to deal with hate speech." These are issues of *cyberspace* and *comparative or international law*, respectively.

At the next meeting, representatives from the university's laboratory school (K through eighth grade) and its child care center ask whether hate speech directed against children and other special populations stands on a different footing from that directed against adults. This question, which has to do with *children and their status*, raises the question of whether an institution like yours has the ability—perhaps duty—to regulate hate speech.

If hate speech directed against children and other especially vulnerable groups presents a stronger than usual case for protection, is this true, as well, when the hate speaker is unusually empowered, say a teacher, lawyer, or social worker speaking to a student or client? This raises the issue of *heightened duties of care* that certain speakers may owe to refrain from hateful speech. Thus, your staff proposes that the next meeting consider whether the university's policy should place additional duties on teachers, university psychologists, and the university's lawyers to refrain from hate speech in the course of their duties.

These hypotheticals trace, essentially, the structure of this book and the major issues that constitute the hate speech controversy. Chapter 1 addresses qualitative issues—the harms of hate speech—while Chapter 2 discusses quantitative issues, in particular its frequency. Chapter 3 then takes a step back and considers theories of racism and hate speech. What are we to make of hate speech, what forces propel it, what functions does it serve?

Next, four chapters, constituting Part Two, particularize the discussion, beginning with a chapter on four especially hateful words. The succeeding chapters consider the case of hate speech against children, campus hate speech, and hate in cyberspace.

Part Three takes up certain special symbols, speakers, and shows. It includes chapters on flags, mascots, and monuments; on lawyers who hate; on talk shows; and on hate speech against whites.

The concluding section—Part Four—examines the experience of other nations in dealing with hate speech; takes a look at common arguments against hate speech regulation; and concludes with a look at the future of this entire issue.

The conventional view is that the legal system has not been kind to the party advocating hate speech regulation. And, it is true that in a number of settings, including municipal hate ordinances and campus speech codes, American courts have proven hostile to attempts to curb this form of utterance. Yet, in a wide range of cases and settings, U.S. courts have approved efforts to curtail or punish disparaging speech aimed at racial and other minority groups. And, as will be seen, other Western countries that share our traditions have gone even further than we in curbing hateful speech and incitement. American courts and lawmakers, at least in certain times and places, have been open to the possibility that speech aimed at certain unchangeable characteristics, such as race, may rightfully be curbed. The jury, as they say, is still out. The public, too, has yet to make up its mind. In the meantime, the American population of color continues to grow and will reach 50 percent of the citizenry around mid–century. Racial harmony may appear a more urgent value as our nation becomes more multicultural and multiracial. If so, proposals to restrain hate speech may grow in frequency and insistency.

How should society respond? Have you ever been the victim of hate speech? How did you feel? Have you ever, in a moment of anger, perhaps, been the speaker of hate speech? How would you have felt had someone called you to account for what you did? Is hate speech a serious problem? Does it cause real harm? That is the topic for Chapter 1. But before we begin in earnest, one preliminary question remains, namely the scope and intention of this book.

Who Is This Book For?

This book is written for the reader with an open mind who is interested in informing himself or herself about the many perspectives from which one may view the hate speech controversy. The book is not written for anyone who believes the controversy is simple, or may be resolved if one only knows one piece of information. In short, the reader who is satisfied to learn that hate speech exacts great costs from its victims and is then prepared to say "It is bad for minorities, so I oppose it; Bring on the regulators," will probably not find this book satisfying, for the book shows that there is much more to the debate than that. Similarly, readers who are predisposed to find that a certain line of precedent (but not others) stands in the way of hate speech regulation, so that they can say, "See, I thought

so; nothing can be done about hate speech (except perhaps pious denunciation)," will also not find this book what they want. The book
is aimed, in short, at students and policy makers who wish to understand a genuinely hard problem in all of its complexity, who know
that solutions will not be simple and that no approach will satisfy
everybody. Speech, like the problems we use it to address, will always remain contested. Nevertheless, we can approach contestation
well or ill, intelligently or not, with full information or with the par-
tial kind. The book is aimed at informing the debate; in some respects, it will succeed if it ends up making the search for resolution
harder, not easier.

RELATIONSHIP BETWEEN HATE SPEECH SCHOLARSHIP AND CRITICAL RACE THEORY

We are well-known critical race theorists, as are many others who
take hate speech seriously and come down on the side of doing
something about it. Yet, many others who take this position are liberals, mainstream civil rights scholars, or, in a few cases, principled
conservatives. The same is true of opponents of hate speech regulation—they include both people on the left and on the right side of
the political spectrum. Critical race theory is distinctive from some
other areas of social analysis in paying close attention to the terms in
which law, common discourse, and the media address issues of race
and power. Thus, many (but not all) critical race theorists are interested in the problems of hate speech, stereotyping, and media imagery of people of color. But the correspondence is not perfect. Some
humanistic film studies scholars, for example, write about media images of minorities in terms that are almost interchangeable with
those a critical race theorist might use.

In other words, readers searching for an introduction to critical
race theory, the new movement in the law that sprang up in the wake
of the civil rights movement of the 1960s and 1970s and that searches
for new solutions to our nation's racial predicament, will learn quite
a bit about it in this book. They should, of course, supplement their
reading by consulting one of the standard works on that movement
(including some by the two of us).

STRUCTURE OF THIS BOOK

This book consists of fourteen relatively short chapters, illustrated by hypotheticals, examples, and boxes containing quotes from judicial opinions, divided into four parts. The first part discusses hate speech in general—how much exists, whom it victimizes, how much damage it causes, and how different schools of thought see it and the problem it presents. Part Two discusses particular examples of hate speech, as well as issues having to do with certain speakers, settings, or victims. Part Three continues that discussion by addressing particular symbols, such as sports mascots, speakers, and shows. Part Four surveys some broader issues, including what other Western industrialized countries, such as Canada, Germany, Sweden, Italy, and England, have done to curb hate speech. It also discusses the future of hate speech regulation. Each chapter ends with questions for discussion, exercises designed to sharpen understanding, and lists of recommended readings. At the end of the book, the reader will find excerpts from international treaties, conferences, and reports, and a glossary of terms.

NOTES

1. Exodus 21:17. The punishment was harsh: death.
2. Exodus 22:28.
3. Leviticus 19:14.
4. Leviticus 19:17.
5. Proverbs 29:8, pointing out that scornful men bring a city into a snare, but that the wise turn away wrath.
6. 88 Wash.2d 735, 565 P.2d 1173 (1977) (en banc).
7. Ibid. at 741, 565 P.2d at 117.
8. *Collin v. Smith*, 575 P.2d 1197, 1200 (7th Cir.), *cert. denied*, 439 U.S. 916 (1978).
9. 17 Harv. C. R.–C.L. L. Rev. 133 (1982), authored by Richard Delgado.

PART ONE
WHAT IS HATE SPEECH?

I

WORDS THAT WOUND:
THE HARMS OF HATE SPEECH

WHAT IS HATE SPEECH?

Many people speak loosely about hate speech, without specifying what they mean or distinguishing the various types of utterance that might be under consideration. This is a sure recipe for analytical unclarity and policy disaster.

One can consider hate speech along various axes, including direct and indirect, veiled or overt, single or repeated, backed by authority and power or not, and accompanied by threat of violence or not. One can also consider hate speech based on the characteristic of the person or group at which it is aimed, such as race, sex, sexual orientation, or national origin. Hate speech can be targeted against one individual ("Smith, you goddamn African American, you are a . . . "). It can be directed against a small group (such as a black fraternity at a college campus). Or it can be aimed at a group in general ("I hate Xs; they should be thrown out of this country"). It can be delivered orally, in writing, or on the Internet. It can even take tangible form, such as a monument, flag, or sports logo.

Finally, one should differentiate hate speech in terms of who is doing the speaking—a teacher, a passerby, a public speaker, three hoodlums surrounding a small victim on a dark night, or an educated, genteel author who writes about the "X problem," making clear that the problem with Xs is not the way they are treated but their culture or genes. As will be seen, different forms of hate speech correspond to the various kinds of remedy that writers and policy boards have been proposing. For example, direct, face-to-face hate speech based on race ("You____, go back to_____!; you don't belong on this campus, you ignorant monkey!") is often remedied by means of tort actions or campus codes backed up by administrative penalties. Hate speech accompanied by threats, assaults, or dramatic symbolic behavior such as cross-burning is often considered a crime punishable under a hate crime statute.

The different types of hate speech threaten different kinds of harm. The one-on-one (or many-on-one) kind can be the most shocking. It can cause serious psychological and physical harm, irrespective of whether the speaker also physically strikes or harms the victim. General hate speech—for example, a learned address by an educated bigot explaining why blacks or Jews cannot advance beyond a certain point—ordinarily does not cause immediate damage, even if overheard by one who understands that the passage is about him or her. The harm is long-term, as society internalizes and later acts on the message, for example by adopting immigration rules aimed at keeping the group out of the country.

The harms of face-to-face hate speech have been the most closely studied, although recently, subtle, or educated, hate speech and its effect on the fabric of society and the life chances of the groups it tarnishes has come under scrutiny. Finally, a small number of writers have focused on the harms of hate speech to the speaker himself or herself. The following sections address each of these issues.

INDIVIDUAL HARMS OF HATE SPEECH

The harms of hate speech include its adverse impacts—sometimes devastating ones—on the victim, the speaker, and society at large. The harms vary, of course, according to the type of hate speech. The more diffuse kind—for example, "All niggers are inferior and should go back to Africa"—is apt to be more harmful to society in general. The more targeted variety—"You goddamn nigger, go back to Africa"— harms society as well, particularly cumulatively, but its principal impact is felt by the individual victim.

> ### Taylor v. Metzger, 706 A.2d 685 (N.J. 1998).
>
> Racial insults are in no way comparable to statements such as, "You are a God damned . . . liar," which [a standard guide] gives as an example of a "mere insult." Racial insults are different qualitatively because they conjure up the entire history of racial discrimination in this country. [Citing Richard Delgado, Words that Wound: A Tort Action for Racial Insults, Epithets, and Name-Calling, 17 Harv. C.R.–C.L. L. Rev. 133, 157 (1982).]

Physical Harms

Hate speech is not merely unpleasant or offensive. It may leave physical impacts on those it visits, particularly when uttered in one-on-one situations accompanied by at least an implicit threat—that is, by someone taller, larger, older, or more powerful than the victim or in a position of authority vis-à-vis him or her. The same is true when the hate speaker is a member of a group engaged in taunting a single member of a disempowered minority faction. Then, the response is internalized, as it must be, for talking back will be futile or even dangerous. In fact, many hate crimes have taken place when the victim did just that—spoke back to the aggressor and paid with his or her life.

The immediate, short-term harms of hate speech include rapid breathing, headaches, raised blood pressure, dizziness, rapid pulse rate, drug-taking, risk-taking behavior, and even suicide.[1] The stresses of repeated racial abuse may have long-term consequences, including damaged self-image, lower aspiration level, and depression.[2] Scientists suspect that the high blood pressure many African Americans suffer is associated with inhibited, constrained, or restricted anger, in addition to genetic factors.[3] American blacks exhibit higher rates of high blood pressure and higher death rates from hypertension, hypertensive disease, and stroke than do similarly situated whites.[4] Further, darker-skinned blacks experience a higher degree of felt stress than do their lighter–skinned counterparts, a correlation that may be a product of the greater discrimination[5]—the many "little murders," in the words of one social scientist—the former suffer.[6]

PSYCHOLOGICAL HARMS

In addition to the immediate physical harms—flinching, clenching, tightening of muscles, adrenaline rush, and the other somatic consequences of a sudden verbal assault—hate speech can cause mental and psychological effects. These include fear, nightmares, and withdrawal from society—what Joe Feagin and his collaborator call an impotent despair.[7] The victim of hate speech, especially the one who fears more of the same, may behave circumspectly, avoiding the situations, places, and company where it could happen again. Needless to say, this "cultural mistrust," a mild form of healthy paranoia, has implications for both the mental health and professional chances of minority workers.[8] Other victims will respond with anger, either internalized or acted-out (neither of which is calculated to make things better).[9] They are also likely to curtail their own speech, so as not to provoke more ridicule, put-downs, or revilement. Self-esteem may wither.

Victims may reject identification with their own race, the very feature that brought about the verbal attack.[10] Or, conversely, they may affect a kind of false bravado, in which they try to convince themselves "It doesn't get to me—I just let it roll off my back." Alternatively, the person may rationalize—the speaker was just ignorant, or targeted him or her not because of race but some other feature. ("I guess he just didn't like teenagers, the tie I was wearing, or the competition I posed for the next promotion at work.")

Some victims may take refuge in alcohol, drugs, or other self-defeating escapes.[11] This is true not only for blacks; three recent studies of Mexican Americans have found that experience with discrimination is associated with increased levels of stress, suffering, depression, and life dissatisfaction.[12] Finally, social scientists who have studied the effects of disrespectful treatment and labeling have demonstrated that speech that communicates low regard for an individual because of race tends, over time, to create in the victim the very traits of inferiority that it assigns.[13]

Scholars who have studied the effects of racism and racist epithets on children believe that youthful victims are among the most easily damaged by racial epithets and name-calling. Children as young as three develop consciousness of race; they know, furthermore, that race makes a difference, and that it is better to be of some races than others.[14]

Minority children who hear stereotypes of their group as stupid, ugly, lazy, or untrustworthy will face hurdles that white children do not confront in growing up confident, happy, and poised. Children who bear the brunt of such language can respond in one of two ways. They can respond aggressively, such as by shouting back at or striking the one who insulted them. Or, they can behave passively and pretend to ignore the aggression. Neither response is successful. Children who behave aggressively in school or elsewhere are marked as troublemakers, adding to their alienation and rejection. Behaving passively is little better. Children who behave passively in the face of their own scapegoating turn the harm inward; robbed of confidence and a sense of ease, these children become defensive, morose, and introverted. This effect is compounded when the parents, who may suffer discrimination themselves, bring their problems home so that they have less energy to devote to their children.[15]

TANGIBLE AND ECONOMIC HARMS

The harms of hate speech go beyond damage to the psyches and bodies of its victims. It can also affect their pecuniary prospects and life chances. Recent studies show that minority students at white-dominated universities may earn lower GPAs and standardized test scores as a result of the stress of studying and living in racially charged environments.[16] The person who is timid, bitter, tense, or defensive as a result of frequent encounters with racism is likely to fare poorly in employment and other settings, as well.[17] Claude Steele's pioneering experiments with "stereotype threat" show that the bearers of stereotypes perform poorly when placed in competitive situations that remind them of society's expectation that they will fail.[18] Even achievement of high occupational and professional status does not insulate a person of color from the harms of racial treatment and prejudice. Such a worker, despite a prestigious title, is apt to suffer a lingering fear that he is still an outsider, that when the chips are down, his white co-workers will disregard his opinion and expertise. Moreover, the worker or professional of color who works his or her way up the career ladder is apt to live and operate in largely white circles. Unlike the trash collector or worker in a food processing plant who lives in a dominantly minority neighborhood and works in a setting with other people of color, the black accountant or Latino lawyer may live, work, and interact mainly with whites. They will thus have more opportunities to encounter race and racism than their blue-collar counterparts—even though it is apt to be of the subtle, genteel variety.[19] Finally, racism closes off career options. Many minority youths are apt to favor careers, such as the Army, the post office, public school teaching, or social work, where prejudice is low, rather than ones—business, accounting, journalism—where prejudice is much more likely to affect one's chances.[20]

Is a racial insult or epithet more serious than one based on other characteristics, such as weight, age group, or physical appearance? Yes. Unlike those other personal characteristics, a person can do nothing to change his or her race. Moreover, race cuts closer to the core of a person's identity than does physique, age, or hair color. Thus, an insult like "You damn nigger. Why don't you . . . " is apt to cause more distress and be less easily shrugged off than "You damn woman driver (student driver, old fart driver), why don't you get off the road!" The driver may feel bad about the insult, especially if it was deserved. But the driver knows that he or she spends only part of the day driving and that in other areas of life he or she may be unusually competent.[21]

Also, racial insults and name-calling evoke and call up a specific history—including violence, lynching, Indian wars, and signs barring Latinos and blacks—that ones based on fatness or clumsiness do not. The recipient of a racial epithet is likely to know of this history and recognize the cultural weight—and maybe the veiled threat—behind it.[22]

HARMS TO THE PERPETRATOR AND TO SOCIETY AS A WHOLE

Finally, racial hate speech harms the perpetrator and society as a whole.[23] Bigots suffer when their narrow, categorical thinking etches in a little deeper. They fail to develop a universal moral sense that extends to all persons. They can easily develop a mildly paranoid mentality with respect to the group they routinely disparage. (If they are so bad, perhaps they will do bad things to me and my friends.) They will fail to learn one of life's most useful lessons—that people of other races and types are just like my own; some good, some bad.[24]

Society at large suffers, as well, when hate speech goes unpunished. It is a visible, dramatic breach of one of our most deeply felt ideals,

> ## Beauharnais v. Illinois, 343 U.S. 250 (1952).
>
> Illinois did not have to look beyond her own borders or await the tragic experience of the last three decades to conclude that willful purveyors of falsehood concerning racial and religious groups promote strife and tend powerfully to obstruct the manifold adjustments required for free, ordered life in a metropolitan, polyglot community. From the murder of the abolitionist Lovejoy in 1837 to the Cicero riots of 1951, Illinois has been the scene of exacerbated tension between races, often flaring into violence and destruction. In many of these outbreaks, utterances of the character here in question, so the Illinois legislature could conclude, played a significant part.

that "all men are created equal." A society in which some, but not all, must run a gantlet of racial abuse and stigmatization scarcely exemplifies this ideal. A racial insult conveys to all who hear or learn about it that equality and equal respect are of little value. Even those who do not take part in the system of racist speech may find themselves demoralized when they realize how often social norms of equality and brotherhood are breached and how far we are, as a group, from living in an egalitarian, humane society.[25]

Racism, including the verbal kind, also contributes to a class system, one in which some regularly confront hurdles and roadblocks that others do not in obtaining a job, taking out a loan, or simply walking down the street.[26] At a minimum, every person of color expends an enormous amount of energy dealing with discrimination—including the many daily decisions of what to confront and what to let go.[27] It goes without saying that American democracy is, by its nature, antithetical to a class society.

The injuries inflicted by racist hate speech are neither minimal nor unserious. Social scientists who have studied hate crime know that the effects are more long–lasting than they are when the same crime is committed without a racial or similar motivation.[28] Any crime shatters one's self-confidence and sense of personal security. A person who is assaulted and robbed on the sidewalk in front of his or her home will take months, if not years, to recover. But one who is assaulted and robbed by a perpetrator who shouts racial abuse at the same time and makes clear that the victim was selected because of race will brood about the event longer and take longer to return to a normal level of self-confidence in going about the world. The same is true of hate speech.

QUESTIONS FOR DISCUSSION, CHAPTER 1

1. Should diffuse hate speech ("All blacks are culturally and intellectually inferior, don't belong at the university, and should go back to Africa") be considered hate speech at all? Note that most campus codes address only the one-on-one, targeted kind.
2. Suppose that an African American or Latino whom you know tells you that hate speech doesn't really bother him or her. He or she "just lets it roll off my back," or says it's the speaker's problem, not his; he is too busy to worry about what ignorant people might say. Why might someone take that position? Would he take hate speech so casually if it were directed against his own child?
3. Is hate speech based on race any worse than a taunt or insult based on physical appearance or weight?
4. Some say that our legal and political system does not and should not recognize groups or classes. What does hate speech say about the wisdom of that course?
5. Suppose you are a member of a group whom others despise and vilify regularly. The rest of the time you are able to go about your life without incident. How much would you be willing to pay to eliminate the first condition?

CLASS EXERCISE

Pair up with another person of a different race than yourself. Then, for the purpose of this exercise, switch racial identities. For example, if you are white, play the part of a black or Latino; if a person of color, play the part of a white.

Enact two or three recurring situations, such as renting a hotel room, being stopped by the police while driving, buying something in a store, or hailing a taxi. Then trade roles and racial identities and do the same thing. At the end, critique each other's performance. Do whites know how blacks (for example) are spoken to? Did you learn anything about daily communication patterns and how they differ when the other person is white or nonwhite?

Recommended Reading, Chapter 1

Leonard Berkovitz, *Aggression—Its Causes, Consequence and Control* (1993).

Herbert Blauner, *Race Prejudice as a Sense of Group Position*, 1 Pol. Social. Rev. 3 (1959).

Center for Democratic Renewal, *Verbal Violence: Hate Speech Threatens Democracy* (1999).

Ellis Cose, *The Rage of a Privileged Class* (1993).

Arnoldo de Leon, *They Called Them Greasers* (1983).

Joe R. Feagin and Karyn D. McKinney, *The Many Costs of Racism* (2003).

Joe R. Feagin and Melvin P. Sikes, *Living with Racism* (1994).

George Fredrickson, *Race* (2002).

Laura Lederer and Richard Delgado, eds., *The Price We Pay: The Case Against Racist Speech, Hate Propaganda, and Pornography* (1995).

Mari J. Matsuda, Charles R. Lawrence, Richard Delgado, and Kimberle Crenshaw, *Words that Wound: Critical Race Theory, Assaultive Speech, and the First Amendment* (1993).

Roland Merullo, *Hatred and Its Sly Legacy*, Chron. Higher Ed., Dec. 1, 2000, at B10.

Charles C. Moskos and John Sibley Butler, *All That We Can Be* (1996).

Patricia Williams, *The Alchemy of Race and Rights* (1991).

Robert A. Williams, *The American Indian in Western Legal Thought: The Discourses of Conquest* (1990).

NOTES

1. See, e.g., Richard Delgado and Jean Stefancic, *Must We Defend Nazis? Hate Speech, Pornography, and the New First Amendment*, 5–10 (1997); Joe R. Feagin and Karyn D. McKinney, *The Many Costs of Racism*, 6–38, 65–93 (2003) [hereinafter, *Many Costs of Racism*]; Joe R. Feagin, Kevin E. Early, and Karyn D. McKinney, *The Many Costs of Discrimination: The Case of Middle-Class African Americans*, 34 Ind. L. Rev. 1313, 1323–1328, 1346–1357 (2001) [hereinafter, *Many Costs*].

2. E.g., *Many Costs*, supra, at 1328–1346, 1354–1356.

3. *Defend Nazis?*, supra, at 6; *Many Costs*, supra, at 1350–1352.

4. *Defend Nazis?*, supra, at 6.

5. Ibid.

6. *Many Costs*, supra, at 1333.

7. Ibid. at 1328–1334.

8. Ibid. at 1323 et seq.

9. Ibid. at 1323–1328.

10. Ibid. at 1334–1335; *Defend Nazis?*, supra, at 5, 10.

11. *Defend Nazis?*, supra, at 6, 91–92, 133.

12. *Many Costs*, supra, at 1335.

13. *Defend Nazis?*, supra, at 5, 7, 9.

14. *Defend Nazis?*, supra, at 6, 8; Debra Van Ausdale and Joe R. Feagin, *The First R: How Children Learn Race and Racism* (2001).

15. *First R*, supra; *Defend Nazis?*, supra, at 8, 10; *Many Costs*, supra, at 1354–1357.

16. See Chapter 6, this volume; text and notes immediately supra.

17. *Defend Nazis?*, supra, at 5–7.

18. Claude M. Steele and Joshua Aronson, *Stereotype Threat and the Intellectual Test Performance of African Americans*, 69 J. Personality and Soc. Psychol. 797 (1995).

19. See Ellis Cose, *The Rage of a Privileged Class* (1993).

20. See, for example, the extensive writing of scholar Charles Moskos on this subject.

21. *Defend Nazis?*, supra, at 5–10.

22. Ibid. at 4–10; *Many Costs*, supra, at 23–25, 52–53. On this history, see Juan Perea et al., *Race and Races* (2000).

23. *Defend Nazis?*, supra, at 4, 7.

24. Ibid. at 7.

25. Ibid.

26. Ibid. at 7–8.

27. Ibid.; *Many Costs of Racism*, supra, at 39–64, 119–146.

28. Frederick M. Lawrence, *The Punishment of Hate: Toward a Normative Theory of Bias-Motivated Crimes*, 93 Mich. L. Rev. 320, 342–343 (1994).

2

QUANTITATIVE ISSUES: HOW FREQUENT IS RACIAL VILIFICATION?

The previous chapter considered qualitative issues. How serious is hate speech? How damaging? To what interests? Is it more injurious for some groups than others? And, is it worse than invective or ridicule aimed, for example, at a person's height or weight? Now it is time to consider quantitative matters. How frequent are hate speech and violence? What forms do they take, and who are the victims?

Figures compiled by social scientists show, unsurprisingly, that the groups victimized by hate speech most frequently are ones whose stigma is obvious to a casual glance, for example, a noticeably gay person, a very dark, black male, or a very indigenous-looking Latino.[1] Looked at from the perspective of the perpetrator, most cases of hate crime and speech are opportunistic. That is, not everyone who bears an animus against, say, blacks, will say something disparaging when confronted by one. It all depends on whom the perpetrator is with, how vulnerable and alone the victim appears, and what the perpetrator has been doing or thinking lately. Some settings discourage the expression of racial vitriol; in others, hate speakers feel freer to express themselves.[2]

The most frequent victims of hate speech and crime, according to the available statistics, are African Americans (especially young males) and other minorities of color, and gays and lesbians who are "out" and make no secret of their sexual identities.[3] White people do report a substantial fraction of the hate *crimes* that the Federal Bureau of Investigation tabulates annually;[4] but a much smaller proportion of hate *speech*—perhaps because the English language contains relatively few terms of contempt for whites. (See Chapter 4 on common racist terms; Chapter 11, on hate speech against whites.)

IS HATE SPEECH INCREASING OR DECREASING IN SOCIETY?

National statistics on hate crime (a close cousin of hate speech) and figures compiled by social scientists suggest that hate speech is increasing, particularly (but not exclusively) on college campuses. This is what social science would predict. The "social competition" theory of racism holds that this form of behavior increases during times of social stress, when whites and groups of color compete for jobs, positions, and other scarce resources.[5] Competition also intensifies when the numbers are nearly equal, as they are now becoming in the national population mix. With the approach of the year 2050, when nonwhites will begin to surpass the number of whites, many whites are increasingly apprehensive about what that shift will mean for them. Social scientists also know—this is the "interest convergence" hypothesis—that racism is often held in abeyance during times when international appearances require it, such as during the Cold War, when the United States needed to project a peaceful, egalitarian image in order not to provide political capital to our enemy, the Soviet Union.[6] Today the United States lacks powerful foreign competitors, so the need for humane treatment for domestic minorities is not so acute as it is during wartime or periods of international competition. All these reasons suggest why, despite claims to the contrary,[7] hate speech apparently is rising and likely to continue to do so for some time.

WHO DISCRIMINATES?

Racism is said to correlate inversely with social and educational class, with the highly educated being less apt to be racists of the rawest sort, and less well-educated working-class people more so. Somewhat surprisingly, therefore, college and university campuses in recent years have been hotbeds of racial slurs, epithets, and graffiti.[8] The average black undergraduate at a white-dominated campus (that is, one unlike Howard, Morehouse, or Fisk, where African Americans preponderate) experiences a racial remark or slur several times in a typical school year.[9] If one counted the many code words, often spoken with a knowing expression or curled lip, that, like "you people" or "inner-city culture," carry heavily negative connotations, the frequency of exposure might approach one or more a day.

SPECIAL PROBLEMS FOR THE LAW

The ubiquity and incessancy of racially abusive speech pose a problem for the law, as will be seen in Chapter 4. Most legal remedies, like tort suits and criminal prosecutions, are designed to redress individual, dramatic acts that cause severe disturbance or harm in the victim. With racial hate speech, we have a different situation. Each harm is, perhaps, tolerable, or at any event, not life-threatening. But the cumulative effect of dozens, if not hundreds, of such incidents is very great, damaging a victim's life prospects, self-esteem, feeling of confidence and security, and, sometimes, physical and psychological health.[10] Moreover, discrimination has a multiplier effect. The suffering of one black or Latino or Asian is communicated to others in that community, who suffer vicariously and arm themselves emotionally for the time when it will be their turn.[11] The law has just begun to address harms like these in areas such as sexual harassment and the law of hostile environment.

THE RELATIONSHIP BETWEEN HATE SPEECH AND HATE MOVEMENTS

Quantitative issues of a different sort arise in connection with the broad social dimensions of hate speech. Scholars such as Alexander Tsesis and George Fredrickson have called attention to the way in which hate movements, such as apartheid in South Africa, Indian extermination, slavery, and the Holocaust, were preceded by campaigns of verbal abuse.[12] Whom we will oppress, we first demonize. The demonization rationalizes what comes later: The group deserved what they got. Movements like these arose not because an occasional German, U.S. Southerner, settler, or South African said something unkind about (or to) a black, Jew, or Indian. It was the cumulative effect of months and years of denigration that made the physical mistreatment, relocation, discriminatory law, or death natural and palatable. Indeed, according to Tsesis, hate speech that is systematically developed over time poses even a greater threat than when it creates an immediate "clear and present danger"—the category of speech that the law does permit to be punished.[13]

AN EVERYDAY COMPARISON

Readers may find a common childhood experience illustrative of the predicament of a minority person subjected to a tide of verbal abuse. Many young people in the middle years of school, when children first become intensely conscious of each others' appearance and dress, experience what it is like to be teased or taunted for some characteristic—a gait, a way their hair grows, a speech mannerism—not easily controlled. For such a person, each school day can bring new bullying, sarcasm, or crude remarks. School can become a torment. Some may even consider dropping out, or lashing out in anger. Children with deviant traits who are taunted and excluded by their peer groups are like minorities isolated and reviled because of their race—except that those children, unlike the minorities, will probably outgrow the trait (or at least the circle of bullies) by the simple process of growing up.

With the advent of the Internet, opportunities for disseminating hate speech multiply. Racists and white supremacists can talk with and reinforce each other. White supremacist Web sites and chat groups whip the users up into a frenzy in which they believe that whites are the oppressed group and that society is in danger of being overrun by ignorant, welfare-loving minorities with designs on white women. The Internet also allows the ignorant and the prejudiced to send cowardly, anonymous messages to those whom they despise, such as officers of black student organizations or Jewish or Arab-American students at major universities. Chapter 7 discusses these issues in greater detail.

THE SOCIAL CONSTRUCTION THESIS

Another way to look at both the qualitative and the quantitative side of racial depiction and abuse is by means of what has come to be called the social construction thesis.[14] For many scholars and students today, reality—social reality, at any rate—is a construct. The world of experience does not come to us as a given; rather we construct, interpret, and imbue it with meaning through the ways we sort, categorize, experience, reflect on, and describe it.[15]

Most scientists take the same position with respect to race. Although persons whom we conventionally designate as black, brown, white, or Asian do exhibit minor physical traits in common, these are trivial in comparison to those we all share. On a level of genes, the fundamental building blocks of life, blacks and whites, for example, share at least 99.99 percent of their genetic material. Moreover, scientists say the small variations between them, which determine such things as hair texture and skin color, cannot possibly contribute to differences with respect to complex human traits like personality, intelligence, or moral behavior.[16]

Races, then, are not fixed, biological, or objectively real. Instead, it is we who have decided to notice and endow with great, imagined significance the few, comparatively minor differences that people of various groups exhibit. Moreover, the categories we create overlap in ways that ought to perplex the uncritical believer in the objectivity of race: The differences between racial groups are much less than the ones within each group. The difference, that is, between the average black and the average white is much less than that between the lightest and the swarthiest white, and similarly on the black side.[17]

What role do racial depiction and labeling play in the social construction of race? A prime one. For without an interlocking system of jokes, scripts, tales, stories, plots, and name-calling, color would be a mere curiosity. No more than we do with hair color, eyebrow shape, or albinism, we would not associate negative qualities and judgments with it. It would not be a misfortune to be born black or brown, any more than it is to be born with freckled skin or curly hair.[18]

So, consider the social construction—largely carried out by words—at play in being, let us say, black. How much is it worth to endure all that goes along with that construction? This would include racism in school, at work, and when you tried to get a loan. It would include being scorned and feared by most whites. It would include being followed around in stores, being the last person on the bus to have a fellow passenger sit beside you, being suspected of intellectual inferiority in school or college because you undoubtedly got in as a result of affirmative action. It would include attractive people of other races (or even your own) refusing to date you. It would include confronting the glass ceiling at work, if you were even given a chance to work. It would include dying about seven years earlier than a white person of your circumstances and education, because of inferior medical treatment and the stress of constantly dealing with racism.

Words play a central role in the creation of all these hurdles. Other people acquire the idea of one's inferiority not because one is in fact inferior but because of what they have heard, read, or seen in the behavior of others toward you and people like you. How much would it be worth to go through life without such a burden? Writer Andrew Hacker describes a yearly experiment in which he asks his undergraduate students (mostly white) what they would pay in the following situation: One day, they wake up and learn that they were supposed to have been born black. A government agent arrives at the door and explains that a mistake has been made. They will now have to go back to the color for which they were originally designed. Tomorrow, an operation will be conducted that will render them black, and they will go through the rest of their lives that way. Their memories, consciousness, personality, and intelligence will remain just as before; they will just be contained in a black body.

The agent apologizes profusely for the mistake and is prepared to offer recompense. How much would each student want? Hacker reports that over the years, the figure has remained roughly the same: $1 million a year for life.[19] More recently, other writers have been addressing aspects of the same question. In a landmark book entitled *Black Wealth/White Wealth: A New Perspective on Racial Inequality*, Melvin L. Oliver and Thomas H. Shapiro examine the financial condition of black and white households. They find that the median black household has a net worth of near-zero, while that of the average white family is in the many tens of thousands of dollars. Many whites inherit substantial estates; the average black, little or nothing. These figures, of course, include only the quantifiable costs of being black; they exclude the many inconveniences, slights, and depressing experiences associated with it—that which, added to the shorter life span and lower earning capacity, caused Andrew Hacker's students to want considerably more than a yearly portion of what Oliver and Shapiro calculated.

Of course, not all black or brown misery can be laid at the doorstep of speech and social construction. Before that system came about, slavery held blacks in chains, and then a system of Jim Crow laws denied them rights of citizenship and access to public services and integrated education. But it is racial depiction and imagery that maintain the system of white-over-black in this society, now that those more tangible barriers have been lowered. It is difficult to argue that the cost to the average person of color of being spoken of (and to) and depicted, constantly—in the press, TV, movies, and everyday conversation—as inferior, stupid, dangerous, lazy, and morally debased is not high, indeed.

QUESTIONS FOR DISCUSSION, CHAPTER 2

1. If you are a woman, what situations would (and do) you avoid if you wish to avoid verbal harassment or taunting?
2. If you are a member of a racial or sexual minority, what situations are ones you have learned to be wary of if you wish to avoid hate speech and name-calling?
3. Have you ever uttered what could be considered hate speech? If so, why?
4. Minorities report much more hate speech than whites believe takes place. Why do you think this is so?
5. Like a single bite from a piranha, one racial insult or epithet is not extremely damaging; but hundreds, endured over a long period of time, are. How should the law treat the piranha—the utterer of the single, unanswered racist remark or slur?

CLASS EXERCISE

Form a group of six or seven. Then ask one of you to step aside for a moment while the others confer. Then, invite the designated person to return to the group, which in his or her absence has selected a single, minor trait to comment on. Go around the circle, commenting on that trait. For example: Person A: "Bill's hair really looks funny today." Person B: "Yes, he seems to have trouble combing it." Person C: "Maybe he doesn't have a good mirror at home." And so on. Make sure to select a minor trait; make sure, as well, that your comments are not vicious.

Then, go around the circle, taking turns bearing the brunt of group criticism.

At the end, discuss how you felt about being the object of (pretended) group criticism.

RECOMMENDED READING, CHAPTER 2

Jannette L. Dates and William Barlow, eds., *Split Image: African Americans in the Mass Media* (1990).

Howard J. Ehrlich, *Campus Ethnoviolence and the Policy Options* (1990).

Andrew Hacker, *Two Nations: Black, White, Separate, Hostile, Unequal* (1992).

Melvin L. Oliver and Thomas H. Shapiro, *Black Wealth/White Wealth: A New Perspective on Racial Inequality* (1995).

Michael Omi and Howard Winant, *Racial Formation in the United States* (second edition, 1994).

Arthur G. Pettit, *Images of the Mexican American in Fiction and Film* (1980).

Andrew E. Taslitz, *Hate Crimes, Free Speech, and the Contract of Mutual Indifference*, 80 B.U. L. Rev. 1283 (2000).

Jon Wiener, "Racial Hatred on Campus," *Nation*, February 27, 1989, at 260.

NOTES

1. We are grateful to the National Institute Against Violence and Prejudice which, over the years, has provided invaluable studies and reports on the frequency of hate speech and crime, including much of the material cited in this chapter. The institute, formerly housed at the University of Maryland, and its

chief researcher Howard J. Ehrlich, Ph.D., are the most definitive sources, along with the annual FBI statistics on crime and hate crime, for empirical information on hate offenses. See, e.g., Howard J. Ehrlich, *Campus Ethnoviolence and the Policy Options* (1990).

2. The leading authority for this view is Lu-in Wang, professor of law at the University of Pittsburgh, who in a series of law review articles and an upcoming book has forcefully expounded and documented this position.

3. See supra.

4. See, e.g., Federal Bureau of Investigation, U.S. Dept. of Justice, Hate Crime Data Collection Guidelines; Hate Crime Statistics Act, 28 U.S.C. § 534 (Supp. V 1993); *Discounting Hate: Ten Years After Federal Officials Began Compiling National Hate Crime Statistics, the Numbers Don't Add Up*, Intelligence Report (Southern Poverty Law Center), winter 2001, at 6.

5. See Gordon Allport, *The Nature of Prejudice* (1954), a classic work on this and other theories of the origin of prejudice.

6. See Derrick Bell, *Brown v. Board of Education and the Interest-Convergence Dilemma*, 93 Harv. L. Rev. 518 (1980); Richard Delgado and Jean Stefancic, *Critical Race Theory: An Introduction*, 16–20 (2001).

7. See Chapter 3, notes 4 and 5.

8. See also Chapter 6 (on campus racism and hate speech codes).

9. See Richard Delgado, *Campus Antiracism Rules: Constitutional Narratives in Collision*, 85 Nw. U. L. Rev. 343 (1991).

10. Ibid.

11. See Joe R. Feagin et al., *The Many Costs of Discrimination*, 33, 138–139 (2001).

12. See George Fredrickson, *Racism* (2002); Alexander Tsesis, *Destructive Messages* (2002).

13. *Destructive Messages*, supra.

14. See Richard Delgado and Jean Stefancic, *Critical Race Theory: An Introduction*, 7–8, 155 (2001).

15. Ibid. at 155.

16. See, e.g., Ian F. Haney Lopez, *The Social Construction of Race*, 29 Harv. C.R.–C.L. L. Rev. 1 (1994).

17. Ibid.

18. E.g., Richard Delgado and Jean Stefancic, *Images of the Outsider in American Law and Culture*, 77 Cornell L. Rev. 1258 (1992).

19. See Andrew Hacker, *Two Nations: Black and White, Separate, Hostile, Unequal* (1992).

3

THEORIES OF RACISM
AND HATE SPEECH

With some knowledge of both the extent and quality of hate speech, the reader might wonder what accounts for it. Ordinary, everyday conflict and irritability might come to mind. From a radio played too loud to an automobile that cuts us off when we want to make a turn, people annoy other people all the time. And when they do, we often say something about it. "You idiot. Why don't you watch where you're going?" "You inconsiderate jerk. Why don't you turn that darned thing down?" And, when we're really mad, we might easily lapse into saying something personal to the individual who has so vexed us. ("You stupid teenager, turn that radio down," or "You idiot lady driver. Why don't you watch where you're going?")

This sort of readily understandable anger probably accounts for a small fraction of racist hate speech. The victim is addressed in racial terms ("You goddamned Mexican, why don't you look where you're going?"), but the immediate cause of the remark is not the other person's race but his or her conduct (for example, inartful driving). When the incident ends or the speaker apologizes, the one who suffered the accusation is satisfied and moves on.

At other times, the racist remark comes out of the blue, without apparent provocation, or else goes far beyond what one might expect in that situation—perhaps one of unintentional affront, such as a jostled elbow on a busy sidewalk. Or it is anonymous, such as graffiti written on a building housing black students or a black organization on a campus, an unsigned racist flyer or leaflet, or an E-mail message sent to all the blacks, Latinos, Jews, or gay/lesbian members of a campus or living group. Or it may take the form of educated, carefully crafted remarks of a public speaker disparaging a race or people.

What explains these latter, more serious, and, unfortunately, more prevalent forms of hate speech? A number of authorities have put forward different, partially overlapping, theories.

INTEREST CONVERGENCE AND CRITICAL RACE THEORY

Critical race theory considers racism ubiquitous in American life and law, where dominant norms of color blindness and neutrality mask an ugly undercurrent of insistent inequality and unequal treatment.[1] It emphasizes the voices, experiences, and perspectives of those at "the bottom of the well" over those whose daily life brings few, if any, experiences with hard-core prejudice.[2] Critical race theory contains two strands. One is a discourse strand that focuses on the system of thoughts, categories, images, and language by which American society constructs racial reality. The other, older and more radical strand emphasizes the material side of race and the way our system of racial categorization serves the interests of the dominant group.[3] For this group, even civil rights law often subordinates the minorities it is supposedly designed to benefit.

Both branches of critical race theory, particularly the discourse analysts, take hate speech very seriously. For them, it is a principal means by which society constructs and maintains racial hierarchy. It teaches minorities "their place." And, it conveys to all the message that equality and equal dignity are of little value (or that certain groups are so valueless, by reason of their nature or their culture, that equal treatment of them would be meaningless—like treating a proud redwood tree and a useless scrub pine the same).

Thus, countless critical race authors have weighed in against hate speech, arguing that it causes great harm; that while regulating it may cause some small diminution in the scope of free speech, the speech is essentially worthless while the interests sought to be protected are central to democracy.[4] They take on, and answer, each of the claims hate speech's defenders put forth. And, they have made some headway. Courts and legislative bodies read and respond to critical litera-

> ### Monteiro v. Tempe Union High School District, 158 F.3d 1022, 1039 (9th Cir. 1998).
>
> In her amended complaint, Monteiro alleged that her ninth-grade daughter and other similarly situated African-American students attended a school where they were called "niggers" by white children, and where that term was written on the walls of the buildings in which they were supposed to learn civics and social studies. It does not take an educational psychologist to conclude that being referred to by one's peers by the most noxious racial epithet in the contemporary American lexicon, being shamed and humiliated on the basis of one's race, and having the school authorities ignore or reject one's complaints would adversely affect a Black child's ability to obtain the same benefit from schooling as her white counterparts. . . . It is the beginning of high school, when a young adolescent is highly impressionable and is making decisions about education that will affect the course of her life. . . . [A] school where this sort of conduct occurs unchecked is utterly failing in its mandate to provide a nondiscriminatory educational environment. Accordingly, we find that the complaint sets forth allegations that satisfy the first factor of the test for a Title VI violation.

ture on the need to control hate speech. Not all agree with the crits, of course. But some do, citing these writers as authority for a measure or ruling that strikes down particular examples or types of hate speech. Some of these writers and judicial opinions are cited in boxes throughout this book.

PROBLEMS WITH CRITICAL RACE THEORY

Some might question whether critical race theorists give too much weight to the hate speech problem. No one knows to a *certainty* that hate speech is increasing in frequency and severity; any increase might be due to better reporting or greater willingness of victims to come forward. Moreover, the harms of hate speech may be exaggerated. At the time, the incidents may seem serious and disturbing to the victim. But most people get over affronts and insults; in time, perhaps hate speech victims will do so as well.

Further, hate speech may serve certain vital and legitimate functions—safety valve, bellwether, opportunity for minorities to speak back or toughen up.[5] Finally, the crits may overlook the reformative power of the First Amendment, the very instrument they wish to encumber. Each of those objections has generated answers by the critical race theorists, some of which are mentioned below and in a later section (see Chapter 13).

THE ACLU ABSOLUTIST POSITION

The diametrically opposite position is the one embraced by the national organization of the American Civil Liberties Union. While a few local branches have broken away from the party line that forbids any restraints on speech, the national organization, led, for many years, by law professor Nadine Strossen, has taken the position that restraints of any kind on hate speech are unwise and unconstitutional.[6] This position sees racist hate speech as simply one of the legitimate (if wrongheaded) voices we must be prepared to tolerate in a liberal democracy. Like the opposite forms of statement—minorities and gays are normal, noble, the same as anyone else, and so on—they express an opinion. If we disagree with that opinion, fine. But we must be prepared to defend the right to offer it as staunchly as we defend the right of a Martin Luther King Jr. or Mahatma Gandhi to assert the fundamental equality of all humanity.[7]

The absolutist position is appealing because it admits of no exceptions to the regime of free speech—no decisions to make, no balancing, no judgment calls. If an official rule or practice limits speech, it is unconstitutional, period. Speech is one of our most highly valued liberties, and the foundation of many others. A government that begins limiting speech takes the first steps toward tyranny and thought control.

The constitutional argument is discussed later in this book (see, for example, Chapter 4). For now, note that courts have agreed with the

ACLU in some situations—for example, with respect to far–ranging campus speech codes—but not in others (for example, relief under the tort laws or the hostile environment doctrine).

<h2>PROBLEMS WITH THE ACLU ABSOLUTIST POSITION</h2>

The ACLU absolutist position suffers a number of weaknesses. One embarrassment is that the system of free speech has already suffered multiple rents, tears, and exceptions. As a later chapter shows, society has tolerated or created dozens of exceptions to free speech whenever it endangers the interests of an empowered group.[8] Why not a further one for some of the least powerful and most vulnerable members of society, such as eighteen-year-old black or gay undergraduates set upon by bigots while walking home late one night from the campus library?

Faced with the increasing difficulty of maintaining an absolutist position about something (free speech) that is not absolutely protected elsewhere, the ACLU lately has modified its position. Instead of insisting that hate speech limitations and prohibitions are unconstitutional, they have been urging that they are unwise:

- The "pressure valve" argument holds that allowing racists to blow off steam harmlessly is better than forcing them to hold things in, with the result that they may explode in violent, much more harmful ways later on.[9]
- The "best friend" argument holds that free speech has been minorities' best friend and a staunch ally in their fight for freedom. If minorities knew their own best interest, they would refrain from encumbering such a potent weapon.[10]
- The "more speech" argument holds that the best approach to speech we don't like is more speech—talking back to the aggressor. This supposedly will empower the victim, educate the utterer of hate speech, and strengthen the system of free speech rather than weaken it.[11]
- The "reverse enforcement" argument holds that curbs against hate speech will inevitably boomerang against minorities. They will end up enforced, not against neo-Nazis, bigots, and white supremacists, but against speakers of color

who say mildly reproachful things about whites or the white establishment.[12]

Each of these arguments is paternalistic—based on the supposed best interest of those it seeks to protect. If minorities knew where their own best interest lay, they would agitate not for hate speech controls, but the opposite. They would embrace the ACLU's absolutist view of free speech. All the ACLU's assertions have answers, as well, which the reader will meet in greater detail in Chapter 13. For example, social scientists write that unpunished hate speech makes the speaker *more*, not less, likely later to do or say something harmful to minorities.[13]

THE CONSERVATIVE "TOUGH LOVE" POSITION

An emerging conservative position opposes controls on hate speech for reasons that are more or less the opposite of the ones the ACLU advances. The conservative position deplores hate speech, considering it crass and uncivilized. But conservatives (who in the main detest paternalism, considering it an affront to individual dignity) place their response to hate speech on different grounds. For them, hate speech is unfortunate, but most of the proposed remedies are even worse. They:

- suppress a useful bellwether that should not be driven underground;[14]
- encourage minorities to dwell on minor slights and victimization;[15]
- promote classism, since the gutter language of a blue-collar worker or campus carouser is punished while the genteel language of the educated elite is not;[16]
- offer a cure that is worse than the disease, because it institutionalizes censorship, an even worse evil than hate speech itself.[17]

All these objections, too, have answers. What is useful to observe now is that the conservative position, like the ACLU approach, lacks a coherent theory of what hate speech is. Lacking a deep insight into its nature and extent, its arguments against intervention are shallow and lacking in substance.

Interest Convergence
and the Optimal Level of Racism

A further approach to racism and hate speech is the view of some critical race theorists that hate speech is not a harm to be confronted, but a tacitly acknowledged good. For this view, hate speech serves to keep minorities one-down. Defensive and demoralized, they never are able to dig in and feel truly at home in an environment, say a college campus. They spend their time and energy introspecting, licking their wounds, and combating low-level daily hassling and assaults on their dignity and self-confidence, instead of confronting more important issues such as minority recruiting, more professors of color, or an ethnic studies major (all measures that would be quite expensive for the college or university to institute).[18]

In this view, the optimal level of racism is not zero, but some low level that permits minorities to exist on campuses and corporations—the contrary would be unthinkable—but maintains them in a compliant, anxious, not-too-demanding condition. High-grade racism would be anathema to such an institution and the white liberals who run it. Crude fraternity parties featuring performers in blackface or giant plywood replicas of South Sea islanders with bones through their noses would create a commotion. The press would come. TV camera crews would interview students about how they felt. The minority community would demand intervention and the assurance that this sort of thing did not happen again. Because of the bad publicity, next year's minority enrollment might drop.[19]

Problems with the Radical View of
Racist Hate Speech as a Societal Benefit

One problem with the view that low-level racism and hate speech (not the flagrant, gross variety) are social goods is that this view is almost as demoralizing as the hate speech it seeks to explain. If administrators, on some level, act as though low-grade racism and hate speech confer institutional benefits, it is hard to know what minorities—who, of course, receive no benefit from them—should do. The materialist strand of critical race theory, which sees the twists and turns of black fortunes as dictated by the changing interests of white elites, has

received criticism from liberals, both white and black, for just this reason. Still, if the economic-materialist view of history and the way
racial dynamics work is true, it is no answer to say "I don't like that;
it makes me feel discouraged." Rather, the answer may be to work
harder and inform complacent whites about the role of hate speech so
that no one will be inclined to tolerate it.

The View from the Bottom:
Classism in the Campaign Against Hate Speech

A further view of hate speech takes the position that racial slurs and
epithets are often the normal vocabulary of working–class whites,
who mean nothing (or very little) by it.[20] Swearing, profanity, impo-
lite language, scatological terms, earthy jokes, and blasphemy are very
common at construction sites and among people who work with their
hands, the argument goes. Hate speech rules and laws, then, can operate unequally, punishing the innocent speech of a blue-collar worker,
while leaving untouched the genteel, but much more damaging, words
of an educated racist writing, for example, about the supposed innate
inferiority of African American people.[21]

Problems with the Classist View

One difficulty with this view is that a real class analysis reveals that
unregulated hate speech can just as easily divide the working class by
stimulating animosity between skinheads, construction workers, blue-
collar whites and their black and brown counterparts. Hateful speech
may be, for a few people, their ordinary form of discourse—although
the reader should ask how likely it is that someone, even from a
working-class family, would not know that "nigger" is today a word
of serious opprobrium and calculated to offend every African American who hears it. (Except, perhaps, when spoken by one African
American to another as a friendly slang greeting.) Finally, does not
everyone in American society, rich or poor, need to learn to speak re-
spectfully? If so, a requirement that all abide by basic norms cannot

be classist. In any event, classism is a form of discrimination aimed at the poor. Since minorities, on the average, are much poorer than whites, a rule aimed at protecting them cannot be classist. It may fall more heavily on uneducated whites than on ones with a high level of education, but that is not the same as classism.

"Every Society Demonizes Somebody; Hate Is Universal"

Another view of hate speech and prejudice holds that hate is, unfortunately, universal. Every social group creates at least one enemy, internal or external, whom it despises, hates, or convinces itself is inferior. In some European countries it is gypsies. In parts of Ireland, it is Catholics. In India, the untouchables. In some parts of Vermont, French-Canadians. Early European storytellers, lacking much acquaintance with colored populations, created villains and witches who were short, swarthy, and gnarled, or white but gnome-like. For this view, we should relax—hate speech is as universal as the common cold, and little more dangerous. In fact, if we did not have some unfortunate group to demonize, we might discharge anger and hostility in even more unfortunate ways.[22]

Problems with the Hate-Is-Universal View

One difficulty with the view that hate speech is ubiquitous is that it makes the familiar mistake of confusing an *is* with an *ought*. Many forms of behavior—theft, rape, mayhem, slavery—have been practiced since time immemorial. This does not mean that we should give up trying to reduce their frequency. Recent work on the psychology of hatred, far from normalizing it, shows that every society that commits genocide or other mass atrocity on another population first engages in a campaign of propaganda and belittlement aimed at the group. The demonization acts as a rationalization for the Holocaust, extermination, relocation, or other cruel treatment that follows.[23]

State v. Buggs, 581 N.W.2d 329, 344 (Minn. 1998).

"Race may be America's single most confounding problem, but the confounding problem of race is that few people seem to know what race is." Ian F. Haney López, *The Social Construction of Race: Some Observations on Illusion, Fabrication, and Choice*, 29 Harv. C.R.–C.L. L. Rev. 1, 5–6 (1994). In part, what makes race a confounding problem and what causes many people to not know what race is, is the view that the problems of race are the problems of the racial minority. They are not. The problems of race belong to all of us, no matter where our ancestors come from, no matter what the color of our skin. Thus, concluding that race is not an issue in this case because juror 32 is not a member of a racial minority, misses the point. Race is an issue.

THE LIBERTARIAN POSITION: TOTAL FREEDOM, NO GOVERNMENTAL INTERFERENCE

A final position is the libertarian one that holds that, as deplorable as hate speech is, controls on what one can say (or think) are even worse. They would require governmental interference into private behavior. This should be left to individual discretion. If certain individuals abuse that discretion, the only recourse is for others to shun them or turn a deaf ear to their bigoted rantings. This view, which maximizes individual liberty, distrusts giving any governmental agent—court, legislature, college conduct-code committee—the authority to dictate personal behavior.[24]

PROBLEMS WITH THE LIBERTARIAN POSITION

One difficulty with the libertarian position is that hate speech, according to the best evidence, does not merely inflict momentary injury to feelings. As Chapter 1 showed, it causes a host of damages to health, life prospects, and self-confidence. Every libertarian concedes a role for social intervention when an individual threatens serious harm to another. Hence, the hands-off libertarian position would seem to apply only to the mildest, least reprehensible forms of hate speech, not the ones with which this book is mainly concerned.

Relation to Remedies and Courses of Action

Each of the many views of what hate speech is brings consequences for what society should do about it. That is, the question of remedy inevitably presupposes some view of the conduct one is trying to deter, punish, or provide recompense for. As the reader will see in later chapters on legal issues, the severity and intentionality of conduct play important parts in the selection of a means of redress.

Relation to Hate Crimes

A word here is in order about a related issue not treated in any detail in this book, namely hate crimes.[25] A hate crime is one, such as assault, battery, arson, rape, kidnapping, or murder, that is committed with a racial motivation. The perpetrator selects his or her victim because the person is white, black, Asian, Latino, or, under some statutes, gay or lesbian. A typical hate crime law punishes such a crime more severely than when it is committed without racial motivation. For example, if Jones spies Mary Yen, a small Asian woman, and mugs her because he believes that as a small woman, she is an easy mark, Jones commits no hate crime. (But he does, of course, commit an ordinary crime—robbery, maybe assault as well—for which he can be sent to jail.) If he selects his victim *because* she is Asian (perhaps thinking that Asians have no business being in this country or are responsible for destroying the American automobile industry), he may be charged with a more serious hate crime.[26]

Hate crimes are different from hate speech. They are, often, more serious, injuring the victim's security, well-being, and sense of safety. And they do not raise constitutional issues in the way hate speech does. Speech is a constitutionally protected activity, mugging someone is not. Accordingly, legal remedies for hate crimes have raised fewer, and less severe, constitutional objections from civil libertarians, absolutists, and libertarians, although a few objectors have questioned whether the punishment of hate crimes does not inevitably punish thought and speech. (The argument is that a prosecutor who charges Jones in the situation mentioned above can prove his or her case only by introducing evidence to the jury of what Jones thinks or says about Asians. For example, when depriving Mary of her purse, he may have said, "Goddamn gook. You steal our money and jobs. Take that!"). Courts have given little weight to this objection.

QUESTIONS FOR DISCUSSION, CHAPTER 3

1. Racism is said to be economically inefficient—employers who discriminate are at a disadvantage (they must hire from a smaller pool) compared to those who do not—so that the market should, over time, drive out racism. Is the same true of hate speech? If so, why does it seem to be increasing, not decreasing?

2. Might a low level of racism benefit a white-dominated institution—say, a college campus—when a high level would not? Might the optimal level of racism, in other words, be not zero, but some small, but constant, level?

3. If race and races are socially constructed, rather than objective, fixed, and biologically determined, what part does hate speech play in that construction?

4. Is hate speech one of those unfortunate facts of life (like bad music or bad jokes) that we must tolerate because of the First Amendment?

5. Does focusing on hate speech just cause minorities to see themselves as weak and victimized, rather than as taking advantage of all the opportunities that lie before them?

6. "One person's hate speech is another person's uncomfortable truth." Does hate speech lie in the eye of the beholder?

7. "Hate speech might be unpleasant and uncomfortable, but giving the government the power to punish speech would be even worse." What do you think of this position?

CLASS EXERCISE

Enact the following: A very young undergraduate from a small, rural town tells her T.A., a foreign graduate student, something the T.A. finds extremely offensive. (For example, "I wish you could speak decent English. I can't understand you. Aren't you supposed to be American?") The T.A. files a complaint, under a campus hate–speech code, which is heard before a committee consisting of one administrator, one student, and one professor.

Role A: The defendant

Role B: The T.A.

Roles C, D, E: The hearing committee

RECOMMENDED READING, CHAPTER 3

Gordon W. Allport, *The Nature of Prejudice* (1954).

Anthony Appiah and Amy Gutmann, *Color Conscious: The Political Morality of Race* (1996).

Derrick Bell, *Race, Racism, and American Law* (fourth edition, 2000).

K. Crenshaw et al., eds., *Critical Race Theory: Key Writings that Formed the Movement* (1995).

Richard Delgado and Jean Stefancic, *Must We Defend Nazis? Hate Speech, Pornography, and the New First Amendment* (1997).

Michel Foucault, *Power/Knowledge* (1980).

Erving Goffman, *Stigma: Notes on the Management of Spoiled Identity* (1963).

Nat Hentoff, *Free Speech for Me—But Not for Thee: How the American Left and Right Relentlessly Censor Each Other* (1992).

Irwin Katz, *Stigma—A Social Psychological Analysis* (1981).

Joel Kovel, *White Racism: A Psychohistory* (1970).

Charles R. Lawrence III, *The Id, the Ego, and Equal Protection: Reckoning with Unconscious Racism*, 39 Stan. L. Rev. 317 (1987).

Mari Matsuda, *Public Responses to Racist Speech: Considering the Victim's Story*, 87 Mich. L. Rev. 2320 (1989).

Ethnic Notions (Marlon Riggs, director, PBS 1986).

Lu-in Wang, *The Complexities of "Hate,"* 60 Ohio St. L.J. 799 (1999).

NOTES

1. See Richard Delgado and Jean Stefancic, *Critical Race Theory: An Introduction*, 6–9 (2001).

2. Ibid. See also Derrick Bell, *Faces at the Bottom of the Well* (1992).

3. See Richard Delgado, *Two Ways to Think about Race*, 89 Geo. L.J. 2279 (2001).

4. See, e.g., Mari Matsuda, *Public Responses to Racist Speech*, 87 Mich. L. Rev. 2320 (1989).

5. See Richard Delgado and Jean Stefancic, *Must We Defend Nazis? Hate Speech, Pornography, and the New First Amendment*, 95–121 (1997).

6. See, e.g., Nadine Strossen, *Regulating Hate Speech on Campus: A Modest Proposal?* Duke L.J. 484 (1990).

7. Ibid. *See also* Nadine Strossen, "Legal Scholars Who Would Limit Free Speech," *Chronicle of Higher Education*, July 7, 1993, at 1–3.

8. Libel, defamation, false advertising, copyright, state secrets, plagiarism, words of threat, and disrespectful speech uttered to a police officer, judge, or other authority figure are just a few examples.

9. *Defend Nazis?* supra, at 98–99.

10. Ibid.

11. Ibid.

12. Ibid. at 101.

13. Ibid. at 100.

14. Ibid. at 110, 114–115.

15. Ibid. at 110, 115–116.

16. Ibid. at 110, 117–118.

17. Ibid. at 110, 118–119.

18. See Richard Delgado, *Campus Antiracism Rules: Constitutional Narratives in Collision*, 85 Nw. U. L. Rev. 343, 380 n.319 (1991).

19. Ibid.

20. See *Defend Nazis?* supra, at 10, 117–118.

21. Ibid.

22. See text and notes 9–10, supra.

23. See Chapter 2, on the relation between hate speech and hate movements.

24. Nat Hentoff and Nadine Strossen have taken this position from time to time.

25. See Lu-in Wang, *Hate Crimes Law* (1994 and supps.).

26. Ibid.

PART TWO
WORDS, SPEAKERS, AND TARGETS

4

THE STRANGE CAREERS OF FOUR SPECIAL WORDS

Alcorn v. Anbro Engineering, Inc.,
2 Cal.3d 493, 86 Cal.Rptr. 88, 468 P.2d 216 (1970).

Although the slang epithet "nigger" may once have been in common usage, along with such other racial characterizations as "wop," "chink," "jap," "bohunk," or "shanty Irish," the former expression has become particularly abusive and insulting in light of recent developments in the civil rights movement as it pertains to the American Negro.

Although the number of words and combinations of words that may (depending on the setting) constitute hate speech is infinite, certain words are only—or almost only—calculated to wound and offend. In this category fall words like *fag, lezzie, cunt, nigger, spic, gook, kike,* and *Tonto.* Although the origin, use, and treatment of the word nigger has been well documented in Randall Kennedy's book of the same name,[1] other words have not received such thorough examination. This chapter considers four such words: *chink, kike, spic,* and *wop,* and the roles they have played in court proceedings.

A SPECIAL FORM OF DISPARAGEMENT

You are on your way to work. An urban dweller, you choose to take public transit. The bus is crowded; you are reading the morning paper, minding your own business. You overhear conversations, but pay little attention to their content—it is none of your business. Suddenly, you hear someone say, "I hate that (blank)!" Now, fill in the blank with an epithet. If the blank was *brown-noser,* the sentence would leave your memory as quickly as you heard it. If it was *asshole,* you would most likely continue to read your paper (although you might flinch); it is still none of your business. If the blank was *bitch,* you would probably notice and find the word greatly offensive. Now, fill in the blank with a racial epithet. "I hate that *chink!*" Instantly, the conversation is your business; it is that of everyone on the bus within earshot. People freeze in astonishment or avert their eyes. "I hate that *kike!*" You glance around and wonder if Jewish people are within earshot. You wonder how they feel, as others wonder if you are Jewish. "I hate that *spic!*" You form a strong disapproval about the speaker. Your peaceful morning has been shattered. Everyone who heard the word is now uncomfortable. You have trouble reading your paper. Out of all the conversations you hear on the bus every day, this one will stick in your mind. You will tell co-workers about a not-so-ordinary sentence you heard from a person you did not know on an ordinary day, on an ordinary bus you took to work.

What makes racial epithets special, different, and noticeable? What is it about *chink, kike, spic,* and *wop?* Are they just words? Randall Kennedy's book, *Nigger: The Strange Career of a Troublesome Word,*[2] examined both the social history of "the filthiest, dirtiest, nastiest word in the English language,"[3] and the effect of "a peculiar, resilient, ever-changing fixture [on] the American jurisprudence of epithets."[4] Kennedy concluded that *nigger* is not inherently insulting. Its meaning, like that of any other word, is not "crystal, transparent and unchanged"; it "may vary greatly in color and content according to the circumstances and the time in which it is used."[5] Indeed, by allowing and even encouraging its use, society can convert *nigger* "from a negative into a positive appellation,"[6] thus "yank[ing] *nigger* away from white supremacists."[7]

Lee v. Ventura County Superior Court, 9 Cal.App.4th 510, 11 Cal.Rptr.2d 763 (1992).

Approximately 10 years ago, the California Supreme Court publicly censured a superior court judge for his use of racial epithets, including the word, "nigger." (*In re Stevens* (1982) 31 Cal.3d 403, 404, 183 Cal.Rptr. 48, 645 P.2d 99.) Ironically, today, we are compelled to rule upon an African-American's request for court authorization to change his name to "Misteri Nigger." As we shall explain, the judiciary should not lend the Great Seal of the State of California to aid appellant in his social experiment. The proposed surname is commonly considered to be a racial epithet and has the potential to be a "fighting word."

Appellant, a 60-year-old educator, filed an application seeking court approval of a surname that he claims is intended to achieve social justice, i.e., to ". . . steal the stinging degradation—the thunder, the wrath, shame and racial slur—from the word nigger." He theorizes that his use of the name, with court approval, could be used to conquer racial hatred. He concedes the proposed surname is "the most provocative, emotionally-charged and explosive term in the language." His opening brief states that the "[n]ame change to me personally means nothing; not even a sacrifice. It is a minor thing."

Appellant claims that by taking the surname, "Nigger," he will take the sting out of the word. We do not question appellant's sincerity in seeking the official name change. However, appellant's premise is, at the very least, suspect. His quest for social justice should not be viewed in a vacuum. "One feature of strong insults and epithets is that they tend to shock those at whom they are directed and others who hear." (*Greenwalt, Insults and Epithets: Are They Protected Speech?* (1990) 42 Rutgers L. Rev. 287, 291.) We presume that at least some

(Continues)

> ### Lee v. Ventura County Superior Court, 9 Cal.App.4th 510, 11 Cal.Rptr.2d 763 (1992). (continued)
>
> African–Americans would not be in agreement with appellant's methods and might suffer embarrassment and shock by his use of the epithet as his official name.
>
> "The use of the term 'nigger' has no place in the civil treatment of a citizen by a public official." (*City of Minneapolis v. Richardson* (1976) 307 Minn. 80, 239 N.W.2d 197, 203.) This rule is broad enough to preclude judicial approval of appellant's use of the name "Misteri Nigger," even at his own request. We stress that we are aware of appellant's stated motive that the name change will lessen racial bias and tension. As indicated, we question the accuracy of appellant's appraisal. At the same time, we unequivocally wish the word would simply fall out of use in the English language.

As Kennedy did with the word that titles his book, this chapter will look at the social and legal history of four other racial epithets: *chink*, *kike*, *spic*, and *wop*. This study may shed new light on his startling conclusion that the best way to defang hate words is to repeat them often.

SOCIAL HISTORY: ORIGINS, USES, AND MEANINGS

Chink

Chink, as a racial epithet, has been traditionally viewed as a derogatory term for a Chinese person, a Chinaman.[8] But lately, the term has expanded beyond describing people of purely Chinese descent to include all people of Asian descent.[9] Most authorities agree that *chink* developed from a simple alteration or mispronunciation of another word, such as Ching or Chinese.[10] Another holds that it derives from mispronunciation of the word Chung-Kuo, which means China in Chinese,[11] and yet another that *chink* is inspired by the Chinese word for Chinese, namely Joong.[12] Finally, some believe that *chink* derives

Taylor v. Metzger, 706 A.2d 685, 698 (N.J. 1988).

Thus, different racial groups can react disparately to racial slurs [and going on to cite cases of blacks and Mexicans subjected to racist epithets]. . . . Due to this distinction, we hold that in an intentional infliction of emotional distress claim arising out of an allegation of racial harassment, the plaintiff's race must shape the objective inquiry into the severity of the distress.

from the Chin'g dynasty, which ruled China during the first major period of Chinese immigration into America.[13] *Chink* is used not only as a noun describing a person of Asian heritage, but also an adjective. For example, *chink* noise is a description of Asian languages, with their fast pace and tonality.[14] One can go out for *chink* food.[15] Variations of the word include *chinkey, chinkie,* and *chinky.*[16]

The word *chink* is unique among epithets due to its numerous legitimate meanings—a dent or crease in an object, the sound of two objects hitting each other, or a gap in a theory.[17] Unlike *nigger, kike, spic,* and *wop,* if one were to overhear the word *chink* spoken by another, one would not automatically know that the speaker is uttering a racial epithet. But if used to refer to a person, *chink* has no other use than as a derogatory term for Asians.

In the latter guise, *chink* was first used in the mid-1800s,[18] most likely by the British around the time of the colonization of Hong Kong.[19] The book *Old Colonials,*[20] written in 1882, recognized that even though the term *chinkie* was commonly used by the British, the term was not merely an identifier, but a vulgarism.[21] By the turn of the century, with the explosion of Chinese immigrants, *chinks* were common in the United States and a major component of the American expansion into the West.[22] With the growth of Chinese-operated businesses, *chink* became a rallying cry for white unions.[23] *Chinks* were seen as threats to the white community; supporting them would hurt the "white institution."[24] Union workers were *skilled,* not like those incompetent *chinks.*[25] In addition to supplying labor during the expansion of the American West, the Chinese were also the backbone of the canning industry of Alaska in the early 1900s[26]—so much so, that when manual labor in fish canning gave way to canning machines, the new machines became known as the "Iron *Chinks*."[27]

Chinks were not merely competition for white businesses, they were seen as unfit to mix with white society.[28] During 1912, Reverend T. Albert Moore of the Methodist Social and Moral Reform Department urged the case for separation: "the question of whether Chinese restaurant keepers and laundrymen should be allowed to employ white women" was "one of the most vital ones before the country."[29] He advised that "only girls of the lowest type" would work for the Chinese.[30] "[T]he results of the close intimacy of this class of white girls and their Oriental employers in daily work was appalling."[31] He speculated that "[m]any disastrous things have occurred when young girls have been employed by Chinks ... we should bring to bear on the Chinese the way of our civilization. Every time anything occurs, punishment should be meted out."[32] The use of *chink* was by then common, appearing as practically the accepted term to describe the Chinese.[33] Politicians across the nation would back the popular stance against Asian voting rights, or risk being perceived as supporters of "evil" and "dirty" *chinks*.[34] *Chinks* appeared on posters and in cartoons with features like those of monkeys.[35]

While not a term freely used by dignified speakers in the second half of the 1900s, *chink* still remained in common use. During the early years of World War II, Asians were repeatedly called *chinks* and seen as foreigners who should go back "home."[36] As World War II continued, however, being a *chink* lost some of its sting; the other option was being a *Jap* and being sent to internment camps.[37] Later, during the Vietnam War Asians, even those who served in the armed forces, were again seen as foreigners.[38]

Even today, racial violence visits *chinks* in the name of fallen white soldiers. In 1989 Jim Loo, a Chinese American, was killed by assailants who called him *gook* and *chink* and blamed him for the death of American soldiers in Vietnam.[39] In 1992, a Vietnamese student at the University of Miami was beaten to death by several white youths who called him *chink* and *Viet Cong*.[40] In the 1980s, Detroit autoworkers were losing their jobs due to Japanese competition. A group of these workers blamed a *chink* stranger for taking their jobs and beat him to death.[41] In 1992, in Coral Springs, Florida, a Vietnamese American college student, Luyen Phan Nguyen, was chased by a white mob who yelled *chink*, and killed him.[42] In 1995, a middle-aged Chinese American woman was beaten by people who yelled, "[f]—k you chink, go back to your country."[43] In San Francisco, a Chinese American business owner opened a Burger King franchise, which immediately sparked community resistance.[44] People living in the vicinity protested the change in "neighbor character" and subjected the *chink* to a barrage of vandalism, graffiti, and protests.[45] In 2002, in an upscale southern California neighborhood, a varsity high school athlete, Kenny Chiu, was stabbed to death in his parents' driveway on his way home from visiting friends. An anti-Asian epithet was found scratched into the family's S.U.V. parked nearby.[46]

The unfair competition stereotype coupled with the model minority myth creates resentment on the nation's campuses, as well.[47] "*Chink, chink,* cheating *chinks*! Stop the Yellow Hordes. Stop the Chinese before they flunk you out" scream graffiti on one campus's walls.[48] Students at U.C.–Berkeley reported seeing similar graffiti,[49] and flyers posted on the lockers of minority students at Boalt Hall Law School screamed: "A town meeting will not save you . . . *chinks*. Your failures are hereditary and can't be corrected by these liberals. Look around Boalt Hall[,] besides the few hand picked affirmative action professors this is a quality law school. . . . When I see you in class it bugs the hell out of me because you['re] taking the seat of someone qualified."[50] At the University of Connecticut, Asian students were spat on, called *chinks, gooks,* and *Oriental faggots,* punched, mooned, and humiliated during a university-sponsored dance.[51]

In 1996, an Asian Pacific American residence was spray-painted with "fucking chinks." The same year, two Dartmouth College students—Korean American and Chinese American males—found racial slurs, including "chink bastards," "bitch," and "faggot," written on the front door of their dormitory room. "Chink" and "Fuck yo [sic] chinks" were scrawled across a computer screen and inside a refrigerator in the Asian American Activities Center at Stanford University. A Laotian American high school girl was taunted by her fellow students with swastikas and the phrases "hippy chink," "demon girl," and "white pride" scrawled onto her truck, and demands to "Go back to China, you chink." One teacher mocked Asian Pacific Americans by mispronouncing his "R's," pretending to be bucktoothed, and uttering unintelligible words while asking the victim, "Did you understand that?" One young student of his found the environment so hostile that she decided to complete her education at home. [52]

Kike

Kike[53] is a "vulgarly offensive name for a Jew."[54] The *Oxford English Dictionary* lists no other definitions. Unlike *chink*, *kike* has a singular meaning. Of the many theories on the origin of *kike*, the most plausible is that put forth by Leo Rosten in *The Joys of Yiddish*.[55] Rosten explained that the word derives from the Jewish word for circle, *kikel*. As immigrants came to the United States through Ellis Island at the turn of the twentieth century, they were required to sign their names. Being illiterate, most signed an "X," but Jewish immigrants would usually sign with a circle, since they saw an "X" as representing the horrors of crucifixion and a symbol of Christian oppression. As a result, immigration inspectors referred to Jewish immigrants as *kikel* (for circle), which was shortened to *kike*.[56] Another theory holds that *kike* has its origin in the common endings of personal names of Eastern European Jews, –*ki* or –*ky*.[57] Others believe that the term derives from the German word *kieken*, which means to peep. Jewish clothing manufacturers were said to peep or spy on fancy European clothing designers to make cheap knockoffs.[58] A less well-supported theory holds that *kike* followed a progression of other racial epithets: *hike* for Italians and *mike* for Irishmen.[59]

Most authorities agree that the word first appeared in the United States during the early 1900s, when its main use was as a term of opprobrium by WASPs for Jews.[60] But *kike* was also commonly used by established German Jews to describe their newcomer Eastern European counterparts[61] and by Jews against members of their group who violated middle-class standards.[62] "Stop acting like a kike" was a frequent warning to noisy, badly behaved children who offended the middle-class mores of the bourgeois Jews.[63] Although some Jewish authors still use the term in their writing to quote the hateful speech of others, few refer to other Jews by that term.[64]

Throughout history, antisemitism has been linked to a belief that Jews are to blame for the problems of the world. The most famous antisemite, Adolf Hitler, maintained that no form of filth or profligacy was not caused by a Jew.[65] "He graphically proclaimed that anyone cutting into an abscess invariably would find 'like a maggot in a rotting body, often dazzled by the sudden light—a kike.'"[66] American hatred of Jews derives from the belief that *kikes* are driven only by greed and gain their wealth from taking from those less fortunate than they.[67] The use of the word *kike* inherently carries with it an element of accusation.[68] Opponents of an anti-pornography ordinance in Cambridge, Massachusetts, posted leaflets throughout the neighborhood demanding, "Help stop commie *kikes* . . . from telling us what we can read."[69]

Even against the backdrop of the Holocaust, antisemites today accuse *kike* women of "[sleeping] with the Nazis [in World War II] so that they could survive and make a profit."[70] During World War II, well-wishers warned refugee organizations to leave Jews out of their lobbying efforts due to "the prevalence of antisemitic feelings in Congress."[71] Dartmouth College at one point excluded Jews of the "*kike*" type from admission.[72] And not to be left out, Ku Klux Klan members ranted, "No Koons, Kikes, or Katolics!"[73]

Literature is replete with examples of persecution of Jews featuring the word *kike*. In the book *Passover*, a Jewish cop investigating the murder of Jewish women interviews the community. The family believes that the murder was motivated by religious bias, but the cop has his doubts. Family members respond to his disbelief by saying, "We're making it up, right? We're always making it up . . . when someone wants to hurt a Jew." As the cop continues through the neighborhood, he hears calls of *kike* coming from several people and finally begins to suspect racial motivation. [74] Even though the cop did not believe that Jews were being persecuted, he knew that *kikes* were.[75]

In "Be-Dad," a Jewish baseball player, Bernie Mandlebaum, was up to bat at a critical moment. Mandlebaum's coach, Murphy, screams out, "Jam it, ye *kike*!" Bernie does; he hits a three-run home run. Murphy is overcome, weeps tears of joy, and cries out, "Oh, Bernie! Oh, Bernie! I forgive ye for bein' a Jew!"[76] In *Men Without Women*,[77] Ernest Hemingway imagined three Roman soldiers having a drink together after work. The soldiers' jobs were to impose punishment upon criminals for the Roman Empire. Their discussion focused on one particular criminal who had been punished that day, a man named Jesus. They marveled how Jesus never begged them to stop even as they were nailing his hands and feet to the cross. They discussed this with their bartender, a Hebrew man named George. As the soldiers leave, they told the bartender to put the bill on their tab. The bartender asked if he could have any of the money today. The soldiers replied no. Once they exited the bar, they commented, "George is a *kike* just like all the rest of them."[78] From the rebellious Jesus Christ to an unassuming Jewish bartender, *kike* has come to represent a history of belief that Jews are to blame.

Spic

As a derogatory word for Mexicans, Mexican Americans, and Puerto Ricans, spic[79] is thought to have developed in the early 1900s.[80] Since then, the term has expanded to encompass other Hispanic groups, including Central Americans, South Americans, and Caribbeans.[81] At the end of the 1800s, *spic* was commonly used to describe Italians; perhaps the term grew out of the term spaghetti, a traditional Italian dish.[82] Today, this use is no longer common, making its use for Latinos the dominant one.[83] Another theory holds that *spic* derived from the phrase "No *spic* da Ingles," [84] highlighting early Hispanics' heavy accents.[85] Occasionally, *spic* has also meant the Spanish language.[86] One book gave an example of a person who studies Spanish: "I've had two years of *spic*."[87] Hemingway wrote, "I wish I could talk *spik*. . . . I don't get any fun out of asking that *spik* questions."[88] No matter the origin, *spic*, like *greaser*, *wetback*, and *beaner*, currently is a highly offensive term for Latinos.[89]

Spic probably came into its current use with the wave of Mexican immigrants entering the United States from the early to mid-1900s.[90] Then, Mexicans were seen as a necessary evil, due to the need for docile servants and cheap labor. One U.S. border patrolman stated, "a lot of fellows got tied with a *spiggity* women. . . . I married a *spiggity* and I choose her from any dammed white woman. She'll do as she's told—never go out to a show unless I tell her to, and she'll be faithful, too."[91] The border patrolman was not so fond of Mexican men, though. Those other *spics* were used to perform needed labor; they were a rough crowd.[92]

While Latinos originally were welcomed as a source of cheap labor, the 1980s saw a change in American attitudes. White America began to fear that Latinos were taking jobs away from them, even though the jobs that a majority of the newcomers performed were ones that whites would consider below them. The anti-immigration movement gained strength. Racial literature opposing immigration trumpeted, "We need a real border. . . . We get the Spics. . . . Deportation—they're all going home."[93] Neutral observers wrote that "[N]on-Hispanics in the United States fear that the country's rapidly growing Hispanic population will not adopt the language, customs, and viewpoint of the dominant, English-speaking culture. Some of these people fear that their way of life will be replaced by the 'foreign ways' of Hispanic Americans."[94]

During the redistribution of Philadelphia voting districts in the 1990s, one legislator worried that political power might fall into the hands of the Latino community: "Look, I'm a white mother fucker from Philadelphia. And I don't want no more ... *Spics* in my district."[95] In the movie *Saturday Night Fever*, the lead character, played by John Travolta, recognized that two Latino dancers should have won a dance contest over him and his partner; they were simply better dancers.[96] Travolta's character commented, "The *spics* should of won."[97]

The fear of Hispanic engulfment has spread to college campuses.[98] At Boston College minority students received E-mails deploring "Monkeys and Apes" and informing them that "BC is for white men ... not *spicks*."[99] Students at prestigious Boalt Law School were called *spics*.[100] Latin American students at Smith College were told that *spics* need to "quit complaining or get out."[101] When Bernhard Goetz shot and killed a group of minority youths who approached him asking for money, his motivation was to "rid his neighborhood of spics. . . ."[102] A New Jersey man was charged with murder after killing a Latino boy as part of a game in which he got points for using his car to "pick off spics. . . ."[103] Before the Columbine High School killings, the infamous teen duo discussed their hatred of *spics* as reason for their actions.[104]

Even Latinos of high status are not immune from name-calling. When television talk show host Geraldo Rivera went to Jonesville, Wisconsin, to tape a Ku Klux Klan rally, a Klansman called him a *spic*. A fight broke out, and both men were arrested.[105]

Wop

A derogatory term for Italians, *wop* is thought to have first appeared during the late 1800s, probably as a corruption of the Italian word guappo (pronounced *wah-po*), which in the Neapolitan dialect means handsome man.[106] In the Sicilian dialect, guappo means a bold and handsome man, sometimes a bully.[107] (The closest American word would be the slang term *dude*.)[108] Among Italians, the term was not thought of as derogatory; following the peak of Italian immigration in the late 1800s, guappo would often be overheard in the banter among immigrants.[109] The last syllable in guappo was subsequently dropped by English speakers, leaving the term *wop*.[110]

Another theory on the origin of the term holds that *wop* stands for one who is without papers. Immigration officials would write WOP ("with out papers") on documents sending immigrants back, and the term caught on.[111] Whatever its origin, the term *wop* carries a decidedly disparaging connotation. The earliest example of *wop* in literature comes from the book *Courts and Criminals*,[112] which describes Italians as living a life of crime:

> Curiously enough, there is a society of criminal young men in New York City who are almost the exact counterpart of the Apaches of Paris. They are known by the euphonious name, "W[o]ps" and "Jacks." These are young Italian-Americans who allow themselves to be supported by one or two women, almost never of their race. These pimps affect a peculiar cut of hair, and dress with half-turned-up velvet collar, not unlike the old-time Camorrist [the Camorra being the Neapolitan version of the Mafia], and have manners and customs of their own. They frequent the lowest order of dance-halls, and are easily known by their picturesque styles of dancing, of which the most popular is the "*Nigger.*" They form one variety of the many "gangs" that infest the city, are quick to flash a knife as the Apaches, and, as a cult by themselves, form an interesting sociological study.

Even social scientists and other professionals assigned negative traits to *wops*, finding them "educationally deficient, socially backward, and bizarre in appearance."[113] A 1921 article in the *Journal of the American Medical Association* explained that the symptoms of Italian immigrants "did not result from any physical malady but only from their general belief that the United States . . . is due . . . to provide for them the rest of their lives."[114] A mid-twentieth-century report by an apothecary in Colorado denied evidence of lead poisoning by workers at a smelting plant on the ground that the alleged victims were lying *wops*, not trustworthy white men.[115] While old-stock Americans opposed the immigration of Italians, they did recognize the value of the cheap labor *wops* provided:

> One faction claims that the superior classes like ourselves, in fact the great British stock, had ought to produce as many kids as possible, to

keep in control of this great nation and maintain the ideals for which we and our ancestors have always stood, while these lower masses hadn't ought to spawn their less intellectual masses. But then again, there's them that hold and maintain that now we've cut down immigration, we need a supply of cheap labor, and where get it better than by encouraging these Wops . . . to raise as many brats as they can?[116]

Italians were considered stupid and criminals. Nobody would care if a *wop* died or was killed in lynching parties, mob beatings, and riots.[117]

As time passed, Italian Americans became better integrated as white Americans. Yet, the term *wop* has not been forgotten. During the mid-1900s baseball players were called *wops*, the most famous being Joe DiMaggio, "a helluva good *wop* center fielder."[118] The Italian enemy soldiers of World War II were called *wops* by American soldiers.[119] Richard Nixon, as president, even used the word when referring to federal judge John J. Sirica.[120] In 1990, the Italian fraternal organization Sons of Italy requested that the California Department of Motor Vehicles recall the many vanity license plates issued with the term *wop* inscribed on them, urging that the term is "deeply offensive to most Italian-Americans."[121]

SUMMARY

The terms *chink*, *kike*, *spic*, and *wop* today embody a history of disdain toward Asians, Jews, Latinos, and Italians. All four terms find their origin in the early 1900s, and even then such terms demonstrated a negative attitude toward foreigners. Being referred to by such derogatory terms is like "receiving a slap in the face."[122]

Increasingly, those who use such terms in the belief that they are not harmful quickly learn otherwise. An Oklahoma state representative, upon "discovering that cups being handed out by a local chamber of commerce were made in China, said he doesn't like things made by 'Chinks.'"[123] After his audience rebuked him for his use of the term, he insisted that "the word wasn't a racial slur, it's just short for Chinese. . . . If I'd wanted to offend them I would have called them 'slopes.'"[124] He later apologized.

Another incident arose when an all-white fraternity at the University of Virginia decided to give a party with a Fiji Islander theme.[125] In keeping with the theme, the fraternity, an equal opportunity offender, posted a sign near the door warning that no "short *wops*" would be allowed to enter.[126] After a public outcry by campus minority groups, the fraternity president complained, "It bothers us that we have to defend ourselves against racism when we know we are not racist."[127] In his song, "They Don't Care About Us," Michael Jackson sings, "Jew me, sue me, everybody do me, kick me, *kike* me, don't you black or white me."[128] After a public outcry, Jackson apologized: "Unfortunately, my choice of words have unintentionally hurt the very people I want to stand in solidarity with. I just want you all to know how strongly I am committed to tolerance, peace and love, and I apologize to anyone who might have been hurt."[129]

Today, the harm of such racial epithets is being recognized. Scrabble, a popular board game, has recently deleted them from its dictionary.[130] A high school in Illinois changed its team name from Chinks to Dragons.[131] Perhaps the comical lines of Monty Python's song "Never Be Rude to an Arab" sum the new attitude up best:

> *Never be rude to an Arab,*
> *An Israeli, or Saudi, or Jew.*
> *Never be rude to an Irishman,*
> *No matter what you do.*
> *Never poke fun at a Nigger,*
> *A Spic, or a Wop, or Kraut.*
> *And never poke fun at . . . (BOOM!!!)*[132]

Chink, kike, spic, and *wop* are harmful because of the history of hate they embody and the continued animosity they symbolize. Using such words compounds racial tension and violence.

JUDICIAL TREATMENT OF RACIAL EPITHETS

Let us now examine how the terms *chink, kike, spic,* and *wop* have been treated in court proceedings within the United States. As will be seen, the overwhelming majority of such cases have concerned charges of bias or hate.[133]

The Constitution

The First Amendment of the Constitution has seen some of its most enduring challenges come from the use of racial epithets.[134] We will examine three examples: fighting words, libel, and hate crimes.

Fighting Words

One category of speech not protected by the First Amendment is fighting words. Not an "essential part of any exposition of ideas, [such words] are of such slight social value as a step to truth that any benefit that may be derived from them is clearly outweighed by the social interest in order and morality."[135] The fighting-words doctrine is said not to ban the content of speech, but merely a particular—inflammatory—mode of expression.[136] Are racial epithets, standing alone, without more context, fighting words? In *Terminiello v. City of Chicago*, the Supreme Court defined fighting words as ones "likely to produce a clear and present danger of a serious substantive evil that rises far above public inconvenience, annoyance, or unrest."[137] The majority opinion ruled that a Chicago statute that criminalized speech that breached the peace was overbroad, since much speech is inherently provocative and challenging. The majority required that the words constitute a "clear and present danger."[138] Thus, the decision never reached whether the words in the particular case were of the fighting variety. Those words were, "Yes, send the Jews back to Russia, Kill the Jews, Dirty *kikes*," while a mob stood waiting.[139] The dissent was astonished that the majority did not understand that such speech presented a clear danger.[140]

Libel/Defamation

Another category of unprotected speech is libel or defamation—untrue, damaging statements made against another.[141] The courts have been unwilling to find that calling someone a racial epithet, not even "slimy *kike*"[142] or a *chink*, stated a cause of action for libel.[143] The courts have usually required some kind of tangible injury before granting relief. Indeed, in one case, *Goetz v. Kunstler*, the plaintiff sued for defamation when the defendant told others that the plaintiff was racist.[144] The court denied the claim when evidence showed that the plaintiff had said, "[T]he only way we're going to clean up this street is to get rid of the *spics*. . . . "[145]

Hate Crimes

Courts once demonstrated hostility toward hate crime statutes as an intrusion on free speech. "For example, if A strikes B in the face he commits a criminal battery. However, should A add a word such as *nigger, honkey, jew, mick, kraut, spic,* or *queer,* the crime becomes a felony, and A will be punished not for his conduct alone—a misdemeanor—but for using the spoken word. . . . [T]he necessity to use speech to prove this intentional selection threatens to chill free speech."[146] The Supreme Court has not followed this lead, holding that statutes that punish bias-motivated crimes are permissible under the Constitution.[147] Since hate crime statutes merely increase punishment in light of the mental state of the perpetrator—something that is very common in the criminal law—they easily withstand First Amendment scrutiny.[148] Numerous hate crime statues have been enacted across the nation,[149] and cases applying hate crime statutes have found that the use of a racial epithet by a criminal has been highly probative of racial bias-motivation.[150]

INTENTIONAL INFLICTION OF EMOTIONAL DISTRESS

Other times, courts consider legal actions against hate speakers not to raise significant constitutional problems. Intentional infliction of emotional distress is a tort action for emotional and emotionally related physical damages. To prevail, the plaintiff must prove conduct that is "outrageous in character, and so extreme in degree, as to go beyond all possible bounds of decency and to be regarded as atrocious, and utterly intolerable in a civilized community."[151] The distress must be "so severe that no reasonable [person] could be expected to endure it."[152] Liability "does not extend to mere insults, indignities, threats, annoyances, petty oppressions, or other trivialities"; instead conduct must violate every standard of decent behavior.[153]

Most courts refuse to find that the use of a single racial epithet, by itself, constitutes intentional infliction of emotional distress. In *Leibowitz v. Bank Leumi Trust Company of New York*, an appellate court found that when an employee was repeatedly called *kike* at work, this did not suffice for summary judgment on a charge of intentional infliction of emotional distress.[154] The court noted that "the use of any religious, ethnic or racial slur must be strongly disapproved and condemned," but "the fact that we view the alleged conduct as being deplorable and reprehensible does not necessarily lead to the conclusion that it arose to such a level that the law must provide a remedy. It is manifestly neither practical nor desirable for the law to provide a remedy against any and all activity which an individual might find annoying."[155] The dissent disagreed and submitted that "the law should never suffer an injury and damage without a remedy" and "[I]t will be for the trier of the facts to determine whether such injuries were actually suffered, and whether the conduct of the defendant was such that it may be said that it went beyond all reasonable bounds of decency."[156]

In *Tarino v. Kraft Foodservice*, a district court found that when a party was repeatedly called *wop* by another, that such remarks "are regrettably all too common," and "[g]iven their currency, reasonable people must learn to endure them."[157] Courts have determined that some additional atrocious behavior must occur to sustain a claim of intentional infliction of emotional distress.[158] California courts have been an exception to this general rule. In *Jones v. Hirschberger*, the court recognized that "use of a racial epithet can support a cause of action for intentional infliction of emotional distress,"[159] because such epithets "have the purpose to disparage, to demean, to humiliate and to hurt."[160]

EMPLOYMENT

In the area of employment discrimination, Title VII is the leading federal statute. Title VII, and its state-law equivalents, prohibit discrimination on the basis of race or sex with respect to the "compensation, terms, conditions, or privileges of employment."[161] Under them, employees can sue for discrimination, a hostile work environment, or disparate treatment.

A hostile work environment exists "[w]hen the workplace is permeated with discriminatory intimidation, ridicule, and insult that is sufficiently severe or pervasive to alter the conditions of the victim's employment."[162] Conduct that is "merely offensive" and "not severe or pervasive enough to create an objectively hostile or abusive work environment—an environment that a reasonable person would find hostile or abusive—is beyond Title VII's purview."[163] Title VII "comes into play before the harassing conduct leads to a nervous breakdown."[164] "Harassed employees do not have to be Jackie Robinson, nobly turning the other cheek and remaining unaffected in the face of constant degradation. They are held only to a standard of reasonableness."[165] The use of racial epithets must be so severe that it creates a pervasive environment; language that merely shows disrespect and prejudice is not enough.[166]

To establish a pervasively hostile atmosphere, a victim must prove more than a few isolated incidents of racial animosity.[167] It must appear either that a single incident was extraordinarily severe, or that a series of incidents was "sufficiently continuous and concerted" to have altered the conditions of her employment.[168] Rarely is one racial epithet enough.[169] In *Risinger v. Ohio Bureau of Workers' Compensation*, the district court had found that being called *chink* on one occasion was not enough to find a hostile work environment.[170] On review, the Sixth Circuit did not disagree, but found that the district made an improper factual finding. The victim had been called *chink* on more than one occasion so that a hostile workplace could be inferred.[171] While no "magic number" of epithets must appear, the use of repeated racial epithets must be sufficiently pervasive to create an abusive milieu.[172] For example, an employee who was referred to as *spic* several times by several employees established a "concerted pattern of harassment" in violation of Title VII.[173]

Where a racial epithet is hurled by a boss or supervisor, courts have been more willing to find a hostile work environment. "Perhaps no single act can more quickly alter the conditions of employment and create an abusive working environment than the use of an unambiguously racial epithet . . . by a supervisor in the presence of his subordinates."[174] A "reasonable Puerto Rican would find a workplace in which her boss repeatedly called her a 'dumb *spic*' and told her that she should stay home, go on welfare, and collect food stamps like the rest of the '*spics*' to be hostile."[175] And, in a major recent decision brought under a state statute similar to Title VII, the California Supreme Court affirmed a finding of discrimination in a case brought by seventeen Latino workers subjected to years of abuse and slurs at

> ## Aguilar v. Avis Rent A Car System, Inc.,
> ## 21 Cal.4th 121, 980 P.2d 846, 87 Cal.Rptr.2d 132 (2001).
>
> For the reasons that follow, we hold that a remedial injunction prohibiting the continued use of racial epithets in the workplace does not violate the right to freedom of speech if there has been a judicial determination that the use of such epithets will contribute to the continuation of a hostile or abusive work environment and therefore will constitute employment discrimination.

the hands of the Avis Corporation and three supervisors.[176] The court also found that imposing liability for hate speech did not violate the First Amendment.

When racial epithets are wielded by fellow employees, liability attaches to employers only if the victim can show that the employer knew or should have known about the harassment and failed to remedy the situation.[177] When an employee complained of being called a *spic* by a fellow employee and the supervisor did nothing, a Title VII violation was found.[178] Of course, when an employee is called *spic* by both fellow employees and supervisors, employer liability is highly likely.[179]

When a racial epithet is not directly targeted at a particular employee, it can still satisfy the requirement of a hostile work environment. "[A] racial epithet need not be directed at a plaintiff in order to contribute to a hostile work environment."[180] Where the term *spic* was used in the presence of a Latina employee, this created a hostile work environment even though the epithet was not directed toward her.[181] Even when the term *chink* was used in front of a black employee, it contributed to a hostile work environment for that worker.[182] But where a fellow employee used the term *kike*, not referring to the plaintiff nor in her presence, no hostile environment was found.[183] "[I]t is a fact of life that social, ethnic, religious, and racial distinction are frequently drawn. The Archie Bunkers of this world, within limitations, still may assert their biased view. We have not yet reached the point where we have taken from individuals the right to be prejudiced, so long as such prejudice does not evidence itself in discrimination."[184] One court went even farther: "[Racial epithets] may provide ventilation for suppressed hostility and fear. Comradeship among soldiers and fellow workers is often based upon insults designed in part to disguise affection."[185]

To prove disparate *treatment* under Title VII, an employee must prove that he or she was subject to a materially adverse employment action (that is, firing, non-hiring, non-promotion) due to intentional discrimination.[186] Intentional discrimination is proven if the employee can show that the action was taken because of the employee's race.[187] Court cases have required more than just the use of racial epithets by a superior to show intent. A plaintiff must show that the discrimination "actually played a role in the employer's decisionmaking process and had a determinative influence on the outcome."[188] Intent was found in a case where an Asian professor was not promoted, and suffered other actions, after a supervisor had stated on a prior occasion, "two *Chinks*" in the pharmacology department are "more than enough."[189] But intent was not found in another firing even though the employee had been called a *wop* by supervisors on numerous occasions.[190] Use of *chink* to refer to an employee was merely a stray remark, "unconnected to the process by which the [plaintiff's] hours and job assignments were controlled."[191]

The courts, on the other hand, have had no problem when an employer punishes an employee for using a racial epithet. Whatever protection such speech has outside the workplace, it does not receive the same protection within it. Allowing otherwise would pose great difficulty for an employer attempting to maintain a non-hostile work environment.[192]

USE OF RACIAL EPITHET BY WITNESS IN COURT

The decision whether to admit or exclude evidence in a trial is left to the court's discretion; evidence should only be excluded if its prejudicial effect outweighs its probative value.[193] In *Bullard v. Florida*, a Florida district court restricted the use of a racial epithet by a witness when describing an event.[194] The district judge ruled that the word *chink* in witness testimony would be irrelevant and do nothing more than outrage a jury. The appellate court disagreed:

It is up to the witnesses, including the accused, to tell their versions of the facts and up to the jury to decide what is believable and what really occurred. It is not up to the judge to edit, censor or in any way change a witness's testimony. So what if the words allegedly said are inflammatory? So what if distasteful language, or gruesome pictures or horrid accounts are put in front of the triers of the facts? If those circumstances are what a witness says occurred then so be it. A courtroom is often not the place for the genteel. It is a place where raw human emotions, grisly and morbid accounts and disgusting filthy language are often brought forth. If the facts include these distasteful elements then they do. It's the facts which count, not the sensibilities of the persons hearing them.[195]

Taylor v. Metzger, 706 A.2d 685 (N.J. 1998)

In 1972, plaintiff Carrie Taylor began working as a sheriff's officer in the office of the Burlington County Sheriff. On January 31, 1992, Taylor, who is African American, was at the Burlington County Police Academy for firearms training. . . . While there, she encountered defendant Henry Metzger and Undersheriff Gerald Isham. Taylor said hello, and, in response, Metzger turned to Isham and stated: "There's the jungle bunny." Isham laughed. Plaintiff believed the remark to be a demeaning and derogatory racial slur, but she did not reply. She became a "nervous wreck," immediately began crying, and went to the bathroom.

In this case, defendant's remark had an unambiguously demeaning racial message that a rational factfinder could conclude was sufficiently severe to contribute materially to the creation of a hostile work environment. The term defendant used, "jungle bunny," is patently a racist slur, and is ugly, stark and raw in its opprobrious connotation. . . . See Mari Matsuda, Public Response to Racist Speech, 87 Mich. L. Rev. 2330, 2338 (1989) ("However irrational racist speech may be, it hits right at the emotional place where we feel the most pain.")

In the case of a defendant charged with arson, the defendant argued she lacked specific intent to commit the charged crime because she was intoxicated at the time of the events. During detention after arrest the defendant was placed in the same room as a Latina prisoner. The defendant called the prisoner a *spic*. The court allowed the use of the term *spic*, over defendant's objections, finding that the ability of the defendant to identify the race of another person and the "clarity of [the] speech" by which she did it rebutted an intoxication defense.[196]

In *State v. Henke*, the court found that defendant's use of *chink* to refer to a man he had assaulted was admissible because its probative value outweighed any prejudicial effect when the term was used to show motive for the assault.[197] In *Port Drum Co. v. Evans Cooperage of Houston, Inc.*, the court found that allowing evidence that the defendant called the plaintiff a *kike* in a breach of contract claim would be overly prejudicial, when the probative value of the evidence was low. When the jury could already determine the defendant's "malice" toward the plaintiff from the defendant's own testimony that he "disliked" the plaintiff, thought the plaintiff was "incompetent," and "wanted to get even in the future," admitting the use of *kike* "would have been cumulative" and had an "inflammatory effect."[198] Apparently, the court believed that *kike* represents little more than ordinary dislike toward another.

USE OF RACIAL EPITHET BY COURT OFFICIAL

By Judge
The California Supreme Court held that a certain Judge Stevens's repeated use of the term *spic* when referring to Hispanics, with counsel and court personnel during in-chambers conferences, warranted public censure, even though evidence demonstrated that Stevens performed his judicial duties fairly and free from actual bias.[199]

By Attorney
Where a plaintiff's attorney made false claims that the defense attorney called the plaintiff a "dirty *spick*," the court found moral turpitude warranting professional sanction.[200]

By Jury

Courts have found that where a jury was motivated by racial bias, this so offends fundamental fairness that a defendant is entitled to a new trial.[201] Claims that a juror used a racial epithet can show bias, but the defendant bears the burden to prove that the language was used and evidenced racial bias.[202] In *Commonwealth v. Laguer*, the court found that racial bias was not proven when, out of four jurors who testified, two testified the term *spic* was used during deliberations and two others that they did not recall it. The court found that the two jurors who recalled *spic* being used were not credible since their accounts of who said the term were contradictory. A dissent argued that even though the juror accounts were in contradiction, such testimony tended to prove that the term was used and showed bias no matter who used it.[203]

SENTENCING AND CULPABILITY

Victimization by racial epithets has also affected defendants at sentencing or played a part in determining their culpability. "[E]vidence about the defendant's background and character is relevant [at sentencing] because of the belief, long held by this society, that defendants who commit criminal acts that are attributable to a disadvantaged background, or to emotional and mental problems, may be less culpable than defendants who have no such excuse."[204] In *Karis v. Calderon*, the Ninth Circuit found that defense counsel failed to adequately investigate a defendant's troubled childhood and present such evidence in mitigation during the penalty phase following a conviction of first-degree murder and rape.[205] The court found that evidence that the defendant's stepfather "never treated [the defendant] like a son, and called him 'you little *wop*' more often than he called him by his name . . ." was "substantial and wrenching evidence" of the defendant's "violent and abusive childhood" and would be "highly relevant to mitigation."[206]

While courts might find that childhood reactions to being called a particular racial epithet can reduce culpability, they do not always give the same leniency to adults. In *State v. Tran*, an Asian male killed a Caucasian male after the latter had called him and his friends *chinks*. The jury and court affirmed that being called an "unkind word" was "certainly . . . not sufficient provocation to deprive an average person of his self-control and cool reflection," and sustained a second-degree murder charge, rejecting the possibility of manslaughter.[207]

An ex-boyfriend stabbed his ex-girlfriend's new Asian boyfriend because he felt that the new man reflected poorly on him. He later stated in a police interview that the officer would have done the same thing if he had "caught his woman with a *chink*."[208] Another defendant stabbed a man he had recently met in the chest and cut his neck to steal the man's money and drugs. The defendant later told a friend that he had killed a *chink*.[209] In a brutal gang beating, "The defendants set out with their friends to inflict serious harm on unsuspecting persons who had caused them inconvenience. They ambushed [the victim] and brutally beat him with crude weapons. Afterwards, the group drove to a nearby fast food restaurant, ate hamburgers and reveled in the success of their 'hunt.' [A defendant] recalled his encounter with [the victim] two years earlier, adding that this time he was 'fucking him up . . . getting him good.' [Another defendant] boasted that he 'got them good,' 'bashing that mother fucker.' The next night he said he 'fucked up them *Spics* with a hammer.'"[210] Needless to say, these remarks played a large part in finding the assailants guilty.

Governmental Immunity

Many government employees receive official immunity from suits when performing government duties. But no such exception applies if the employee acts outside the scope of his employment, for example with malice toward another. In *Piro v. Franklin Township*, the court defined malice as the "willful and intentional design to do wrong" and found that a city employee who referred to a citizen as a *wop* acted with malice and was not protected by governmental immunity.[211]

Military

When a superior officer's "conduct falls below the standards a soldier has every right to expect" in dealing with a subordinate, the officer is stripped "of the mantle of special protection afforded to him by Congress."[212] In one case, a military court found that if a superior officer called a subordinate something so "profane and insulting as *kike*, *wop*, *nigger*, *spick*, *polock* and *jap*," the superior officer would temporarily lose his "cloak of authority."[213] In *United States v. Johnson*, the court went even further to find that when a black subordinate was called *boy*, the context made the word the equivalent of *nigger*. Upon proof that the subordinate assaulted an officer after being called *boy*, the court dropped the charge from assault on a superior officer to simply assault.[214]

IMMIGRATION

Asylum

Political asylum can be granted under the discretion of the U.S. attorney general if it is determined that an alien is a refugee.[215] A refugee is defined as one who is unable to return to his country of origin "because of persecution or a well-founded fear of persecution on account of race, religion, nationality, membership in a particular group, or political opinion."[216] The mere use of racial epithets is not enough to demonstrate persecution. In *Zviagilsky v. Naturalization Service*, the petitioner alleged that he had received death threats in the Ukraine, had been repeatedly called a *kike*, and that the government failed to remedy the threats. While the U.S. court believed the petitioner's allegations, they found that, "[t]he discrimination and mistreatment he complains of are at the hands of private individuals and exist in all societies. . . . The failure of a government to stop acts of hatred before they occur can hardly be viewed as persecution."[217] By contrast, in *Korablina v. Immigration and Naturalization Services*, the court found that physical attacks on the petitioner's relatives, who were referred to as *kikes* by the attackers, plus a belief that government provided no protection, were enough to show persecution and that the petitioner's treatment was no "minor disadvantage or trivial inconvenience."[218]

Deportation

Under Section 340(a) of the Immigration and Nationality Act, a person who has been admitted to citizenship of the United States may be denaturalized if he or she willfully concealed or misrepresented material facts in order to procure naturalization. In *United States v. Sokolov*, a court found that an immigrant's representation that he had "not written one single fascist or pro-facist line" was a material misrepresentation when in fact the immigrant was employed by the Nazis as a propagandist and had written numerous works referring to the evils of *kike* world domination and called for the destruction of *kikes*.[219]

UNCLEAN HANDS

When a party to a contract dispute sues for specific performance, courts sometimes require that the party come in with "clean hands" before it will grant specific performance or other equitable remedies. In *Briggs v. Sylvestri,* the court found that a contracting party who called the other a *wop*, although blameworthy, did not do enough to suffer unclean hands.[220]

COPYRIGHT

The doctrine of fair use in copyright law allows subsequent authors to make limited uses of a copyrighted work. The doctrine embodies First Amendment claims under copyright. In *New Era Publications Int'l v. Henry Holt and Co.,* the court found that when a quotation is used by an author merely to "free ride on the creative talents" of another, fair use will not be found. But where the quotation is used to demonstrate a quality of the original writer, the use will be fair. The court concluded that a quote of L. Ron Hubbard's *Asia Diaries,* "The trouble with China is, there are too many *Chinks* here," was used to "show Hubbard's bigotry, bias and coarse lack of taste,"[221] and thus was more than mere expression. The Second Circuit found that such a distinction for fair use was not necessary, but still found the quote was fair use.[222]

CHILD CUSTODY

In *Rivera v. Argot,* a child custody case where one parent was alleged to have called his child a *spic*, the court concluded, "a court may not assume that because a child will encounter prejudice in one parent's custody, their best interests will be served by giving [the child] to the other parent." The court ordered joint custody on the theory that both parents were fit, "that no couple, divorced or intact, agrees on every aspect in the upbringing of a child," and that this child needed two loving parents. Is it not remarkable how little weight the court gave to the effect of being called *spic*, especially by a parent?[223]

FAIR HOUSING AND SCHOOLS

A defendant was found to violate a state Fair Housing Act when he refused to rent due to an applicant's race and told a hearing officer that real estate agents were bringing in "too many . . . *spics*."[224] In another case, a school was found to violate a similar statute when an Asian student complained about being called *chink* only to have the school send him home, ostensibly for his own protection, rather than solve the problem.[225] A federal court found that the school failed to provide the student a "learning environment free from racial and national origin discrimination."[226]

Later cases have amplified on this "hostile environment" doctrine, borrowed from employment law. In a case discussed elsewhere (see Chapter 5), an Arizona school was held potentially liable for tolerating student-on-student verbal harassment including the word "nigger." And a recent decision (*Davis v. Monroe County Board of Education*) agreed, in a case dealing with gender, not race discrimination. A dissent warned that the principle the court embraced could allow students to sue their schools for tolerating student-on-student hate speech, and further warned that colleges and schools are now even more likely than before to enact speech codes.

NON-JUDICIAL REMEDIES

Not every response to hate speech takes the form of filing an individual action in court. As discussed elsewhere in this book (see Chapter 8), minority groups disgusted with a racist logo, symbol, or sports mascot have staged protests, organized boycotts, or challenged the right of the organization licensing, for example, a racist shirt to hold an exclusive, federally protected trademark. Minority organizations upset with media stereotyping have formed a national coalition to press for a greater minority presence on television and a reduction in harmful stereotypes. Earlier, a national Mexican American organization threatened to file a

> ## Aguilar v. Avis Rent A Car System, Inc., 21 Cal.4th 121, 980 P.2d 846 (1999).
>
> A jury found that defendants had engaged in employment discrimination, in part by permitting plaintiffs to be the target of racial epithets repeatedly spoken by a fellow employee. In addition to awarding damages, the trial court issued an injunction prohibiting the offending employee from using such epithets in the future. Defendants argue that such an injunction constitutes a prior restraint that violates their constitutional right to freedom of speech. For the reasons that follow, we hold that a remedial injunction prohibiting the continued use of racial epithets in the workplace does not violate the right to freedom of speech if there has been a judicial determination that the use of such epithets will contribute to the continuation of a hostile or abusive work environment and therefore will constitute employment discrimination.

$610 million lawsuit against the Frito-Lay Corporation for using Frito Bandito, a cartoon figure, advertising its corn chip products. Although the suit was never filed, the campaign raised consciousness of the harmfulness of racist logos and cartoons and spurred later efforts by shareholders to work "from the inside" to temper corporate policies and advertising that created a racially offensive climate for viewers.

RACIAL EPITHETS: A LEGACY OF VIOLENCE

As the above cases show, *chink*, *kike*, *spic*, and *wop* have had long and checkered careers. And in egregious cases, courts provide redress for those victimized by them. While judges might not agree on how to deal with such troublesome words, they do agree the words cause harm.

Although some courts are reluctant to impose the full power of the judiciary against speakers of racially harmful words because of the be-

Harris v. Forklift Systems, Inc., 510 U.S. 17 (1993).

The Magistrate found that, throughout Harris' time at Forklift, Hardy often insulted her because of her gender and often made her the target of unwanted sexual innuendos. Hardy told Harris on several occasions, in the presence of other employees, "You're a woman, what do you know" and "We need a man as the rental manager"; at least once he told her she was "a dumb ass woman."

A discriminatorily abusive work environment, even one that does not seriously affect employees' psychological well–being, can and often will detract from employees' job performance, discourage employees from remaining on the job, or keep them from advancing in their careers. Moreover, even without regard to these tangible effects, the very fact that the discriminatory conduct was so severe or pervasive that it created a work environment abusive to employees because of their race, gender, religion, or national origin offends Title VII's broad rule of workplace equality.

lief that this would impair freedom of speech, racial epithets exhibit a history unlike that of other scathing words. Such words embody hate, but their hate is reinforced by a history of social practice and subjugation. Protecting them does not add to the freedom of speech, nor does punishing those who utter them subtract from it. As mentioned in the opening passages of this chapter, one recent author holds that not all uses of racial epithets are meant to be—and are—harmful. But a Mexican who enjoys being called *spic* or does not mind it has an easy recourse—not to file a complaint. Others, who feel they have been harmed, deserve their day in court.

TAKING OWNERSHIP VERSUS STOPPING WOUNDS

Randall Kennedy, in his book *Nigger*, cited examples where *nigger* was not used to harm.[227] Kennedy supported such uses as a way of taking ownership of the term away from those who would use it to harm.[228] His hopes for the word *nigger* resemble in some respects what the homosexual community has done with the term *queer*. The slogan "We're here, we're queer, get used to it" suggests an indifference to being called queer. It also suggests that it is non-queers, rather than queers, who must change to accommodate the new usage.[229] Kennedy hoped that white supremacists will come to lament, "I resent you people using that word. That's our word for making fun of you! We need it!!"[230]

Can this approach work with *chink*, *kike*, *spic*, and *wop*? Unlike *nigger*, Asians, Jews, Latinos, and Italians rarely use these epithets among themselves. There is no *nigga* equivalent in the terms used to describe Asians, Jews, Latinos, and Italians. What's up, my (blank)? While filling the blank with *nigga* could be conceivable in today's society, filling in the blank with *chink*, *kike*, *spic*, or *wop* seems out of place and wrong. *Nigger* was developed as a racial epithet in the 1700s; *chink*, *kike*, *spic*, and *wop*, in the 1900s. Is the use of racial epithets an evolution? Is it a positive one? Perhaps we must wait another two hundred years until the day a Jew says to another Jew, "What's up, my *kike*?" Or, this may never happen. In the meantime, the wisest course is to stop these words and the harm they cause now. *Chink*, *kike*, *spic*, and *wop* have no meaning but to promote exclusion, no use but to incite racial supremacy and hate.

QUESTIONS FOR DISCUSSION, CHAPTER 4

1. Many legally cognizable harms—for example, threat, defamation, harassment, conspiracy, deceptive advertising, fraud, and many others—turn on the speaking of certain words. Why, then, do some resist recognizing a new harm for hate speech?

2. As this chapter and Chapter 1 have shown, the law already affords relief to the victim of hate speech under a number of existing torts (causes of action), such as intentional infliction of emotional distress, defamation, assault, and hostile environment. Why, then, not a new, freestanding remedy— "racism as a tort"?

3. When courts afford relief for racist language, are they providing a remedy for the language spoken, or for some other, underlying harm for which the language was just an accompaniment or outward manifestation?
4. Can a term like *nigger*, *spic*, or *kike* ever have an innocent, or noninjurious, meaning?
5. Can the same words ("You _____") spoken by one person or in one setting be extremely offensive or damaging, but less so when said by another, in a different situation?
6. How could a plaintiff ever prove damages if there is no broken arm or other observable injury to show?

CLASS EXERCISE

Name and write on the blackboard as many damaging words as you can for:

African Americans
Latinos
Asians
Indians
Gays and lesbians
Whites
Women

When you run out of words, examine the size and contours of each list. What patterns emerge?

RECOMMENDED READING, CHAPTER 4

Jack Balkin, *Free Speech and Hostile Environments*, 99 Colum. L. Rev. 2295 (1999).
  Bob Jones University v. United States, 461 U.S. 574 (1983).
  Brown v. Board of Education, 347 U.S. 483 (1954).

Roland F. Chase, *Recovery and Damages for Emotional Distress Resulting from Racial, Ethnic, or Religious Abuse or Discrimination*, 40 A.L.R.3d 1290 (1971).

Richard Delgado, *Words that Wound: A Tort Action for Racial Insults, Epithets, and Name-Calling*, 17 Harv. C.R.–C.L. L. Rev. 133 (1982).

Thomas Emerson, *The System of Freedom of Expression* (1970).

Stanley Fish, *There's No Such Thing as Free Speech, and It's a Good Thing, Too* (1994).

Kent Greenawalt, *Speech, Crime, and the Uses of Language* (1989).

Steven J. Heyman, *Righting the Balance: An Inquiry into the Foundations and Limits of Freedom of Expression*, 78 B.U. L. Rev. 1275 (1998).

Randall Kennedy, *Nigger: The Strange Career of A Troublesome Word* (2002).

Calvert Magruder, *Mental and Emotional Disturbances in the Law of Torts*, 49 Harv. L. Rev. 1033 (1936).

William L. Prosser, *Handbook of the Law of Torts*, § 1, at 3–4, § 10, at 36, § 54, at 327–328 (fourth edition 1971).

William L. Prosser, *Intentional Infliction of Emotional Distress: A New Tort*, 37 Mich. L. Rev. 874 (1939).

R.A.V. v. St. Paul, 112 S. Ct. 2538 (1992).

Restatement (Second) of Torts § 46 (1965).

University of Pennsylvania v. E.E.O.C., 110 S. Ct. 577 (1990).

U.S. Constitution, First Amendment.

Jamie L. Wacks, *A Proposal for Community-Based Racial Reconciliation in the United States through Personal Stories*, 7 Va. J. Soc. Pol. & L. 195 (2000).

Notes

1. Randall Kennedy, *Nigger: The Strange Career of a Troublesome Word* (2002).
2. Ibid.
3. Ibid. at 175–176.
4. Ibid. at 112.
5. Ibid. at 55 (quoting *Towne v. Eisner*, 245 U.S. 418, 425 [1918]).
6. Ibid. at 175.

7. Ibid.

8. Richard A. Spears, *Forbidden American English*, 34 (1990); *Oxford English Dictionary*, second edition (1989).

9. Leslie Dunkling, *A Dictionary of Epithets and Terms of Address*, 71 (1990); Richard A. Spears, *Slang and Euphemism* (1981).

10. Irving L. Allen, *Unkind Words*, 21 (1990).

11. Kim Pearson, Interactive Dictionary of Racial Language (found at http://kpearson.faculty.tcnj.edu/Dictionary/dictionary.htm).

12. Tony Thorne, *The Dictionary of Contemporary Slang* (1990).

13. Bill Sing, ed., *Asian Pacific Americans: A Handbook on How to Cover and Portray Our Nation's Fastest Growing Minority Group*, 49 (1989).

14. Such *chink* noise is traditionally mocked in cartoons and movie stereotypes of Chinese or Japanese characters. Ilhyung Lee, *Consciousness and Minority Scholars*, 33 Conn. L. Rev. 535, n.209 (2001).

15. Michael Sean Quinn, *Patrick's Case*, 5 Tex. J. Women & L. 101, 107 (1995).

16. See Pearson, supra.

17. See *Oxford English Dictionary*, supra (less common meanings of *chink* include a convulsive gasp for breath, a crack, pieces of money, short for the flower Chinkerinchee, to open or crack, or to twist).

18. See *Slang and Euphemism*, supra.

19. "We ...had a good passage to Hong Kong. When we arrived, the first Chinese war with Britain had broken out, and there was every appearance of plenty of fun to be shortly had with the *Chinkies*." William J. Barry, *Up and Down*, 51 (1879).

20. For other early uses, see Boxall, *Bushrangers*, 241 (1899) ("They rode straight to the Chinese camp at Wombat, 'to give the Chinkies a lesson.'"); *Munsey's Magazine*, Volume XIV, at 536 (1901) ("The leader suggested the 'chink,' and to the one Chinese laundry . . . the little band departed."); *Westminster Gazette*, September 6, 1905, at 6 ("The farmers getting a reward of [one pound] for each 'Chinkey' they turn over to the police"); *War Slang*, Athenaeum, August 8, 1919, at 727 ("'Chinks' for Chinese laborers."); J. S. Fletcher, *Ravensdene Court*, 173 (1922) ("'A Chink?' 'He means a Chinaman,' I said."); D. H. Lawrence, *Kangaroo*, 351 (1923) ("Brother Brown and Chinky and all the rest; the Indians in India, the nigger in Tranvaal."); *Chamber's Journal*, 552 (1926) ("The towns, small or large, possessed from one to hundreds of 'Chink' laundries."); R. Hyde, *Passport to Hell*, 229 (1936) ("The little Chinks hated the Boche like hell."); J. Durak, *Coast to Coast 1967–68*, 99 (1969) ("We used to have a couple staying with us. Chinks, they were, medical students."). For further examples, see Interactive Dictionary, supra.

21. Alexander J. Boyd, *Old Colonials*, 233, (1882).

22. In a story about the frontier days of America, a frontiersman remarks, "There's ce'tainly something doing at the Silver Dollar this glad mo'ning. Chinks, greasers, and several other kinds of citizens driftin' that way, not to mention white men." Upon arriving at the Silver Dollar, the author described the scene: "It was filled with a motley crowd of miners, vaqueros, tourists, cattlemen, Mexican, Chinese, and a sample of the rest of the heterogeneous population of the Southwest." William MacLeod Raine, *Bucky O'Connor*, 51–52 (1910).

23. "For these unions, class identity was synonymous with white racial identity: Union shops were white and anti-Asian; non-white shops were nonunion." *See* Florence C. Lister and Robert H. Lister, *Chinese Sojourners in Territorial Prescott*, 31 J. S.W. 1, 17, 43 (1989); Marion Crain, *Colorblind Unionism*, 49 UCLA L. Rev. 1313, 1322 (2002).

24. See Lister, *supra* (White store shops would post signs asking, "Do the Chinese support the schools: Nit! Do the *chinks* spend their money where they make it? Nein! Are they a credit to the country or an honor to the town? Nixey! Then why not send your clothes to a *white institution*? Hey? The Prescott Steam Laundry invites your patronage. D. M. Clark, Proprietor [*emphasis added*]).

25. A union magazine described unionized white food service industry workers as "Skilled, Well-paid Bartenders and Culinary Workers Wear Them [clean garments]. Chinks, Japs and Incompetent Labor Don't." Dana Frank, *Purchasing Power: Consumer Organizing, Gender, and the Seattle Labor Movement, 1919–1929*, 230 (1994). Quoting Dorothy Sue Cobble, *Sisters in the Craft: Waitresses and Their Unions in the Twentieth Century*, 158 (1986), Ph.D. dissertation, Stanford University.

26. Debora L. Threedy, *Fish Story: Alaska Packers Association v. Domenico*, Utah L. Rev. 185, n.171 (2000).

27. "The reliance of the canning industry on manual labor existed until 1905, when a machine that prepared salmon for canning was first introduced. The machine, in a striking example of the racism of the period, was called the 'Iron Chink'" (emphasis added). It could do the work of thirty to forty Chinese laborers and was a significant improvement in the efficiency of the canning process. See Threedy, supra.

28. Constance Backhouse, *The White Women's Labor Laws: Anti-Chinese Racism in Early Twentieth-Century Canada*, 14 L. & Hist. Rev. 315, 339 (1996) (citing "White Girls in Chinese Cafes," *Regina Leader*, September 25, 1912, at 12; "White Women and Chinese Employers," *Regina Daily Province*, September 24, 1912, at 7).

29. Ibid.

30. Ibid.

31. Ibid.

32. Ibid.

33. See, e.g., "War on Opium—Chink Receives Term in Prison," *Moose Jaw Evening Times*, Oct. 1, 1910, at 8; "Chinks Lose Car of Goods," *Regina Morning Leader*, Apr. 7, 1911, at 12; "Montreal Police Raid Chinatown—Twenty Chink Gamblers Arrested," *Regina Daily Province*, Sept. 24, 1912, at 7; "Chink Follows Pick-Pocket and Gets Back $1,400 Wallet," *Regina Evening Province*, Sept. 17, 1916, at 3; "Distributes Opium through West Canada–Chink Arrested at Moose Jaw," *Regina Daily Province*, Oct. 17, 1912, at 10; "Chinamen in Rush Lake Wreck–Three Coaches Derailed and Fifteen of the Chinks Injured," *Regina Daily Province*, Nov. 20, 1912, at 4.

34. "California became the leader of anti-Asian directives as it responded to the increasing numbers of Asian immigrants residing within its borders. Soon the anti-Asian sentiment became a national phenomenon as popular perceptions of the evil 'chinks' and dirty 'orientals' spread through political campaigns, the media, and education." Su Sun Bai, *Affirmative Pursuit of Political Equality for Asian Pacific Americans: Reclaiming the Voting Rights Act*, 139 U. Pa. L. Rev. 731, n.106 (1991).

35. The book *Nineteen Nineteen* centers on a period immediately following World War I. The author described a Chinese bartender as a "broadfaced Chink with a heart-broken smile like a very old monkey's." John Dos Passos, *Nineteen Nineteen*, 17 (1932).

36. Ronald Takaki, *Strangers From a Different Shore: A History of Asian Americans*, 365 (1989).

37. During Japanese internment, "[p]reviously maligned as the 'heathen Chinee,' 'mice-eaters,' and 'Chinks,' the Chinese were now friends and allies engaged in a heroic common effort against the 'Japs.'" Ibid.

38. During boot camp, racism resulted in the singling out of Asian Pacific American soldiers as *gooks, Japs, chinks*, or *Ho Chi Minh*. Julie Yuki Ralston, *Geishas, Gays and Grunts: What the Exploitation of Asian Pacific Women Reveals About Military Culture and the Legal Ban on Lesbian, Gay and Bisexual Service Members*, 16 L. & Ineq. J. 661, n.51 (1998).

39. See U.S. Commission on Civil Rights, *Civil Rights Issues Facing Asian Americans in the 1990s*, 26–31 (1992).

40. National Asian Pacific American Legal Consortium, *1995 Audit of Violence Against Asian Pacific Americans: The Consequences of Intolerance in America*, 8–9 (third annual report, 1995).

41. This was the well-known case of Vincent Chin. See Robert S. Chang, *Toward An Asian American Legal Scholarship: Critical Race Theory, Post-Structuralism, and Narrative Space*, 81 Cal. L. Rev. 1241, 1252 (1993).

42. National Asian Pacific American Legal Consortium, *1993 Audit of Violence Against Asian Pacific Americans: Anti-Asian Violence, a National Problem* (April 1994), at 8.

43. See National Asian Pacific American Legal Consortium, *supra*.

44. Victor M. Hwang, *Interrelationship Between Anti-Asian Violence and Asian America*, 21 Chicano-Latino L. Rev. 17, 27 (2000).

45. Flyers called for "Chinks and Burger King Out of the Sunset." Ibid.

46. Southern Poverty Law Center, *The Forgotten*, Intelligence Report, spring 2002, at 9–10.

47. See Takaki, supra, at 479.

48. Ibid.

49. Marjorie M. Shultz, *Excellence Lost*, 13 Berkeley Women's L.J. 26, 29 (1998).

50. Garner K. Weng, *How Stella Got Her Character*, 13 Berkeley Women's L.J. 19, 21 (1998).

51. United States Commission on Civil Rights, *Civil Rights Issues Facing Asian Americans in the 1900s*, at 41–42 (1992).

52. *Executive Summary of 1996 Audit*, 5 Asian Pac. Am. L.J. 99, 101 (1998). "I experienced a lot of stuff walking down the street . . . somebody would make a racial comment, like Chink or something or like some sort of racial epitaph, maybe like, go home. . . . I was like . . . this is Michigan. I thought people were supposed to be more open–minded . . . not so ignorant and stuff like that . . . it kind of awakened me . . . that's when I [started] to meet a lot more Asian students like myself . . . and realized that a lot of similar experiences had happened to us." Walter R. Allen and Daniel Solorzano, *Affirmative Action, Educational Equity and Campus Racial Climate: A Case Study of the University of Michigan Law School*, 12 La Raza L.J. 237, 261 (2001).

53. Alternative spelling: *kyke*.

54. See the *Oxford English Dictionary*, supra.

55. Leo Rosten, *The Joys of Yiddish* (1968). Rosten's theory is the only one with a strong weight of oral history. See Pearson, Interactive Dictionary, supra, note 11; Hugh Rawson, *Wicked Words*, 225 (1989).

56. Rosten, supra, at 180.. Rosten's authority for the *kikel* theory is Philip Cowen, who is known as the "dean of immigration inspectors" and was the first editor of the newspaper *American Hebrew*. See Rawson, supra.

57. See *Oxford English Dictionary*, supra.

58. Jonathan Green, *Cassell's Dictionary of Slang* (1998).

59. *Random House Dictionary of English Language* (1966).

60. See *Oxford English Dictionary*.

61. Irving L. Allen, *The Language of Ethnic Conflict* 121 (1983).

62. See Rawson, supra.

63. Paul Jacobs, *Is Curly Jewish?* (1965).

64. See Pearson, supra.

65. Adolf Hitler, *Mein Kampf*, 57 (Ralph Manheim trans., 1971) (1927).

66. Ibid.

67. Sinclair Lewis, *It Can't Happen Here*, 205 (1935). Such hatred can run very deep. In one book, the author described a man "whose twisted life process revolved around a maniacal hatred of Jews [kikes], who is a decaying cesspool of every vile chauvinism and hatred ever invented." See Howard Fast, *The Winston Affair* 27, 86 (1959).

68. See R. L. McCardell, *Show Girl and Her Friends*, 49 (1904) ("And what do you think? He had the impudence to tell me that Louie Zinsheimer was a *kike!*"); O. Henry, *Works*, 1449 (1905) ("Judas . . . I always thought that *Kike's* squeal on his boss was about the lowest-down play that ever happened."); Bronson-Howard, *Enemy to Society*, 290 (1911) ("You keep yer tongue for them as needs it, you kike!"); Grahm, *Poor Immigrants*, 126 (1914) ("I should say for the benefit of English readers that illiterate Russians and Russian Jews are called 'Kikes,' illiterate Italians are 'Wops,' Hungarians are 'Hunkies.' These are rather terms of contempt."); Theodore Dreiser, *Diaries*, 232 (1917) ("Former kikes all, raised to ridiculous heights by wealth!"); F. Hurst, *Humoresque*, 211 (1919) ("A little red-haired kike like her!"); P. Marks, *Plastic Age*, xviii, 201 (1924) ("You go chasing around with kikes and micks."); John Dos Passos, *1919* 164 (1932) ("The little kike behind the desk had never been to sea."); Sinclair Lewis, *It Can't Happen Here*, 204 (1945) ("Why don't you kikes take a tumble to yourselves and get out, beat it . . . and start a real Zion, say in South America?"); Vladimir Nabokov, *Gift*, 179 (1963) ("My better half . . . was for twenty years the wife of a kike and got mixed up with a whole rabble of Jew in-laws."). For further examples, see Interactive Dictionary, supra.

69. Catharine A. MacKinnon, *Pornography as Defamation and Discrimination*, 71 B.U. L. Rev. 793 (1991).

70. Undated letter from S. Weiss of Grand Rapids, Michigan, to Laurie Levenson, professor, Loyola Law School, L.A., a legal commentator on the Rodney King trial (letter on file with Loyola of Los Angeles Law Review).

71. David S. Wyman, *The Abandonment of the Jews: America and the Holocaust*, 14 (1984).

72. Frederick J. Frommer, "Dartmouth Confronts Its Anti-Semitic History," *Valley News* (New Hampshire), November 17, 1997, at 1.

73. During 1928, the KKK hated Jews. In New York, cross-burnings and rallies drawing thousands reminded Catholics and Jews alike that Nassau County was not open to them. The Klan parade in Merrick contained a placard which read "No Koons, Kikes, or Katolics!" William E. Nelson and Norman R. Williams, *Suburbanization and Market Failure: An Analysis of Government Policies Promoting Suburban Growth and Ethnic Assimilation*, Fordham Urb. L.J. 197, 217 (1999).

74. Leon Wieseltier, *Washington Diarist: Machoball Soup*, New Republic, April 24, 1995, at 46 (book review of *Passover*, written by David Mamet).

75. See David Karp, *All Honorable Men*, 74 (1956).

76. John A. Heffernan, "Be-Dad," *McClure's*, June 1912, at 230–231.

77. Ernest Hemingway, *Men Without Women*, 207–213 (1927).

78. Ibid.

79. Alternative spellings: *spick, spik*.

80. See the *Oxford English Dictionary*, supra.

81. Ibid.

82. See Rawson, *Wicked Words*, supra note 55.

83. See *Oxford English Dictionary*, supra (no longer listing *spic* as an Italian).

84. See *Forbidden American English*, supra, at 34.

85. Juan Perea, *Demography and Distrust: An Essay on American Languages, Cultural Pluralism, and Official English*, 77 Minn. L. Rev. 269, 79 (1992). Perea noted the epithet *spic* is one that emphasizes how Latinos speak, as opposed to how they look.

86. See *Oxford English Dictionary*, supra.

87. *American Speech*, 67 (1975).

88. Ernest Hemingway, *Winner Takes Nothing*, 200 (1933).

89. See Thorne, *Contemporary Slang*, supra note 12. See also H. A. Franck, *Zone Policeman*, 88 (1913) ("It was my first entrance into the land of the panamenos, technically known on the Zone as 'Spigoties' and familiarly with a tinge of despite as Spigs."); E. Peixotto, *Our Hispanic Southwest*, 102 (1916) ("The Mexican men they despise and call 'spicks'."); S. Lewis, *Man Who Knew Coolidge*, 116 (1928) ("We need a supply of cheap labor and where get it better than by encouraging these Wops and Hunks and Spigs and so on to raise as many brats as they can?"); William Faulkner, *Knight's Gambit*, 137 (1949) ("I didn't intend that a fortune-hunting Spick shall marry my mother."); F. Scott Fitzgerald, *Tender Is the Night*, 275 (1953) ("'He's a spic!' he said. He was frantic with jealousy."); E. Lacy, *Pity Honest*, ii (1964) ("This is becoming a tough neighborhood full of Spics."); D. E. Westlake, *Nobody's Perfect*, 39 (1977) ("You'd put your kid in school with a lotta niggers and kikes and wops and spics?"). For further examples, see Interactive Dictionary, supra.

90. World Book, "History of Hispanic American Immigration" (found at http://www2.worldbook.com/features/features.asp?feature=cinco&page=html/im migration.htm&direct=yes). Greaser, another derogatory term, entered earlier. See, for example, California's 1855 Vagrancy Act, popularly knows as the Greaser Act.

91. Ernest Peixotto, *Our Hispanic Southwest*, 102 (1916) (interview of Border Patrol officer in El Paso).

92. Ibid.

93. Terri Yuh-lin Chen, *Hate Violence as Border Patrol: An Asian American Theory of Violence*, 7 Asian L.J. 69, 96 (2000).

94. See World Book, supra.

95. Ken Gormley, *Racial Mind-Games and Reapportionment*, 4 U. Pa. J. Const. L. 735, 750 (2002).

96. *Saturday Night Fever* (1977).

97. Ibid.

98. A Latino professor (tenured, full professor) at the University of Colorado at Boulder told the author that his daughter was treated cruelly in Boulder schools and called a "spic." Richard Delgado and Jean Stefancic, *Home-Grown Racism: Colorado's Historic Embrace—and Denial—of Equal Opportunity in Higher Education,* 70 U. Colo. L. Rev. 703, n.701 (1999).

99. *Race Relations on Campus,* J. Blacks Higher Educ., winter 1998/1999, at 142.

100. Lisa Ann Mammel, *Boalt Minorities Get Hate Mail Delivery,* A.B.A. J., May 1995, at 17.

101. Randolph, "Black Students Battle Racism on College Campuses," *Ebony,* December 1988, at 126.

102. *Boalt Minorities,* supra, at 17.

103. *The Case for Abolishing Peremptory Challenges in Criminal Trials,* 21 Harv. C.R.–C.L. L. Rev. 227 (1986).

104. One of those teens, Dylan Klebold, discussed his hatred of "all niggers, spics, Jews, gays, fucking whites," and others he and his confederates believed had abused them or who had failed to defend them. Their hope was to kill as many as 250 people. Nancy Gibbs and Timothy Roche, "The Columbine Tapes," *Time,* December 20, 1999, at 42.

105. See generally "Rivera, Klansmen Arrested in Scuffle," *Advocate* (Baton Rouge, Louisiana), August 17, 1992, at 3A; "Geraldo Won't Be Charged for Punching Heckler," *Advocate* (Baton Rouge, Louisiana), August 31, 1992, at 3A.

106. See Allen, *The Language of Ethnic Conflict,* supra note 61, at 118. See also Spears, *Slang and Euphemism,* supra note 9; *Oxford English Dictionary.*

107. *Language of Ethnic Conflict,* supra, at 118.

108. Ibid.

109. See *Language of Ethnic Conflict,* supra, at 118; Rawson, supra.

110. *Language of Ethnic Conflict,* supra.

111. See Rawson, supra.

112. Arthur C. Train, *Courts and Criminals* (1912). See also George Bernard Shaw, *Apple Court,* 78 (1930) ("What they call an American is only a *wop* pretending to be a Pilgrim Farmer. He is no more Uncle Jonathan than you are John Bull. Magnus. Yes: we live in a world of *wops,* all melting into one another."). See Interactive Dictionary, supra, for further examples.

113. John Higham, *Strangers in the Land: Patterns of American Nativism* 1860–1925, 65 (second edition, 1988).

114. G. P. Benton, "War" Neuroses and Allied Conditions in Ex-Service Men, 77 J. Am. Med. Assoc. 360, 362 (1921).

115. Herman M. Somers and Anne Ramsay Somers, *Workmen's Compensation: Prevention, Insurance, and Rehabilitation of Occupational Disability,*

28–29 (1954). Quoting Alice Hamilton, *Exploring the Dangerous Trades*, 152 (1943). See also Leonard Dinnerstein and David M. Reimers, *Ethnic Americans: A History of Immigration and Assimilation*, 36 (1982), quoted in Mary C. Waters, *Ethnic Options: Choosing Identities in America*, 2 (1990).

116. Sinclair Lewis, *The Man Who Knew Coolidge*, 124 (1928).

117. See Higham, supra. After shooting two *wops*, an accomplice tells the other he shouldn't have done that. The shooter replies, "They're crooks ain't they? They're wops ain't they? Who the hell is going to make any trouble." Ernest Hemingway, *In Our Time,* 17 (1924).

118. Jerome H. Skolnick, *Justice Without Trial* (1966). The year Jackie Robinson integrated major league baseball, Philadelphia Phillies manager Ben Chapman led his players in ugly, racist taunts. Chapman viewed his activity as representing "bench jockeying" in the baseball tradition because "[w]hite rookies, he said, were referred to as wops, dagos, Polacks, and they never complained. Taunting Robinson was no different." Jackie Robinson, *I Never Had It Made*, 16, 59 (1995).

119. R. A. F. Journal, June 26, 1942, at 13 ("The pilots . . . suggested that the '*Wops* were yellow' or that they could not take it through cloud.").

120. Richard Delgado, *Words that Wound: A Tort Action for Racial Insults, Epithets, and Name-Calling*, 17 Harv. C.R.–C.L. L. Rev. 133, n.279 (1982), citing *New York Times*, May 12, 1974, at 1, col. 5).

121. Jack Cheevers, "Vanity Plates: One Man's Slur Is Another Man's Badge," *Los Angeles Times*, August 21, 1990, at A3.

122. Charles R. Lawrence III, *If He Hollers Let Him Go: Regulating Racist Speech on Campus*, Duke L.J. 431, 452 (1990). Even in 1919, it was recognized that *chink, kike, spic*, and *wop* were born of "hatred" and "contempt." Such words demonstrated a "national attitude" toward "foreigners." H. L. Mencken, *The American Language*, 341 (1919).

123. Ilhyung Lee, *Race Consciousness and Minority Scholars*, 33 Conn. L. Rev. 535, n.209 (2001), quoting "Hall of Shame: Statehouse Sophistry," *Insight*, June 10, 1991, at 10.

124. Ibid.

125. Darryl Brown, *Racism and Race Relations in the University*, 76 Va. L. Rev. 295, n.112 (1990).

126. Ibid., quoting *Cavalier Daily* (University of Virginia student newspaper), October 4, 1988, at 1.

127. Ibid.

128. "Sony's Statesmanship," *Wall Street Journal*, June 20, 1995, at A18, quoting lyrics from music video version of Michael Jackson's song "They Don't Care About Us."

129. "Anti-Semitic Lyrics Resurface in New Michael Jackson Video," Jewish Bulletin, February 23, 1996 (found at http://www. Jewishsf.com/bk960223/etmj.htm).

130. The latest *Official Scrabble Players Dictionary* has deleted such racist epithets as *wop*, *spic*, and *nigger*. Jeff Lyon, "Word Police," *Chicago Tribune*, October 9, 1994, at C10.

131. Robert A. Frahm, "Teams Cling to Symbols Despite Indians' Protests," *Hartford Courant*, October 23, 1991, at D1.

132. Monty Python, "Never Be Rude to an Arab," Contractual Obligations Album lyrics found at http://www. Polbox.com/g/genie/montypython/songs/lyrics/ neverberudetoanarab.html.

133. But not always. See, e.g., *Doo Wop Shoppe Ltd. v. Ralph Edwards Productions*, 180 Misc.2d 907 (City Civ. Ct. 1998). *In re Universal Studio Tour*, 93 Lab. Arb. (BNA) 1 (Apr. 5, 2001) ("Doo Wop Singers"). *Rogen v. Ilikon Corp.*, C.A. 1st, 1966, 361 F.2d 260, 266 (["T]he standard of review is a rigorous one and not even one chink in the armor of decision can be vulnerable to the question: taking the facts and inferences most favorable to the losing party, would a trier of fact nevertheless have to find against him?"). *L & F Products v. Proctor & Gamble Co.*, 45 F.3d 709, 33 U.S.P.Q.2d 1621 (2d Cir. 1995). (Plaintiff failed to establish falsity of a commercial message that indicated that Spic 'n Span will clean a surface better than Lysol. Therefore, the district court did not clearly err in determining the commercial was not literally false.)

134. Ordinarily, these challenges are mounted under the free-speech clause. Occasionally a racist university or employer seeks to defend itself by arguing that its religion required them to discriminate against a certain group, usually blacks. These challenges usually fail. See Southern Poverty Law Center, *Legal Brief: Race as Religion*, Intelligence Report, winter 2002, at 53.

135. *Chaplinsky v. New Hampshire*, 315 U.S. 568, 572 (1942).

136. *R.A.V. v. City of St. Paul*, 505 U.S. 377 (1992).

137. 337 U.S. 1, 4 (1949).

138. Ibid.

139. Ibid. at 22.

140. Ibid. (dissent).

141. See *Chaplinsky*, supra.

142. *Greenberg v. Burglass*, 229 So.2d 83 (La. 1969).

143. *Mitchell v. Tribune*, 99 N.E.2d 397 (Ill. App. Ct. 1951). See also *Gomez v. Hug*, 645 P.2d 916, 923 (Kan. App. 1982) (where "fucking *spic*" was not slander per se).

144. 164 Misc.2d 557, 564 (N.Y. App. Div. 1995).

145. Ibid.

146. *State v. Mitchell*, 485 N.W.2d 807, 816 (Wis. 1992), *rev'd*, 508 U.S. 476 (1993).

147. *Wisconsin v. Mitchell*, 508 U.S. 476 (1993).

148. Ibid.

149. See, e.g., Wis. Stat. § 939.645 (penalty enhancement for crimes committed because of race); Fla. Stat. § 775.085(1) (enhancing degree of crime if crime committed because of race); Ca. Pen. Code. § 422 (enhancement for terrorist committed because of race); Wash. RCW 9A.36.080(1)(c) (person is guilty of malicious harassment if he harasses because of race); 18 U.S.C. § 245 (enhancement of attempts to injure based on race).

150. See *State v. Stalder*, 630 So.2d 1072, 1073–74 (Fla. 1994) (racial bias shown when defendant said, "Jewish *kike*" prior to battery); *People v. O'Keefe*, 2002 WL 596805 (Cal. App. 2002) (unpublished) (threat against Jewish organization stating that defendant would finish the job on the *kikes* who survived was subject to enhancement); *State v. Wendt*, 1999 WL 455458 (Wash. Ct. App. 1999) (unpublished opinion) (defendant's statement to police that he couldn't believe he was being arrested for beating up *spics* showed bias); *State v. Haberman*, 22 P.3d 264, 266 (Wash. Ct. App. 2001) (racial bias found where defendant called victim *chink*); *State v. McCallum*, 2000 WL 1201228 (Wash. Ct. App. 2000) (bias found when defendant repeatedly called victim *kike* and a Christ-killing Jew); *People v. Miccio*, 155 Misc.2d 697, 698 (N.Y. Crim. Ct. 1992) (bias found when defendant stated that, "We don't want any *Spics* or *Niggers* in the neighborhood."); *United States v. Ebens*, 800 F.2d 1422, 1427 (2d Cir. 1986) (bias found where prior to killing, defendant called victim a *chink* and blamed *chinks* as the reason he lost his job).

151. Restatement of Torts § 46, comment d.

152. Ibid., comment j.

153. Ibid., comment d.

154. 152 A.D.2d 169 (N.Y. App. Div. 1989).

155. Ibid.

156. Ibid. (dissent). See also *Colon v. Wal-Mart*, 182 Misc.2d 921 (N.Y. Gen. Term 1999), where even though the court found an employee called a customer a *spic*, the court ruled that "an isolated racial epithet will not support a cause of action for intentional infliction of emotional distress."

157. 1996 WL 84680 (D. N.J. 1996).

158. See *Wu v. City of New York*, 934 F. Supp. 581 (S.D.N.Y. 1996) (intentional infliction of emotional distress would lie when, on top of calling him *chink*, police arrested plaintiff without probable cause on the uncorroborated accusation of a city employee and without allowing the plaintiff an opportunity to explain himself).

159. See *Jones*, supra, at 8.

160. Ibid., quoting *Gaiters v. Lynn*, 831 F.2d 51, 54 (4th Cir. 1987).

161. 42 U.S.C. § 2000e–2(a)(1).

162. *Harris v. Forklift Sys., Inc.*, 510 U.S. 17, 21 (1993).

163. Ibid.

164. Ibid.

165. *Tores v. Pisano*, 116 F.3d 625, 631–632 (2d Cir. 1997).

166. *Howard v. National Cash Register Co.*, 388 F. Supp. 603, 606 (S.D. Ohio 1975).

167. *Gilbert v. City of Little Rock*, 722 F.2d 1390, 1394 (8th Cir. 1983).

168. *Perry v. Ethan Allen, Inc.*, 115 F.3d 143, 149 (2d Cir. 1997), quoting *Carrero v. New York City Housing Auth.*, 890 F.2d 569, 577 (2d Cir. 1989).

169. *Sanders v. Village of Dixmoor*, 178 F.3d 869, 870 (7th Cir. 1999).

170. 883 F.2d 475, 477 (1990).

171. Ibid., at 481.

172. See *Carrero*, supra. See also *Pagan v. New York State Division of Parole*, 2002 WL 398682, at 4 (S.D.N.Y. 2002) (being called *spic* three times enough); *Bampoe v. Coach Stores, Inc.*, 93 F. Supp.2d 360, 374 (S.D.N.Y. 2002) (where "continuous" use of *spic* was enough). Compare with cases where not enough racial epithets were hurled to constitute a hostile work environment: *Candillo v. North Carolina Department of Corrections*, 2002 WL 745894, at 6 (M.D.N.C. 2002) (being called *spic* on one occasion enough); *Arroyo v. Westlab Administration, Inc.*, 54 F. Supp.2d 224, 230 (S.D.N.Y. 1999) (where being called *spic* six times in twenty-five months was not enough); *Hockerson v. New York State Office of General Services*, 188 F. Supp.2d 215, 219 (N.D.N.Y. 2002) (one incident of being called *wop* not enough); *Rodriguez v. America Online, Inc.*, 183 F. Supp.2d 1340, 1350 (D.N.M. 2001) (being called *spic* "on a few occasions" was not enough).

173. *Snell v. Suffolk County*, 782 F.2d 1094, 1103 (2d Cir. 1986).

174. *Rodgers v. Western-Southern Life Ins. Co.*, 12 F.3d 668, 675 (7th Cir. 1993).

175. *Tores v. Pisano*, 116 F.3d 625, 632–33 (2d Cir. 1997).

176. See *Aguilar v. Avis Rent A Car Systems, Inc.*, 21 Cal.4th 121, 980 P.2d 846, 87 Cal. Rptr.2d 132 (1999).

177. *Breda v. Wolf Camera & Video*, 222 F.3d 886, 889 (11th Cir. 2000).

178. *Miller v. Kenworth of Dothan*, 277 F.3d 1269, 1273 (11th Cir. 2002).

179. See *Carrero*, supra.

180. *Black v. Zaring Homes, Inc.*, 104 F.3d 822, 826 (6th Cir. 1997).

181. *Collier v. RAM Partners, Inc.*, 159 F. Supp.2d 889, 894–95 (D. Md. 2001).

182. *Gonzalez v. New York State Department of Correctional Services*, 122 F. Supp.2d 335, 344 (N.D.N.Y. 2000).

183. *Levine v. Navapache Hospital*, 1981 WL 241, at 5 (D. Ariz. 1981).

184. Ibid., quoting *Howard v. National Cash Register Co.*, 388 F. Supp. 603, 606 (S.D. Ohio 1975).

185. *Snell v. Suffolk County*, 611 F. Supp. 521, 528 (E.D.N.Y. 1985).

186. *Texas Dep't of Community Affairs v. Burdine*, 450 U.S. 248, 256 (1981).

187. *McDonald v. Santa Fe Trail Trans. Co.*, 427 U.S. 273 (1976).

188. *Reeves v. Sanderson Plumbing Prods.*, 120 S. Ct. 2097, 2105 (2000).

189. *Chuang v. University of California Board of Trustees*, 225 F.3d 1115, 1128 (9th Cir. 2000).

190. *Serritella v. Midwest Dental Products Corp.*, 1996 WL 495563, at 5 (N.D. Ill. 1996).

191. *Nguyen v. Dobbs Int'l Services, Inc.*, 94 F. Supp.2d 1043, 1049 (W.D. Mo. 2000).

192. See *Young v. American Diabetes Association*, 2002 WL 203123, at 4 (6th Cir. 2002) (unpublished) (employee firing due to use of *spic* and *kike* at the workplace was reasonable even though productivity of work was not affected; it still exposed the employer to liability); *Weidner v. Shareholders Services Group, Inc.*, 1998 WL 1184131 (Mass. 1998) (employee fired for use of *spic* at work in presence of supervisor); *Weber v. Department of Transportation*, 2000 WL 1481123 (Wash. App. Ct. 2000) (employee demoted for use of *chink* at work in front of fellow employees); *City of Houston v. Tippy*, 991 S.W.2d 330 (Tex. App. 1999) (employee denied benefits due to misconduct resulting from calling supervisor *wop* in front of fellow employees).

193. See, for example, Fed. R. Evid. Rule 403.

194. 521 So.2d 223, 224 (Fla. Dist. Ct. App. 1988).

195. Ibid. at 226.

196. *Dorst v. Coombe*, 1996 WL 733071, at 3 (E.D.N.Y. 1996).

197. 954 S.W.2d 685 (Mo. Ct. App. 1997).

198. 1994 WL 7243 at 9 (Tex. App. 1994) (unpublished).

199. *In re* Stevens, 645 P.2d 99 (Cal. 1982).

200. *In re* Dixon, 1999 WL 562767 (Cal. Bar Ct. 1999).

201. *Commonwealth v. Laguer*, 630 N.E.2d 618 (Mass. App. Ct. 1994).

202. *State v. Santiago*, 252 A.2d 293 (Conn. 2000).

203. See *Laguer*, supra, note 201.

204. *Boyde v. California*, 494 U.S. 370, 380 (1990).

205. 283 F.3d 1117, 1133–1139 (9th Cir. 2002).

206. Ibid. at 1138–1139.

207. 743 So.2d 1275 (La. Ct. App. 1999).

208. *Zamudio v. State*, 1996 WL 474429, at 4 (Tex. App. 1996).

209. *Starcher v. State*, 1999 WL 642243, at 4 (Tex. App. 1999).

210. *Commonwealth v. Chaleumphong*, 746 N.E.2d 1009, 1017 (Mass. 2001).

211. 656 N.E.2d 1035, 1039–1040 (Ohio App. 1995).

212. *United States v. Allen*, 10 M.J. 576 (A.C.M.R. 1980).

213. Ibid. (internal quotations omitted).

214. 43 C.M.R. 604 (A.C.M.R. 1970).

215. United States Code, Title 8, Section 1158(a).

216. United States Code, Title 8, Section 1101(a)(42)(A).

217. 182 F.3d 934 (10th Cir. 1999).

218. 158 F.3d 1038 (9th Cir. 1998).

219. 814 F.2d 864, 867 (2d Cir. 1987).

220. 1997 WL 280273 at 5 n.4 (Conn. Super. Ct. 1997) (unpublished opinion).

221. 695 F. Supp. 1493, 1512–1513 (S.D.N.Y. 1988).

222. *New Era Publications Int'l v. Henry Holt and Co.*, 873 F.2d 576, 583 (2d Cir. 1989).

223. 1998 WL 1391395 (Pa. Com. Pl. 1998).

224. *Menillo v. Commission on Human Rights and Opportunities*, 1996 WL 601982 (Conn. Super. Ct. 1996).

225. *Engele v. Independent School District No. 91*, 846 F. Supp. 760, 762 (D. Minn. 1994).

226. Ibid. at 767.

227. See Kennedy, supra.

228. Ibid.

229. Kenji Yoshino, *Covering*, 111 Yale L.J. 769, 840–841(2002).

230. See http://freepages.tv.rootsweb.com/~eeyore/simpsons/homer.html, quoting from the episode "Homer's Phobia" from the television show *The Simpsons*, produced by the Fox Television Network) (Homer Simpson, a main character, when discussing gays, "They're embarrassing me. They're embarrassing America. They turned the Navy into a floating joke. They ruined all our best names like Bruce, and Lance, and Julian. Those were the toughest names we had! Now they're just, uh . . ." John, a homosexual replies, "Queer?" Homer Simpson, "Yeah, and that's another thing! I resent you people using that word. That's our word for making fun of you! We need it!!").

5

HATE SPEECH AND CHILDREN: THE SPECIAL CASE OF YOUTH

The arguments for protection from hate speech reach new heights in connection with children. Because of their vulnerable age, children are particularly susceptible to the wounds words can inflict. At the same time, the conventional arguments *against* regulating hate speech lack force when children are concerned. This is true in no small part because kids are hardly able to enter into a dialogue with their attackers, whether an adult or peer. They are scarcely able to "talk back," especially to one who is older or larger. Given these considerations, courts and legislatures have been willing to extend considerable protection to children from the effects of offensive speech.

This chapter first establishes why children are different enough from adults to warrant special protection. While the difference between mature adults and developing children may seem obvious, political and legal theory often has overlooked the important social component in the maturation process that makes hate speech so damaging to children. The chapter next deals with how and in what form children receive hate messages. Finally, it reviews how technology today allows speech to reach a much larger youthful audience, thus magnifying its reach and impact.

What Is a Child?

In 1925, Supreme Court Justice James C. McReynolds wrote, "The child is not the mere creature of the state; those who nurture and direct his destiny have the right, coupled with the high duty, to recognize and prepare him for additional obligations."[1] Put another way, the child is not merely a legal conception, unlike the corporation the law somewhat artificially deems to be a "person" or the animal it deems "property." Neither, however, is the child simply a miniature adult. Rather, the child is a potentiality, in some respects like a lump of clay modeled by many influences into an adult.

Psychologists have long debated the cognitive abilities of children and what they are capable of. Jean Piaget, whose work shaped the field of child development,[2] believed that children advance cognitively in a series of distinct stages, each of which sets the bounds for what the child can do. The child advances successively through each stage; no child can skip one or proceed out of order. In particular, according to Piaget, children cannot understand concepts beyond their stage of development.[3] Piaget's work, based as it is on close observation, has inspired modern-day social scientists such as Mary Goodman, Kenneth Clark, and Debra Van Ausdale and Joe Feagin, who study how children come to understand race. Although some adults seem to assume that children cannot understand concepts such as race and racism,[4] studies have shown that children know more about the adult world than their parents care to acknowledge.[5] Children as young as three know the meaning of race. They also understand what hate speech is. White children are taught to dislike and distrust minorities. They come to believe they are superior to their peers of color and thus continue hundreds of years of racist beliefs. This can be seen in the day-to-day experiences of children.

> Carla, a three-year-old child, is preparing herself for resting time. She picks up her cot and starts to move it to the other side of the classroom. A teacher asks what she is doing. "I need to move this," explains Carla. "Why?" asks the teacher. "Because I can't sleep next to a nigger," Carla says, pointing to Nicole, a four-year-old Black child on a cot nearby. "Niggers are stinky. I can't sleep next to one." Stunned, the teacher, who is white, tells Carla to move her cot back and not to use "hurting words." Carla looks amused but complies. . . . At the meeting

both parents [of Carla]—the father is white, and the mother is half-white and half-Asian—were baffled when told of the incident. The father remarked, "Well, she certainly did not learn that sort of crap from us!" The teacher immediately insisted that Carla did not learn such words at the center. Carla's father offered this explanation: "I'll bet she got that from Teresa. Her dad is . . . a real redneck."[6]

Young minorities are taught to hate themselves, as evinced by stories of children trying to scrub the color out of their skin,[7] favoring light- over dark-colored clay when asked to build a model of a person,[8] and of course the well-known example, set out in *Brown v. Board of Education,* of minority children preferring white dolls to black ones.[9] In that famous case, the Supreme Court ruled segregation in public education was unconstitutional. As one author has put it,

> *Brown* speaks directly to the psychic injury inflicted by racist speech in noting that the symbolic message of segregation affected the "hearts and minds" of Negro children "in a way unlikely ever to be undone. . . . "The message of segregation was stigmatizing to Black children. To be labeled unfit to attend school with white children injured the reputation of Black children, thereby foreclosing employment opportunities and the right to be regarded respectable members of the body politic.[10]

Made to feel inferior to whites, some minority children resort to denial or lying to avoid what they have been made to feel is the truth about themselves.[11]

How do these conceptions get instilled today, nearly fifty years after the *Brown* decision? Much of the blame rests with the words and names children are exposed to while growing up.[12] Because children have fewer coping mechanisms than adults, the words can affect them more deeply than others. A child who reacts with anger will be punished and likely alienated.[13] Internalizing the harm yields no better results, as it undercuts the young person's confidence and motivation.[14]

Messages to Children

Children can be exposed to hate speech in a variety of settings. Coaches, social workers, store employees, even religious leaders can say things that inflict irreparable harm. Imagine the coach who tells his black athlete to "play like you're back in the 'hood"[15] or the social worker who chastises "you people, why can't you ever take advantage of the opportunities we give you?" Or consider the store employee who tells a co-worker, "you've got to watch their kind" when a black child enters. Each of these and countless other examples inflict psychic harm upon the child and shape self-perception as well as perception of others.

Hate to Kids and Their Parents

Many of the cases that arise both inside and outside school concern claims of intentional infliction of emotional distress. The tort of intentional infliction essentially requires that the defendant said or did something intended to be (and that was) emotionally damaging to another person. The best way to explain the concept, and show how hate speech affects children, is to simply consider a few examples.

In *Quinn v. National Railroad Passenger Corporation*,[16] a mother and her two children sued Amtrak for the treatment they received on an aborted trip from Chicago to Los Angeles. While many problems occurred on the trip, including their not being given seats on the train and being kicked off twice, of concern here is what happened after their train left Denver. While Teyan and DaSean Quinn, both children, played on a blanket with two other black children, a white passenger allegedly threatened them. When the conductor arrived, he asked Claudine Quinn, the children's mother, "Who put you people in here?" and, according to another passenger, immediately took the white woman's side in the dispute. Amtrak sought summary judgment on numerous grounds, all of which proved unavailing. As of fall 2003, the case was still pending.

In *Rogers v. Elliott*,[17] two black parents brought suit on behalf of themselves and their children against a Georgia Wal-Mart and several of its employees. According to their complaint, while Mrs. Rogers checked out, she gave her children some candy after the checker had scanned it. As her children walked away, another checker from another line yelled, "Hey, get over here, boy, and pay for this candy."[18] Mrs. Rogers explained that the candy had been paid for and left the store. In the parking lot, the checker again confronted her and, in front of her children, insulted and slapped her. The court dismissed their federal claims against Wal-Mart in part because when the attack took place, they were no longer "shopping at Wal-Mart."[19] The court did leave the plaintiffs the option of pursuing their claims in state court.[20]

Of course, not every case leaves the child this option. In 1990, a white teenager and several friends burned a cross on the lawn of the Joneses, a black family in St. Paul, Minnesota. After being convicted of violating the city's ordinance banning racially hostile symbols and artifacts on public or private property, the teen challenged the constitutionality of the ordinance. The case gained national attention, especially after the U.S. Supreme Court ruled the statute was an unconstitutional intrusion into First Amendment protections of speech.[21] Unlike in other cases where the Court considered the impact of speech on children when balancing First Amendment concerns,[22] the Court made no mention of the effect a cross-burning might have on the Jones children, who saw the cross on fire outside their home.

The Jones family was naturally upset as "the black couple has watched their children's innocence about race go up in smoke."[23] In their own words: "It makes me angry that they [the kids] have to be aware of racism around them, that they notice it more and more."[24] Indeed, the family reported that the incident had changed their oldest son's behavior. "He's had a hard time with it. . . . He's real sensitive to name calling," his mother reported.[25] Yet the Supreme Court's opinions were silent on the effect such symbolic speech has on the children exposed to it.

On the Playground: Hate Speech at School

The courts have confronted a recurring question in connection with schools—when do clothing and symbols cross the line and constitute impermissible hate? The most common examples arise in connection with the Confederate flag. In *Castorina v. Madison County School Board*,[26] the Sixth Circuit Court of Appeals found that school districts could not selectively ban racially sensitive symbols in clothing, for instance allowing black students to wear Malcolm X shirts but prohibiting Confederate flags on shirts.[27] In *West v. Derby Unified School District No. 260*,[28] the Tenth Circuit upheld a school district's antiharassment policy and affirmed its suspension of a student who drew a Confederate flag on a piece of paper.[29]

In re Michael M.,
86 Cal.App.4th 718, 729, 104 Cal.Rptr.2d 10 (2001).

On September 26, 1999, appellant used a permanent black marking pen and wrote the word "Nigger" on the classroom door of the only African American teacher at his school. On the same date, appellant used a black marking pen to write "Kill the Niggers" on the music building of the school.

The teacher testified that she discovered the word . . . on her classroom door on the morning of September 27, 1999. She was shocked, belittled and "almost moved to tears" by the graffiti. She was somewhat apprehensive about going into her classroom. In her experience, the word "nigger" connoted "a little bit" of violence, and she had some family members who had been exposed to violent situations in which the word had been used in connection with their race and color. The victim stated she consulted with a relative who advised her for her own safety to leave school before dusk and not go to the school alone on the weekend.

* * *

The record establishes that the word "Nigger" on the door of the school's only African-American teacher carried with it a violent connotation. The word produced a sense of apprehension, terror, and fear in the teacher. The even more descriptive words "Kill the Niggers," written on the music building where a number of African-American students gathered, was reasonably interpreted as a direct, violent threat to those students.

In *Denno v. School Board of Volusia County, Florida*,[30] the Eleventh Circuit denied relief to a student suspended for displaying a Confederate flag,[31] even when no evidence showed that he had acted with racist intent.[32] While all three cases cited *Tinker v. Des Moines Independent School District*,[33] the Supreme Court case holding that students do not "shed their constitutional rights to freedom of speech or expression at the schoolhouse gate"[34] in allowing students to wear black armbands in protest of the Vietnam War,[35] each came to a different outcome.

In two of the cases, *West* and *Castorina*, the school district's policy came in response to past racial violence. In *West*, this seems to have been an important factor in the decision;[36] but the Sixth Circuit held that "even if [a history of] racial violence . . . necessitates a ban on racially divisive symbols" the school district cannot selectively pick and choose which ones to ban.[37] Thus, the difference between the two cases seems to turn on the selective enforcement of a prohibition in *Castorina*, in which black students were able to get away with behavior white students could not.[38] Thus, each court would seem to uphold a ban on racially offensive material, perhaps regardless of intent, as long as that prohibition is applied to all students.

In *Graham v. Guiderland Central School District*,[39] a black high school student sued the district for being called a *nigger* by her teacher. In response to another student's question as to why gays shouldn't be called "faggots," the teacher pointed to the only black person in the class and said, "Why not call Liz a 'nigger' because that's what she is? Liz, why not tell us what it feels like to be called a 'nigger'?"[40] The student's lawsuit was dismissed because the teacher's remarks did not rise to the level of "extreme and outrageous conduct,"[41] despite the plaintiff's claim that Liz's "youth, and the fact that she was the only African American in the class, rendered her particularly vulnerable to derogatory comments of this nature."[42] Writing in dissent, Judge Cardona argued the case should go forward not only because Elizabeth was the only black student in the class, but also because "[s]he was not an adult, but rather an adolescent."[43]

Not every student suit against a school district is about what was said or conveyed. Sometimes, the issue is what was not allowed to be said. In *Saxe v. State College Area School District*,[44] a guardian, on behalf of his children, sued the school district for not allowing the students to speak out against homosexuality. The school's anti-harassment policy prevented students from talking about their views of the sinfulness of homosexuality and its harmful effects.[45] The Third Circuit held the policy unconstitutional, reversing the district court's decision upholding student protection from harassment. The court said:

In short, we see little basis for the District Court's sweeping assertion that "harassment"—at least when it consists of speech targeted on the basis of its expressive content—"has never been considered to be protected activity under the First Amendment." Such a categorical rule is without precedent in the decisions of the Supreme Court or this Court, and it belies the very real tensions between anti-harassment laws and the Constitution's guarantee of freedom of speech.[46]

In *Davis v. Monroe County Board of Education*,[47] two parents brought suit against their daughter's school district under Title IX's anti-harassment protection. The student, a fifth-grader named LaShonda, and several classmates were subjected to repeated sexual harassment by one of their peers. The boy's conduct eventually rose to a criminal level and he pleaded guilty to sexual battery.[48] Yet the school took no disciplinary action against the boy, even as LaShonda's grades slipped and her father discovered a suicide note.[49] The majority held that the school district "may be liable for their deliberate indifference to known acts of peer sexual harassment."[50]

Montiero v. Tempe Union High School District[51] raised the question whether certain books should be banned from the classroom for their racist content. As the court put it:

More and more frequently we are faced with cases in which two fundamental constitutional rights appear to be at odds. . . . The setting is a freshman English class in Tempe, Arizona, and the competing interests are the First Amendment rights of high school students to receive information or ideas . . . and the rights of those same students to receive public education that neither fosters nor acquiesces in a racially hostile environment.[52]

At issue were *The Adventures of Huckleberry Finn* and *A Rose for Emily* and their repeated use of the word *nigger*.[53] Several African–American students asserted that they suffered psychological injury, and that the school district offered no solution other than studying alone in a study hall during the class discussion.[54] The court threw out the portion of the lawsuit dealing with the books in part because it feared schools would "buy their peace" and avoid any literary works that might cause harm:

White plaintiffs could seek to remove books by Toni Morrison, Maya Angelou, and other prominent black authors on the ground that they portray Caucasians in a derogatory fashion; Jews might try to impose civil liability for the teachings of Shakespeare and of more modern English poets where writings exhibit a similar antisemitic strain. Female students could attempt to make a case for damages for the assignment of some of the works of Tennessee Williams, Hemingway, or Freud, and male students for the writings of Andrea Dworkin and Margaret Atwood. The number of potential lawsuits that could arise from the highly varied educational curricula throughout the nation might well be unlimited and unpredictable.[55]

The court reached this result despite acknowledging that

books can hurt, and that words can hurt—particularly racist epithets. It is now uncontroversial to observe that some of the most lauded works of literature convey explicitly or in a more subtle manner, messages of racism and sexism, or other ideas that if accepted blindly would serve to maintain or promote the invidious inequalities that exist in our world today. We also recognize that the younger a person is, the more likely it is that those messages will help form that person's thinking, and that the feelings of minority students, especially younger ones, are extremely vulnerable when it comes to books that are racist or have racist overtones.[56]

Nonetheless, "it is important for young people to learn about the past—and to discover both the good and the bad in our history."[57] Thus, between the potential for many works to be banned and this important need for history, the court affirmed the dismissal of part of the plaintiff's case.

But the circuit court reversed the trial court's dismissal of a different part of the plaintiff's case. In this other part, the plaintiffs alleged that after their classmates read the assigned books, racial graffiti and remarks, including the word *nigger*, proliferated around the school. The court found that this part of the complaint stated a cause of action for hostile racial environment under a federal statute (Title VI). Because school authorities knew about the torrent of racial vituperation, but did nothing about it, they were liable.

Books, then, must be tolerated, but student remarks need not be—even if they contain the same words.

Broadcasting the Message

Adults can, of course, "speak" to children through a variety of media. Music, television, radio, and now the Internet (see Chapter 7) all touch more people than any individual could hope to do in person. Even bumper stickers, when they contain messages like *"If you don't speak English, get the [expletive] OUT!"*[58] can harm children.[59] Accordingly, the courts have been willing to afford children special protection in some circumstances, even if doing so limits the First Amendment rights of adults. One of the earliest and perhaps best examples comes from *Federal Communications Commission v. Pacifica Foundation*,[60] better known as George Carlin's "Seven Dirty Words" case. Though it does not bear directly on the issue of hate speech, the case does evidence a willingness by the Supreme Court to treat First Amendment issues differently when children are concerned.

In the *Pacifica* case, the U.S. Supreme Court pondered whether the FCC could prohibit a radio broadcaster from airing a comedy monologue laced with obscenities. A New York radio station, owned by Pacifica, aired a twelve-minute portion of a routine performed by Carlin about "the words you couldn't say on the public, ah, airwaves, um, the ones you definitely wouldn't say, ever."[61] As anyone familiar with Carlin's comedy can attest to, the rest of the segment was an expletive–laden rant featuring those very words.[62] After an outraged listener filed a complaint with the FCC, the agency determined the broadcast was improper and could have resulted in administrative action against the station.[63] In affirming the FCC's action, the Court stressed the impact such broadcasts could have on young ears. Indeed, the original complaint was filed by a father whose son was with him in the car when the broadcast came over the airwaves at 2 p.m.[64] The Court wrote:

> broadcasting is uniquely accessible to children, even those too young to read. . . . Other forms of offensive expression may be withheld from the young without restricting the expression at its source. . . . The ease with which children may obtain access to the broadcast material . . . amply justifies special treatment of indecent broadcasting.[65]

The Internet has proven a fertile source for hateful messages directed at children. "Many sites operated by neo-Nazis, skinheads, Ku Klux Klan members and followers of religious cults are growing more sophisticated, offering Web environments that are designed to attract children and young adults."[66] The examples are virtually limitless and growing in number each day. One neo-Nazi Web site used to be drawn in crayon-looking text and provided a link to standard antisemitic Nazi propaganda.[67] Another provided a cartoon of white kids shooting at a poster of a pig that read, "Kill the Jew pigs before it's too late."[68] Still other sites provide variations of popular computer games modified so that the targets are members of minority groups.[69]

Video games, both on the Internet and available for purchase on CD, teach children that violence is acceptable. In recent years games like Mortal Kombat, Tekken, and Duke Nukem have come under fire for the level of violence they depict. These games, however, are objectionable primarily because of their violent content. A new breed of games has popped up, developed by Resistance Records.[70] In one, ethnic cleansing, players can choose to be either a skinhead or Klansman in white robes as they hunt down Jews and "predatory subhumans" portrayed as blacks and Latinos.[71] "During the game, monkey and ape sounds are heard when Blacks are killed, poncho-wearing Latinos say 'I'll take a siesta now!' and 'Ay caramba!' while 'Oy vey!' rings out when Jewish characters are killed. The game features a high level of background detail including various National Alliance signs and posters that appear throughout while racist rock blares on the soundtrack."[72]

Next, Resistance Records was planning to market "Turner Diaries—The Game," an adaptation of William Pierce's apocalyptic race fantasy in which heroic white supremacists deploy space-age weapons to destroy swarms of nonwhites bent on destroying civilization.[73]

Anyone who has purchased a rap or heavy metal CD is familiar with the Parental Advisory Label attached to the cover, designed to warn parents that the music contains violent and/or hateful messages. Similarly, radio stations usually only play edited versions of songs, bleeping out obscene and inappropriate language. Some songs are edited up to sixty times to filter out offensive material.[74] Of course, sensitivity for the concerns of children is not uniform. While a radio station may bleep out a derogatory reference to blacks, a few seconds later an equally offensive reference to gays might go unchecked.[75]

Many musicians complain that their words, though perhaps crude, are not hateful.[76] But labels like Resistance Records buck that trend. Musicians on such labels sign on specifically to perpetuate their hateful messages. Resistance was founded in 1993 in Canada, but soon moved to Detroit to avoid Canada's hate speech laws.[77] A sampling of one song's lyrics tells the story:

> *Kill all the niggers and you gas all the jews*
> *Kill a gypsy and a coloured too*
> *You just killed a kike*
> *Don't it feel right*
> *Goodness gracious, darn right*[78]

A few year later, the National Alliance purchased the label in hopes of using it to attract new youthful members.[79] With good reason. As one observer put it: "With Resistance Records forging ahead as arguably the most lucrative hate enterprise in the country, old-school racists are viewing violent skinhead culture in a new light. As hate rock bands merge into the mainstream heavy metal music arena, white supremacist leaders are coming to see the music as the most powerful recruiting tool to hit their movement in de-cades."[80] One recent white power music festival, Hammerfest, in Bremen, Georgia, drew fans from across the world and four bands from Britain alone. Today, racist music might be recorded in Poland, pressed in the United States, and sold by a Swedish outlet via the Internet. Music gives hate groups not only an international language, but immediate access to youth.[81] Realizing the offensive content of these products—as well as their multi-million-dollar-a-year appeal— one online distributor of such hate music included the following disclaimer:

> Although some of the items available on this site contain offensive, violent or "racist" themes, Micetrap Distribution is merely supplying a service and in no way condones illegal activities or the "acting out" of lyrics contained in this merchandise. . . . If you are offended or opposed to anything contained on my website, close your browser immediately. Simply put, these items are made available for those who seek them only. Rather than attacking ideologies and le-

gal merchandise, I suggest that my opponents should instead refo-
cus their attention onto real issues that plague our society; rape and
sexual abuse, murder, drugs, thefts, assault and other illegal
activities.[82]

Finally, while this chapter has not dealt with hate speech on television, it is noteworthy that the subject was briefly popularized in early
2002. An NBC *The More You Know* service announcement warned
viewers that words can hurt. And an episode of Fox's *Boston Public*
dealt with the study of the word *nigger* in a public high school.[83]

QUESTIONS FOR DISCUSSION, CHAPTER 5

1. Children are, perhaps, more vulnerable to hate speech than
   adults. But are they not also more resilient?
2. Is *Brown v. Board of Education* a hate speech case (about the
   message segregated schooling sends to black schoolchildren)?
   If so, why should we hesitate to afford a remedy for hate
   speech that communicates the same message of inferiority directly, as opposed to indirectly or symbolically? And why not
   for adults, as well?
3. Why did the Supreme Court in *R.A.V.*, the cross-burning
   case, overlook the impact on the family's children?
4. Is hate speech at school worse than that which takes place in
   a non-school setting, say a public park or playground?
5. Should school authorities assign books that contain the word
   nigger?
6. Do violent, racist video games harm children and shape their
   attitudes? Or are they just harmless fun?

CLASS EXERCISE

Consider children's literature and stories like Snow White, Cinderella,
Little Black Sambo, and Little Red Riding Hood. What lessons do
they teach about color and who is good and bad?

RECOMMENDED READING, CHAPTER 5

Bill Berkovitz, "Ethnic Cleansing," Video Game Earmarked for the White "Revolution," online http://workingforchange.com/article.cfm?

Danuta Bukatko and Marvin W. Doehler, *Child Development: A Developmental Approach* (1992).

Kenneth Clark, *Prejudice and Your Child* (1963).

Mary Ellen Goodman, *Race Awareness in Young Children* (revised edition 1964).

Marjorie Heins, *Not in Front of the Children: Indecency, Censorship, and the Innocence of Youth* (2001).

Joint Commission on Mental Health of Children, *Social Change and the Mental Health of Children* (1973).

Meyer v. Nebraska, 262 U.S. 390 (1923).

Jean Piaget, *The Moral Judgment of the Child* (1932).

Pierce v. Society of Sisters, 268 U.S. 510 (1925).

Michael S. Romano, "Putting Up A Filter for the Kids," *New York Times*, April 4, 2002, at A23.

Debra Van Ausdale and Joe R. Feagin, *The First R: How Children Learn Race and Racism* (2001).

NOTES

1. *Pierce v. Society of Sisters*, 268 U.S. 510, 535 (1925).

2. Debra Van Ausdale and Joe R. Feagin, *The First R: How Children Learn Race and Racism*, 5 (2001). "Piaget's theory remains a dominant force in developmental psychology, despite the fact that much of it was formulated half a century ago. Some of the reasons for the lasting appeal are the important acquisitions it describes, the large span of childhood it encompasses, and the reliability and charm of many of its observations."

3. Ibid.

4. Ibid. at 3.

5. Ibid.

6. *The First R*, supra, at 1.

7. Richard Delgado, *Words That Wound: A Tort Action for Racial Insults, Epithets, and Name-Calling*, 17 Harv. C.R.–C.L. L. Rev. 133, 142–43 (1982).

8. Ibid.

9. *Brown v. Board of Education*, 347 U.S. 483, 494–495 n.11 (1954).

10. Charles R. Lawrence III, *If He Hollers Let Him Go: Regulating Racist Speech on Campus*, Duke L.J. 431 (1990); Mari Matsuda et al., *Words That Wound: Critical Race Theory, Assaultive Speech and the First Amendment*, 74 (1993).

11. Delgado, *Words That Wound,* supra, at 143.

12. Ibid. at 146.

13. Ibid. at 147.

14. Ibid.

15. *Any Given Sunday* (1999).

16. 1999 WL 637170 (N.D. Ill.).

17. 135 F. Supp.2d 1312 (N.D. Ga. 2001).

18. Ibid. at 1313.

19. Ibid. at 1315.

20. Ibid.

21. *R.A.V. v. City of St. Paul*, 505 U.S. 377 (1992). In a more recent case (*Black v. Commonwealth*), children's welfare did not play a part.

22. See *F.C.C. v. Pacifica*, 438 U.S. 726 (1978).

23. Don Terry, "Rights Advocates Uncertain About Ruling's Impact," *New York Times*, June 23, 1992, at A16.

24. Ibid.

25. Ibid.

26. 246 F.3d 536 (6th Cir. 2001).

27. Ibid. at 544.

28. 206 F.3d 1358 (10th Cir. 2000).

29. Ibid. at 1365.

30. 218 F.3d 1267 (11th Cir. 2000).

31. Ibid. at 1278.

32. Ibid. at 1275, n.6.

33. 393 U.S. 503 (1969).

34. Ibid. at 506.

35. Ibid. at 514.

36. *West*, 206 F.3d at 1366–67.

37. *Castorina*, 246 F.3d at 544.

38. Ibid. at 541.

39. 256 A.D.2d 863 (N.Y. App. 1998).

40. Ibid. at 863.

41. Ibid. at 863.

42. Ibid. at 864.

43. Ibid. at 865 (Cardona, P.J., dissenting).

44. 240 F.3d 200 (3d Cir. 2001).

45. Ibid. at 203.

46. Ibid. at 209.

47. 526 U.S. 629 (1999).

48. Ibid. at 634.

49. Ibid.

50. Ibid. at 648.

51. 158 F.3d 1022 (9th Cir. 1998).

52. Ibid. at 1024.

53. Ibid.

54. Ibid.

55. Ibid. at 1030.

56. Ibid. at 1031.

57. Ibid.

58. Jim Panos, "Stretching Limits of Free Speech," *New York Times*, May 7, 2000, at 27.

59. Ibid.

60. 438 U.S. 726 (1978).

61. Ibid. at 729 (quoting Carlin's routine).

62. The text of Carlin's routine is included in the Appendix to the Supreme Court's opinion. Ibid. at 751.

63. Ibid. at 730. The FCC, however, did not take any such actions. Ibid.

64. Ibid. at 730.

65. Ibid. at 749–750.

66. Michel Marriott, "Rising Tide: Sites Born of Hate," *New York Times*, March 18, 1999, at G1.

67. Ibid.

68. Ibid.

69. Ibid.

70. Resistance Records is owned and operated by the National Alliance, a white supremacist organization. Both are discussed more fully later.

71. *Racist Groups Use Computer Gaming to Promote Violence Against Blacks, Latinos and Jews*, http://www.adl.org/videogames/default.asp.

72. Ibid.

73. Southern Poverty Law Center, *Games Extremists Play, Coming Soon: Ethnic Cleansing—The Game*, Intelligence Report, winter 2002, at 2.

74. Neil Strauss, "Policing Pop: A Special Report," *New York Times*, August 1, 2000, at A1.

75. Ibid.

76. Ibid.

77. *Deafening Hate: The Revival of Resistance Records: Introduction*, http://www.adl.org/resistance_records/introduction.html; *Hate for Profit*, http://www.adl.org/resistance_records/hate.html.

78. Lyrics from "Third Reich" by RaHoWa, a band on the Resistance Records label.

79. *New Owner: Willis Carto of the Liberty Lobby*, http://www.adl.org/resistance_records/new_owner.html.

80. *Deafening Hate: The Revival of Resistance Records: Introduction*, http://www.adl.org/resistance_records/new_owner.html; *Hate for Profit*, http://www.adl.org/resistance_records/hate.html.

81. Southern Poverty Law Center, *White Pride World Wide*, Intelligence Report, fall 2001, at 24.

82. Micetrap Distribution, http://www.micetrap.net/.

83. The episode first aired on February 25, 2002. The episode was inspired by the publication of *Nigger*, by Harvard law professor Randall Kennedy. See also David D. Kirkpatrick, "A Black Author Hurls that Word as a Challenge," *New York Times*, December 1, 2001, at A15.

6

COLLEGE AND UNIVERSITY STUDENTS: THE CASE OF CAMPUS HATE SPEECH (AND CONDUCT) CODES

College and university students are, of course, older than the very young children considered in the previous chapter. But many of them have yet to reach the age of twenty-one or become financially and emotionally independent of their parents. Moreover, some, particularly seventeen- and eighteen-year-old freshmen, may be traversing the final stages of personality development and are still vulnerable to assaults on their personhood and self-esteem. College hate speech brings all these issues into play, plus a powerful countervailing First Amendment interest, since colleges and universities are places of intellectual and academic inquiry where speech, ideally, should be as free as possible.

Literally hundreds of colleges and universities have enacted some type of hate speech code.[1] Some regulate hate speech directly, by means of a specific regulation designating it as a campus offense and providing some form of sanction. Others regulate it under a general provision—that is, without naming it directly—such as a rule requiring that members of the campus community treat each other with respect or desist from interfering with each other's ability to study, work, or enjoy the privileges of campus life.[2]

Why the great interest in regulating hate speech on campus, and why do campuses often rely on before-the-event regulations, as opposed to (for example) tort actions or suits for harassment or hostile environment brought after the fact? Colleges have not been shy about explaining their reasons. Campus hate speech is ubiquitous, and increasing. As mentioned earlier, the average undergraduate of color experiences hate speech (depending on how narrowly or broadly it is defined) frequently, as often as once a day.[3] These experiences have measurable effects: Students of color may drop out, feeling threatened and demoralized. Others hear about incidents of unredressed hate speech at a given college and choose not to go there. "I have to deal with racism the rest of my life," one said. "Why should I deal with that in college?"[4] An official with the United Negro College Fund recently posited that an upsurge in applications to historically black colleges such as Fisk and Morehouse came from "students who are disgruntled. These students want the chance to develop without the threat of harassment that looms over many of those (white-dominated) campuses."[5] Another study showed that tolerating a hostile environment for minority students caused them to earn lower grades.[6] One professor described the role of "racial microaggressions" in keeping minority students on edge.[7] Professors of color, too, consider the climate of a school in deciding where to apply for a teaching position.

In addition to these consequences, hate speech simply looks bad, especially when it takes the form of mediacentric events, such as the following, that attract the press and TV cameras.

- At a major Western university, concern for the safety of Muslims became a prominent issue when hate-filled messages appeared on the pillars of the campus library and anonymous hate messages were left on the voice recorder of the Muslim Students Association.[8]
- At a famous military academy, five white cadets, clad in white sheets and cone-shaped masks, awoke a black cadet who was sleeping in his room. After shouting obscenities, they fled, leaving behind a charred cross made of newspaper. After reporting the incident, the black cadet suffered further harassment for having gone to the authorities, and later resigned from the academy. The school took no action other than recommending ethnic awareness classes for all cadets.[9]
- At an elite private school, four staff members of a conservative campus newspaper criticized a black professor in print,

then confronted him after class. A campus disciplinary panel found them guilty of disorderly conduct and harassment, and the university president, a Jew, criticized them for "poisoning the campus atmosphere." Unrepentant, the students charged the president with censorship, reverse discrimination, and conduct resembling Adolf Hitler. A state court ordered the students reinstated, but a federal court threw out their suit against the university.[10]

- At an elite public university, fraternity members sponsored a party with a "Fiji Island" theme, as part of which they erected a fifteen-foot-high plywood caricature of a black man with a bone through his nose. Black students picketed, and the university suspended the fraternity and ordered its members to undergo sensitivity training. One month later, an investigator recommended reversal. This time the university apologized and reinstated the group. Minority students were outraged.[11]

- At another elite public university, a drunk fraternity member shouted epithets at a group of passing black students; later a campus disc jockey told black students who had demanded that the station play rap music to go back where they came from. Still later, members of a gay and lesbian group reported that an anonymous caller had left a phone message urging that people like them should be taken out and gassed as Hitler did with the Jews. The campus responded by stepping up awareness training and enacting a policy prohibiting "those personally abusive epithets which, when directly addressed to any ordinary person, are likely to provoke a violent reaction whether or not they actually do so."[12]

- At a top-flight private university in 1988, some students argued over whether the composer Ludwig van Beethoven was mulatto. Later, some of the whites defaced a poster of the composer by adding stereotypically black features. When the incident sparked confrontations between black and white students, the university revised its student conduct code to prohibit words "directly addressed" to a specific person and containing "words, pictures, or symbols that . . . convey . . . hatred or contempt" on the grounds of race or sex. Ten years later, with the country's racial climate changed, a local court struck down the rule. The university decided not to appeal.[13]

Why do events like these happen? What is going on in the minds of the perpetrators? Some mild cases of hate speech may be simple mistakes—the speaker, perhaps a young undergraduate from a remote farming community or an all-white suburb, simply does not know that a certain term or concept is offensive. But ignorance certainly cannot account for more than a small fraction of campus hate speech, including some of the more glaring examples in the list immediately above. A leading authority, Lu-in Wang, wrote that much hate behavior is opportunistic and dependent on context or setting. The perpetrator finds himself in a situation—perhaps in the company of others of his race and seeing a lone member of an out-group—in which he knows that a push, shove, blow, or epithet will go unpunished. It may bring rewards, enabling the hate speaker/actor to bond with his peer group or terrorize the member of the out-group, thereby enhancing his own group's standing. Relatively few hate incidents are planned and intentional, beginning with a perpetrator who consciously decides to go looking for a member of a minority group to oppress. The hardcore, animus-driven perpetrator is the exception, not the rule. Many hate speakers and actors hardly know why they act or speak as they do. They never calculate in advance; they may gain little from the act; afterward, they may be astonished at what they did.[14]

If Professor Wang and the social scientists who take her view are right, changing the campus environment to make clear that hate speech will not be tolerated should go a long way toward preventing its arising in the first place.[15] Given all this, it should come as no surprise that many campus administrators support measures to control hate speech and continue to enact them despite court cases striking particular ones down.

TYPES OF HATE SPEECH REGULATION/CODE

Campus hate speech codes take almost as many different forms as the human imagination is capable of. Some are patterned after the law of tort, prohibiting conduct that violates another's right to be free from intentional infliction of emotional distress, for example.[16] Others forbid interference with another's ability to study, learn, or otherwise enjoy the benefits of his or her campus experience.[17] These "right to an education" measures in some respects mirror the legal doctrine in employment discrimination law known as "constructive discharge." Other codes forbid conduct that creates a hostile environment, while still others prohibit breaches of the norms of civility or mutual respect.[18] Some campuses punish egregious hate speech under a general campus provision requiring civilized conduct; others, under a provision specifically addressed to hate speech.

Most hate speech codes contain a scienter element—that is, that the speaker realize that his or her words were offensive—and another requiring a certain level of effect, such as "severe" disruption of the ability to study.[19] Most are couched in race-neutral language, so that a black who addressed hate speech to a white would be just as remiss as a white who did the reverse. Most punish hate speech that vilifies on the basis of race, gender, religion, sexual orientation, national origin, and disability. A few forbid hate speech based on other characteristics, such as socioeconomic class or veteran status.

Most cover students; others protect any member of the campus community, including visitors at academic functions. A few prescribe what is acceptable speech for faculty. These faculty speech codes, as one might imagine, spark even sharper resistance than ones that apply to students.[20] One state (California) has enacted a statewide statute (the "Leonard law") barring any institution that enacts a hate-speech code from receiving state funds.[21]

LEGAL TREATMENT OF CAMPUS HATE SPEECH CODES

Many hate speech codes are never challenged in court (perhaps because they are rarely applied or appealed). Some are withdrawn when challenged; the campus goes back to the drawing boards and issues a new, narrower code that it hopes will withstand judicial scrutiny. Two decisions by lower federal courts, one in Wisconsin,[22] the other in Michigan,[23] and one by a state trial court near Stanford, California,[24] suggest that many campus codes—unless very carefully drawn—may be vulnerable to challenge as vague, overbroad, or unduly invasive of viewpoint or content. The U.S. Supreme Court has never decided such a case, although it may well have to do so sometime.

How will the Supreme Court rule? Two conflicting decisions suggest different answers. The first cross-burning case, *R.A.V. v. St. Paul* (1992),[25] suggests that hate speech regulations will be in for a tough time. In that case, two white youths were charged with burning a cross on the property of a black family under a local ordinance that forbade expressions of racial contempt or hatred. Observing that the ordinance did not also penalize other expressions of contempt and hate, the Supreme Court struck the law down as a violation of the doctrine of content neutrality. The opinion left open the possibility that an across-the-board rule forbidding all forms of severe interpersonal insult would pass muster.

Only a few years later, the Supreme Court confronted a similar issue in a case of some black youths who had attacked an innocent white youth after watching the movie *Rosewood*, which portrays an incident of racial violence against a black community. Charged under a Wisconsin law that provides enhanced sentences for crimes committed with a racial motivation, the youths challenged their sentence as a violation of their right to equal treatment. The Supreme Court upheld the sentence, noting that while expression is constitutionally protected, action is not. Thus, even though what the youths did was punished more severely than a similar crime committed without motivation would have been, the Court held that the sentence was imposed on account of what they did, not what they thought.[26]

Until the Supreme Court rules on the legality of campus hate speech codes, it would seem that the best course for a university interested in curtailing hate speech would be to combine the two Supreme Court cases. Heeding the mandate of the cross-burning case, *R.A.V. v. St. Paul*, the campus ought to enact a code that is neutral on its face and punishes all types of severe interpersonal insult and invective equally. Then, elsewhere in the code, the campus should enact a provision that all campus offenses (not just ones carried out by means of speech—for example, stealing, destruction of property, trashing, arson, plagiarism, and the like) carried out with racial motivation are subject to enhanced penalties. That way, the campus can end up punishing insults based on, for example, fatness or poor parking ("you idiot, why did you take up two spaces?") mildly, and ones based on race, gender, or sexual orientation ("you fag, you're going straight to hell") more severely.

THE STRUCTURE OF THE CAMPUS
HATE SPEECH CODE CONTROVERSY

The campus hate speech controversy contains a few elements that are not present elsewhere in the discourse on hate speech, in part because hate speech codes, unlike tort or criminal law rules, operate before, not after, the fact. The latter approaches punish speech in familiar ways that cut across large categories of conduct. Like rules against conspiracy, threat, false advertising, and copyright infringement, they punish speech and communication. But they are familiar and uncontroversial; no one today suggests that laws against plagiarism, for example, are unconstitutional, even if sometimes it is a black, brown, or low-income plaintiff who charges a white, privileged defendant with violating a general norm.

Scholars (including us) have pointed out that the campus hate speech controversy features two constitutional narratives in collision.[27] Both narratives, equality and free speech, are deeply rooted in our traditions. Equality proponents point out, with considerable justification, that campus hate speech offends values of equal citizenship and equal dignity.[28] Especially when concerted, hate speech marginalizes its victims and relegates them to second-class roles.[29] But, by the same token, laws against hate speech diminish the free-speech interests of the hate speaker; they limit speech, another value of high importance in our scale of constitutional rights.[30] Without a code of some sort, free speech would violate equality; but, with a code, equality interests intrude on free speech—on what people can say. Striking the right balance between equality and speech is, to say the least, a delicate and value-laden task.[31]

Another feature present in the campus hate speech situation is incessancy. Campus administrators worried about hate speech, and victims filing charges under the codes, are not worried so much about the damage from a single incident as the compounding or aggregate effect of many such incidents.[32] A victim who experienced just one attack of hate speech might laugh it off, or wonder what on earth the speaker meant. The problem is that the victim of hate speech—for example, a black or gay undergraduate—is apt to experience many such offenses, in a nearly daily rain of insults, aspersions, loaded language, anonymous E-mail messages, and social exclusion. Like water dripping on limestone, hate speech scars through its frequent repetition. How to curtail the underlying behavior, not to mention apportion punishment, is a challenging task.

THE BACKLASH: REVERSE VICTIMIZATION
AND THE "DIVERSITY HOAX" ARGUMENT

Not only is the task challenging, it is by its nature misguided, according to some critics of hate speech regulation. These critics argue that hate speech guidelines are political correctness gone amok, that they curtail campus discussion, and that conservative or independent-minded maverick speakers are their main victims. A 1999 book by several graduates and students at the University of California (Boalt Hall) law school argued that hate speech codes, like affirmative action and other liberal measures, constitute a diversity hoax.[33] One aspect of this hoax is that conservative speakers end up silenced in the classroom and elsewhere. They are now the main victims of liberal and civil rights orthodoxy. The minorities have their civil rights laws, hate speech codes, and the NAACP. Conservative students are left alone, or with each other only.[34]

How seriously should we take this argument? Despite the book's laments about political correctness, hate speech seems not at all to have been silenced (see Chapter 2), but is growing in frequency and severity. The same is true for its more sophisticated, civilized counterparts—books such as *The Bell Curve*, call-in radio, and Web sites touting white supremacy are growing in numbers. Most campuses, executive boardrooms, and the officer ranks of the military are predominantly white. White thoughts, ideas, and power are in little danger of being suppressed. How many white readers, for example, could name more than three famous historical figures who are black, Latino, or Asian? Minority persons of the most minimal level of literacy could name many more—as well as dozens of famous figures who are white.

QUESTIONS FOR DISCUSSION, CHAPTER 6

1. Why do campuses—as opposed to workplaces, churches, voluntary organizations, or other settings—find hate speech codes attractive?

2. Campuses that enact hate speech codes can expect to be sued by the ACLU. Yet, if they tolerate a known climate of racial abuse, they can be sued (or at least criticized) for ignoring a hostile learning environment. How should a campus administrator balance these risks?

3. Will diversity awareness seminars and sensitivity training prevent campus hate speech, making a formal code unnecessary? Or are formal rules and the prospect of punishment necessary before the campus community will take seminars and policies seriously?

4. Even if it is never applied, does a campus hate speech code serve an important symbolic foundation, showing that the campus values equality, diversity, and dignity?

5. Should a campus hate speech code be broadly, or narrowly, drawn?

6. Because of their function in generating and testing knowledge and ideas, should colleges and universities be especially reluctant (or eager?) to discourage racist and sexist hate speech?

CLASS EXERCISE

Conduct a mock trial of a campus hate speech code. One group represents the ACLU; another, the university; another, the campus minority student organization that has gained permission to state its position; and still another, a group of campus conservative students who want to present arguments the ACLU is unlikely to raise.

The remainder of the class is the jury, which must vote and give a short statement explaining why it decided as it did—BUT, strictly on the basis of the arguments presented.

RECOMMENDED READING, CHAPTER 6

Lee Bollinger, *The Tolerant Society* (1986).

Charles Calleros, *Preparing for the Worst—and Striving for the Best: Training University Employees to Respond Clearly, Constructively, and Constitutionally to Hateful Speech on Campus*, 26 J.L. & Ed. 41 (1997).

Avern Cohn, *Life on Campus Really Ain't So Bad*, 98 Mich. L. Rev. 1549 (2000).

Richard Delgado, *Campus Antiracism Rules: Constitutional Narratives in Collision*, 85 Nw. U. L. Rev. 343 (1991).

Dinesh D'Souza, *Illiberal Education: The Politics of Race and Sex on Campus* (1991).

Chester E. Finn Jr., "The Campus: 'An Island of Repression in a Sea of Freedoms,'" *Commentary* 17 (1989).

Thomas Grey, *Civil Rights vs. Civil Liberties: The Case of Discriminatory Verbal Harassment*, 8 Soc. Philos. & Pol'y 81 (1991).

Diana Tietjens Meyers, *Rights in Collision: A Non-Punitive, Compensatory Remedy for Abusive Speech*, 14 L. & Phil. 1 (1999).

Michael Olivas, *The Law and Higher Education* (1989).

Robert O'Neil, *Free Speech in the Campus Community* (1997).

Thomas F. Pettigrew, *New Patterns of Racism*, 37 Rutgers L. Rev. 673 (1985).

NOTES

1. See, e.g., Jon B. Gould, *The Precedent that Wasn't: College Hate Speech Codes and the Two Faces of Legal Compliance*, 35 L. & Soc. Rev. 345, 352–353 (2001).

2. Ibid.

3. See Chapter 2; David Glenn, "Scholars Present Data in Hopes of Bolstering Legal Defense of Affirmative Action," *Chronicle of Higher Education*, August 20, 2002 (online edition, on file with author).

4. Isabel Wilkerson, "Racial Harassment Altering Blacks' Chances in College," *New York Times*, May 9, 1990, at A1.

5. Ibid.

6. "Scholars Present Data," supra.

7. Ibid.

8. Jessika Fruchter, "U. Colorado Students Deface Library with Anti-Arab Graffiti," *U. Wire*, September 20, 2001.

9. Richard Delgado and Jean Stefancic, *Must We Defend Nazis? Hate Speech, Pornography, and the New First Amendment*, 49–50 (1997).

10. Ibid. at 50.

11. Ibid. at 53–54.

12. Ibid. at 51.

13. Ibid. at 51–52.

14. See Lu-in Wang, *The Complexities of Hate*, 60 Ohio St. L.J. 799 (1999).

15. See Richard Delgado, *Fairness and Formality*, Wis. L. Rev. 1359 (1985).

16. See, e.g., Mari Matsuda et al., *Words That Wound* (1993), discussing this and other approaches; Gould, *The Precedent that Wasn't.*

17. Gould, supra, at 350–360 (codes based on harassment).

18. Ibid. See also Mari Ricker, "Speech Codes: Just Another Word for Censorship?," *Student Lawyer*, February 1999, at 26.

19. A University of Wisconsin system-wide code one of us helped draft, for example, contained both elements.

20. See, e.g., Robin Wilson, "Wisconsin Scales Back Its Faculty Speech Code," *Chronicle of Higher Education*, March 12, 1999, at A10.

21. See Cindy Enright, "Battle Lines," *Denver Post Mag.* Sec., June 12, 1994, at 8 (on California's Leonard Law).

22. *UWM Post v. Regents, University of Wisconsin*, 774 F. Supp. 1163 (E.D. Wis. 1991).

23. *Doe v. University of Michigan*, 721 F. Supp. 352 (E.D. Mich. 1989).

24. Nat Hentoff, "Against the Odds: A Historic Free Speech Victory," *Denver Post*, May 2, 1995, at 20.

25. 505 U.S. 377 (1992).

26. *Wisconsin v. Mitchell*, 113 S. Ct. 2194 (1993).

27. *Defend Nazis?* supra, at 46–49, 62–66.

28. Ibid. at 47–48, 65–67.

29. Ibid. at 66–68.

30. Ibid. at 62–65.

31. *See* Richard Delgado and Jean Stefancic, *Hateful Speech, Loving Communities: Why Our Notion of "A Just Balance" Changes So Slowly*, 82 Cal. L. Rev. 851 (1994).

32. *Defend Nazis?*, supra, at 66–68.

33. David Wienir and Marc Berley, eds., *The Diversity Hoax: Law Students Report from Berkeley* (1999).

34. Ibid.

7

HATE IN CYBERSPACE

As we begin the twenty-first century, a new medium brings us together like no other. Cyberspace allows any person with a computer and a telephone line to communicate with the rest of the world. This technology, however, is not exclusively a tool for good; anyone with something to say can spread ideas to millions with relative ease. Cyberspace creates opportunities for individuals and groups to spread supremacy and hate more easily, quickly, and cheaply than before. Because the Internet is yet in its infancy, many of the issues regarding its control have not yet been settled. We will first look at the current state of cyberspace and its use by hate groups. Then, we will examine the relationship between cyberspace and the First Amendment. Subsequently, we will examine what protections from hate speech the technology itself affords. Finally, we will consider ways the Internet could be structured consistent with current First Amendment doctrine.

THE NEW MEDIA

Cyberspace, most commonly called the Internet, is a worldwide connection of computers over telephone, cable, and fiber optics lines.[1] These connections allow anyone with access and a computer to send and receive data. While the communication of data over the Internet can take many different forms, some of the most common are E-mail, chat rooms or newsgroups, and the World Wide Web.

From http://www.kukluxklan.net/index18.html

Q. What does the Klan think about interracial marriages? Everything after its own kind. Racial integrity should be no different than the rest of the plant and animal kingdom. Each species remains true to its genetic pattern as God intended. God called this [sic] groupings unified by common traits "good." When the fundamental nature of creation is tampered with, the result is ungodly mutation and confusion. A weed patch does not harmonize with a rose garden. Homogenization of race, language, religion and government is as old as the tower of Babel story. The real evil in the world today is the false god of integration promoted by a godless United Nations and the New World Order. The false teachers of churchianity justify interracial marriages in order to keep the White race blind to administering God's laws. A segregated White race will protect itself from alien idolatries. The enemies of God have lived in their luxuries through sin. They can only thrive on their compost of lies. But God's Word is sure and unchanging no matter what the haters of "kind after kind" may say. The fact that God chose a holy and special people to be above all the races of the earth speaks for itself (Deuteronomy 7:6). Truth is not meant to be warm and fuzzy for liberal minded antichrists. Number 25 is a javelin lesson for race mixing. Get the message? As Yahweh spoke to the children of Israel (the White race), "Ye shall not go in to them (all other races), neither shall they come in unto you: for surely they will turn away your heart after their gods." (I Kings 11:2)

E-mail is short for electronic mail—essentially letters or messages sent by computer. Chat rooms or newsgroups are sites where people can post messages on servers that others can read and respond to in either "real time" or later. Finally, the World Wide Web is a collection of Web sites that are set up by individuals and groups. Web sites can be accessed by anyone with an Internet browser such as Microsoft Internet Explorer or Netscape Navigator. These sites can contain a wide range of material including print, pictures, video, audio, and interactive formats for all to see.

Hate groups have seized upon every tool of the Internet to spread their message. Individuals use E-mail to threaten racial minorities, often by anonymous hate messages.[2] Hate groups use listservs that allow them to send E-mail to each other with a click of the mouse.[3] Chat rooms and newsgroups devoted to racial hatred are rife on the Internet.[4] But by far the World Wide Web has been the most popular tool of hate groups. Supremacist messages litter Web sites promoting racial superiority and attacking certain religions or gays and lesbians.[5] These sites—the Southern Poverty Law Center listed 405 in a recent edition of their newsletter[6]—usually contain the history of the sponsoring group, a mission statement, and text by group members. To attract the reader, symbols and pictures offer eye-catching teasers.[7] Some sites even have free downloadable music with lyrics promoting hate[8] or interactive games that make hating "fun."[9] As a collection of many diverse ideas, it should be no surprise that the Internet is also a collection of many forms of hate.

The Internet has become a popular forum among hate groups because of its ease, effectiveness, low cost, wide reach, and anonymity for the speaker.[10] Imagine that you, the reader, were to start an anti-Asian organization called Asian-Haters whose aim is to have all Asians deported from the United States. You might first contact your local Internet provider and buy "space" on their server where you could store your Web site. After creating your Web page, www.asianhater.com, from free downloadable programs from other Internet sites, you would post it on the Internet. You could contact other sites with similar views and have links placed on their sites connecting directly to your own. When visitors came to your site, they could read materials that you post on reasons why Asians should be deported. You would leave your E-mail address on your site so that visitors could send their E-mail addresses to you. Upon receiving these addresses, you would add them to your listserv and send out weekly updates on your cause. An unlimited number of people could visit your site, and you could send them all electronic letters with one click of the mouse.

As a well-read person, you know that your views are unpopular and would most likely damage your reputation if others knew of them. But on www.asianhater.com, you can broadcast any message in absolute anonymity, just as the respondents to your site can support your cause without their identities becoming known.[11] Using the Internet is much cheaper than posting leaflets, making calls, or taking out advertisements. Time and distance are compressed, so you can reach millions around the world in split seconds. As the founder of Asian-Haters, you might easily choose the Internet over traditional forums such as print, television, or telephone.

Unquestionably, the Internet is a powerful tool that eases the spread of beneficial and hateful ideas alike. Why would one want to regulate it? Those who take this position reason that the glory of the Internet is its lack of regulation.[12] The Internet provides an unlimited forum for free speech that should be encouraged, not controlled.[13] Web sites, even if they promote hate, are incapable of harassing or terrorizing because visitors must seek the information. Ideas reach only those who wish to entertain them.[14] Proponents of regulation point out that the very ease of cyberspace communication argues for its regulation. Cyberhate can polarize communities and damage society.[15] The victim of a hateful E-mail may be unable to respond, because the sender mailed the message from a public terminal or has turned off his computer. While the debate rages, those who oppose regulation will continually seek shelter for their views under the First Amendment, while proponents will point to the high social cost of hate.

THE FIRST AMENDMENT AND CYBERSPACE

Cyberspace has become one of the most efficient forms of communication. With the growth of this new medium, critics have asked whether current governmental responses, developed for more traditional forms of media, are adequate for cyberspace. Does the ease of cyber-communication warrant new forms of regulation? Does one First Amendment fit all, or should that guarantee be applied in an institution-specific manner?[16] First consider how traditional forms of First Amendment protection have been applied to cyberspace. Then ponder attempts to expand regulations to the new technology and their results.

The First Amendment has traditionally protected all speech except when the speech falls in certain unprotected categories, when the regulation is content-neutral, and when the government is the purveyor or facilitator of the messages.

Categories of unprotected speech include threats, harassing speech, fighting words, libelous speech, obscenity, child pornography, and speech that incites imminent lawless actions (see Chapter 4).[17] These forms of speech are unprotected because their social costs have been found to outweigh their benefits.[18] For speech to constitute threats, harassment, fighting words, or libel, it must be targeted at a specific individual. Blanket statements expressing hatred toward certain groups are given free sway, even if individual members of such groups are put at risk.[19] Modern courts have followed this doctrine in cyberspace, affording speech protection except when a hurtful message is directed against identified individuals.[20] Thus, most hate speech on the Internet will not be considered threats, harassment, fighting words, or libel, since it is generally directed broadly and not at a particular person.

Speech that incites imminent lawless action need not be directed toward particular individuals, but the standard required will rarely be met by cyberspace. "Since the speaker and listener are separated and often do not even know each other, it is doubtful that a call to arms on the Internet would result in immediate violence. . . . [I]t is unlikely that someone who reads hate on the Internet will immediately rush out of his home to commit a violent act."[21] First Amendment law dealing with this category of unprotected speech is likely to have relatively little application in cyberspace.

Speech can be regulated through content-neutral rules that promote a significant government interest. These "time, place, and manner" restrictions[22] have been used to protect a finite space from harmful secondary effects.[23] However, time, place, and manner regulations do not translate well into cyberspace because few such spaces find a location there. Secondary effects such as noise, traffic, and loss of privacy simply do not arise in a forum without physical limitations.[24] Nevertheless, one type of content-neutral regulation might visit cyberspace in the future. The Supreme Court has upheld zoning laws that confine sexually explicit shops and theaters to certain areas of town in order to protect against corrosive effects on the surrounding neighborhood.[25] Two Supreme Court justices have suggested the zoning of speech on the Internet to the cyberspace equivalent of "adults-only" districts if adequate technology to do so became available.[26] And of course Internet speech that constitutes a hate crime may be punished just as it would if the speech took a more conventional form.

Speech can also be restricted if the government finances it or it takes place on government property. The government finances speech either when a government employee is the speaker or the government underwrites or endorses a private spokesperson.[27] The courts have upheld regulation of hate speech in these situations, and probably will in cyberspace as well.[28] Where speech occurs on government property that is not considered a "public forum," courts have also allowed speech restrictions.[29] Public universities have become fertile ground for disseminating hate. Professor Arthur Butz of Northwestern University (which receives public funds) uses university resources to promote his Holocaust denial book, *The Hoax of the Twentieth Century*. As a public forum, Northwestern cannot restrict Butz, but it has placed a disclaimer on the site disowning any responsibility for its content.[30] Another campus, the University of Illinois, has banned all non-university–related Web sites on its server. Under this policy, in 1996 it removed a student site that promoted Holocaust denial.[31] Public universities are thus not entirely powerless against hate cyber-speech.

Congress attempted to expand governmental monitoring of cyberspace with the enactment of the Communication Decency Act in 1996 (CDA).[32] Two provisions of the act sought to protect minors from harmful materials on the Internet.[33] The Supreme Court overturned those provisions because it considered the terms "indecent transmissions" and "patently offensive display" contained in the act to be unconstitutionally vague.[34] With the enactment of the CDA, and three subsequent statutes, the Child Pornography Prevention Act of 1996, the Children's Online Protection Act of 1998, and the Children's Internet Protection Act of 2000, Congress joined many commentators—and foreign nations—in recognizing that the Internet is different from other forms of media in that it amplifies ideas in a way no other media can. The first few attempts at Internet-specific regulation failed, but Congress is unlikely to abandon the task. While the Supreme Court can be expected to be wary of broad regulation,[35] it has in the past treated different types of media differently for First Amendment analysis.[36] It is now incumbent on Congress and the cyberspace community to develop regulations against hate that can withstand judicial scrutiny.

From http://www.americanskinheads.com/cartoons/traitorn.jpg

Non-Regulatory Protection: Gatekeeping

While proponents of hate speech regulations wait for Congress and the Supreme Court to work out their differences, self-regulation can do much to discourage hate in cyberspace. Effective gatekeeping can be instituted at both ends of a cyberspace transmission. At the sending end, Internet Service Providers (ISPs) and Web hosts can block access to cyberspace for hate messages. At the receiving end, individuals can filter what comes into their homes and businesses. Even hate groups themselves can put visitors on notice of the nature of their sites. ISPs and Web hosts store and maintain Web sites for the general public. They usually are private companies or public universities. Private providers and hosts can ban certain forms of speech on their servers, but under current legislation are not required to do so.[37] Examples of major providers and hosts that have chosen to ban hate speech are Prodigy, Compuserve, America On-Line, and Angelfire.[38] Of course, self-regulation will not work for groups well-heeled enough to offer their own server.[39]

On the receiving end of cyberspace, individuals can screen the information that comes into their homes or businesses by means of Internet filters or selected search engines. Internet filters are programs a purchaser can download. Various private companies that charge an installation fee create these programs.[40] Once downloaded, the program bars specific Internet content. Filters block content in two ways. First, filtering companies continually search cyberspace for extremist Web sites, chat rooms, and newsgroups. Those who purchase Internet filters pay a yearly fee for updates of content they may wish to block.[41] Second, filters feature a database of language characteristic of hate groups and white supremacists, which they then block from coming through. The second feature is useful for the exclusion of unwanted E-mail, which cannot easily be pre-chosen for blocking. These programs are usually capable of fine-tuning to serve user preferences.[42] Most Internet filters do not target hate speech alone, but also sites with adult content, pornography, violence, or offering illicit drugs. This technology has been especially important to parents of children who surf the net.[43]

While Internet filters can be used in private homes and businesses, their use in public forums such as libraries is still an open question. But certain trends have already been established. Courts have decided that it is unconstitutional to place filters on every computer in public libraries, but neither can individuals nor pressure groups force libraries to install filters on particular computers or content.[44] It is still uncertain whether filtering of some, but not all, computers is constitutionally permissible. In 1998, 14.6 percent of U.S. public libraries used filters on some or all of their computers.[45]

Another way to filter incoming content is through the choice of search engines. Specialized search engines will block out designated content in the search list.[46] While most search engines do not filter, they still reserve the right to block materials for any reason.[47] Public pressure might compel the companies that offer search services to exercise that right. Finally, hate sites themselves can warn visitors of their content. While this has proven successful with Web sites containing pornography, it has not caught on with hate sites. Those who do, expound their hate even in their warning.[48]

Standards and Ratings

A second nongovernmental approach is standards and ratings. Other forms of media have agreed to regulate messages aimed at public consumption and to separate or mark those that are particularly sensitive.[49] General magazines are kept "clean" by market forces, with plastic wrappers used to separate those that cater to adult tastes.[50] Movies are rated for their content, while theaters showing hard-core films are located in special parts of town.[51] The 1-900 number for telephone services with mature content discourages underage callers or at least puts them and their parents on notice of the nature of the calls they are making.[52] Common to these regulations is the way they structure media; they do not ban speech, rather they shape the way it is marketed or presented.

Under current proposals, World Wide Web sites would be rated to protect the unwary net surfer.[53] Technology is already in place that would allow such a system.[54] Web sites are similar to movies in many ways. They both provide a wide range of visual and audio content. Neither medium is directed at any particular individual, just at all those who wish to see it. Ratings allow users to ascertain content before they come into contact with it, just as they allow society to notify users what content it considers harmful. With ratings, parents can protect their children from content they deem unwholesome.

The Web site community could set the standards of cyberspace regulation, as the Motion Picture Association of America and the National Association of Theater Owners, both nongovernmental groups, currently do with movies. Alternatively, individually calibrated filters could screen content. Or, content producers could rate their own sites, with governmentally enforced punishment for gross deviation from agreed standards.

Once content is rated, users will be warned before they view a Web site. They can then simply close the site once they see the rating. Browsers can be equipped with options to eliminate ratings for those who do not desire them.[55] Search engines can be designed to censor and screen out content. No matter the method, users will have a choice. They will know when particular materials are coming, will know what content society finds potentially harmful, and can choose not to allow cyberhate material into their homes.

QUESTIONS FOR DISCUSSION, CHAPTER 7

1. Because Internet technology is in its infancy, should society (and the legal system) be wary of regulating it too harshly? Or do other features of cyberhate call for controls, even though we might otherwise wish to allow the technology to develop unimpeded?
2. With Web sites and chat groups, the user must come to the sender. Exposure to hate, in other words, is voluntary. E-mail is different, however. Should the two media of electronic communication be treated differently for that reason?
3. Have you ever visited a hate Web site? Been sent a hate-filled message? What did you do?
4. Should parents and libraries employ filters, so as to discourage access to hate sites or hard-core electronic pornography degrading to women?
5. If a European country enacts a law punishing electronic transmission of material denying the Holocaust or disparaging Jews, should American courts cooperate in enforcing it?
6. Will the Internet bring people closer together, or push them farther apart?

CLASS EXERCISE

Discuss: What are the vilest things you have seen on the Internet? The most ennobling?

Is the Internet a force for good?

RECOMMENDED READING, CHAPTER 7

Peter J. Breckheimer III, Note, *A Haven for Hate: The Foreign and Domestic Implications of Protecting Internet Hate Speech under the First Amendment*, 75 S. Cal. L. Rev. 1407 (2002).

Center for Democratic Renewal, *Hate on the Internet* (undated).
Lawrence Lessig, *The Future of Ideas* (2001).

Thomas B. Nachbar, *Paradox and Structure: Relying on Government Regulation to Preserve the Internet's Unregulated Character*, 85 Minn. L. Rev. 215 (2000).

Robert O'Neil, *Free Speech in the Campus Community* (1997).

Sonjiv N. Singh, *Cyberspace: A New Frontier for Fighting Words*, 25 Rutgers Computer & Technol. L.J. 283 (1999).

Alexander Tsesis, *Hate in Cyberspace: Regulating Hate Speech on the Internet*, 38 U.S.D. L. Rev. 817 (2001).

The World's Most Offensive Web Site, Journal of Blacks in Higher Ed., Spring 2001, at 36.

Jeffrey R. Young, "Stanford Officials Attempt to Trace Origin of Racist E-mail Message," *Chronicle of Higher Education*, June 18, 1999 (Info. Technol.).

Notes

1. See, e.g., Lawrence Lessig, *The Future of Ideas: The Fate of the Commons in a Connected World* (2001); Lawrence Lessig, *Code and Other Laws of Cyberspace* (1999).

2. In *U.S. v. Machado*, 195 F.3d 454 (9th Cir. 1999), the defendant sent E-mails titled "Asian Hater" to sixty Asian students at the University of California, Irvine. The messages declared his hate for Asians and blamed Asians for all crimes occurring on campus. Machado wrote, "I personally will make it my life career to find and kill every one of you personally." In *U.S. v. Kingman Quon* (unpublished), Kingman Quon sent E-mails to Hispanic professors, students, and employees of universities across the nation. Quon's message accused Hispanics of being too stupid to get jobs or to be accepted as students without affirmative action policies. He threatened to "come down and kill" them. See Anti-Defamation League, *Combating Extremism in Cyberspace: The Legal Issues Affecting Internet Hate Speech* [http://www.adl.com] (2000).

3. Access to listservs can usually be found on the Web sites of hate groups. To subscribe, an individual usually sends an E-mail to a chosen address with "subscribe" in the message box. Once the manager of the listserv receives the E-mail, the subscriber's E-mail enters a list that usually receives monthly, weekly, or daily updates from the hate group. The listserv for the "KKK Magazine and News Report" can be subscribed to at klan-news@usa.net. Another white supremacy group, Stormfront, receives subscriptions at listserv@lists.stormfront.org.

4. Popular sites that allow users to set up and use chat rooms and newsgroups are Yahoo! at http://clubs.yahoo.com, Microsoft Networks at http://communities.msn.com, and NBC at http://clubs.nbci.com. These clubs are easy to set up and free. The Ku Klux Klan is an example of a hate group that has multiple clubs

set up on each of the three main Internet sites. *See* http://clubs.yahoo.com/clubs/thekukluxklanklub, http://communities.msn.com/christianwhiteknightsofthekukluxklan, and http://clubs.nbci.com/kukluxklan.

5. White supremacy groups such as the Ku Klux Klan, Neo-Nazis, Stormfront, Christian Identity Movement, and National Association for the Advancement of White People (NAAWP) have multiple Web sites on the Internet. While a main Web site is set up by a group's leader, multiple sites are also set up by district or state chapters, and individual members. Some of these sites include http://k-k-k.com, http://bbs.stormfront.org, and http://www.naawp.org. Sites attacking Christianity can be found at http://www.anus.com/altar/index.html, http://www.blackplague.org, and http://www.glistrup.com. Anti-gay sites can be found at http://www.christiangallary.com, and http://www.melvig.org. Antisemitic sites not only promote exclusion of the Jewish people, but deny the Holocaust. Some examples are http://www.blacksandjews.com, http://www.ety.com/ HRP, and http://holywar.org. Other hate groups that promote male superiority, the militia, and teach bomb-making can also be found.

6. Southern Poverty Law Center, *Active Hate Sites: On the Internet in the Year 2001*, Intelligence Report, spring 2002, at 38.

7. For example, a Ku Klux Klan site at http://www.k-k-k.com features a picture of an imperial shield and sword, a photo of a burning cross surrounded by white-hooded Klansmen, and the drawing of a baby and parents with the statement, "To be born WHITE is an honor and a privilege."

8. Music is downloadable from certain Web sites. Once downloaded, listeners can listen to the music on their computers or record it onto CDs and tapes by changing the music into WAV format. Some examples of white supremacy Web sites that have downloadable music are http://www.snj. quik.com/sickboy, and http://www.hellbilly.com.

9. For example, at http://www.niggers.com visitors can play an interactive game in which they attempt to place a noose on a moving "nigger."

10. Elizabeth Phillips Marsh, *Purveyors of Hate on the Internet: Are We Ready for Hate Spam?*, 17 Ga. St. U. L. Rev. 379, 387 (2000).

11. Ibid. at 390–394. Example adopted from hypothetical on Society for Cutting and Raping of Every Woman (S.C.R.E.W).

12. See ACLU, *Cyber Liberties*, at http://www.aclu.org/issues/cyber/hmcl. html. The American Civil Liberties Union (ACLU) argues against Internet regulation.

13. Walter A. Effros, *High-Tech Heroes, Virtual Villains, and Jacked-In Justice: Visions of Law and Lawyers in Cyberpunk Science Fiction*, 45 Buff. L. Rev. 931 (1997).

14. See Anti-Defamation League, supra.

15. Steven G. Gey, *Fear of Freedom: The New Speech Regulation in Cyberspace*, 8 Tex. J. Women & L. 183, 185 (1999).

16. Arguing for one First Amendment, see Rodney A. Smolla, *Will Tabloid Journalism Ruin the First Amendment for the Rest of Us?*, 9 DePaul-LCA J. Art & Ent. L. & Pol'y 1, 34 (1998). For institution-specific First Amendment, see

Frederick Schauer, *Principles, Institutions, and the First Amendment*, 112 Harv. L. Rev. 84 (1998).

17. For speech that constitutes threats, harassment, fighting words or libel, see *Chaplinsky v. New Hampshire*, 315 U.S. 568 (1942). For speech that incites imminent lawless actions, see *Brandenburg v. Ohio*, 395 U.S. 444 (1969).

18. *Chaplinsky*, 315 U.S. 568 (1942).

19. See Anti-Defamation League, supra.

20. In *Planned Parenthood of the Columbia/Willamette, Inc. v. American Coalition of Life Activists*, 23 F. Supp.2d 1182 (D. OR 1999), an Internet site listed the names and home addresses of doctors who performed abortions. The site called for the doctors to be brought to justice for crimes against humanity. The names of doctors who had been wounded were listed in gray. Doctors who had been killed by anti-abortionists had been crossed out. The court found this speech to be threatening and not protected under the First Amendment.

21. See Anti-Defamation League, supra.

22. See Gey, supra, at 195.

23. *Ward v. Rock Against Racism*, 491 U.S. 781, 792 (1989) (noise). *Frisby v. Schultz*, 487 U.S. 474 (1988) (residential privacy). *Cox v. New Hampshire*, 312 U.S. 569 (1941) (traffic).

24. See Anti-Defamation League, supra.

25. *Young v. American Mini-Theaters*, 427 U.S. 50 (1976); *City of Renton v. Playtime Theaters*, 475 U.S. 41 (1986).

26. *Reno v. ACLU*, 521 U.S. 844, 886 (1997) (S. O'Connor, J., concurring, joined by Chief Justice Rehnquist).

27. See Gey, supra, at 199.

28. Concerning speech of government employees, the court stated, "Government officials should enjoy wide latitude in managing their offices, without intrusive oversight by the judiciary in the name of the First Amendment." *Connick v. Myers*, 461 U.S. 661, 673 (1994). Upholding a restriction on abortion information provided by government-funded doctors, the court stated, "This is not a case of the Government 'suppressing a dangerous idea,' but of a prohibition on a project grantee or its employees from engaging in activities outside of the project's scope." *Rust v. Sullivan*, 500 U.S. 173, 194 (1991).

29. *International Soc'y for Krishna Consciousness v. Lee*, 505 U.S. 672, 678–679 (1992).

30. See Anti-Defamation League, supra.

31. Ibid.

32. 47 U.S.C.A. § 223 (1996).

33. CDA § 223(a)(1)(B)(ii) criminalizes the "knowing" transmission of "obscene or indecent" messages to any recipient under eighteen years of age; 47 U.S.C.A. § 223(a)(1)(B)(ii). CDA § 223(d) prohibits "knowing[ly]" sending or displaying to a person under eighteen any message "that, in context, depicts or describes, in terms patently offensive as measured by contemporary community standards, sexual or excretory activities or organs," 47 U.S.C.A. § 223(d).

34. See *Reno*, supra, at 864–885.

35. The U.S. Supreme Court has preferred to adopt the marketplace-of-ideas model of free speech—a model that allows beneficial and harmful speech to co-exist, with the truth prevailing. It is willing to allow harmful speech because it believes such speech will be tested and rejected. See Anti-Defamation League, supra. "As a matter of constitutional tradition, in the absence of evidence to the contrary, we presume that governmental regulation of the content of speech is more likely to interfere with the exchange of ideas than to encourage it." *Reno*, 521 U.S. at 885.

36. "The Court has long been in the habit of saying that each medium of mass expression raises particular First Amendment problems." *Reno*, 521 U.S. at 868.

37. See 47 U.S.C.A § 230, Internet Service Providers and Web hosts will not be held responsible for the content of customer Web sites.

38. See Anti-Defamation League, supra.

39. The Ku Klux Klan has created its own server, which the reader can access at http://www.k–k–k.com. Don Black, the creator of the white supremacist group Stormfront, has also created his own server. The server houses not only Stormfront's Web site, but also the Web site of other hate groups. For example, the National Observer, once a Web site on America On-Line, was removed from that server for content that violated America On-Line's Terms of Service under "hate propaganda." National Observer now resides on Don Black's server.

40. At http://afafilter.com, Cyber Patrol can be downloaded for $49.95 with the first year of content updates free. Additional yearly updates are $49.95. At http://www.adl.org, HateFilter can be ordered for $29.95 with a free content update period of three months. A yearly update subscription can be purchased for an additional $29.95. At http://familycow.com/internetfilters.html, Cyber Sentinel can be downloaded for $34.95. Cyber Sentinel does not offer updates; it filters strictly using word content.

41. See text and note immediately supra.

42. For example, Cyber Patrol allows users to choose multiple settings for different levels of access for each particular user. Users can set Internet use to limited times of the day. The filter can also filter outgoing messages. Finally, the filter can take "snapshots" of prohibited content sought and E-mail it to a third party (e.g., parents of children).

43. See 47 U.S.C.A § 230, "It is the policy of the United States . . . to remove disincentives for the development and utilization of blocking and filtering technologies that empower parents to restrict their children's access to objectionable or inappropriate online material."

44. In *Mainstream Loudoun v. Board of Trustees for Loudoun County Library*, 24 F. Supp.2d 552 (E.D. Va. 1998), the court ruled that a county library policy board violated the First Amendment when it required filtering software to be installed on every public library computer in Loudoun County, Virginia. In *Kathleen R. v. City of Livermore*, 87 Cal. App.4th 684 (Cal. Dist. App. 2001), the

court ruled that a parent cannot compel a public library to install filtering software, even on computers used mainly by children.

45. *The 1998 National Survey of U.S. Public Library Outlet Internet Connectivity: Summary Results*, American Library Association Office for Information Technology Policy, American Library Association Web site, Dec. 1998.

46. Cyberspace is a collection of millions of different sites each identified by a specific hypertext transport protocol (http). Most users go into cyberspace not knowing the specific http of the site they wish to visit, or they want a list of http's of sites on a subject they wish to search out. Search engines, which are free Internet-based programs, help users find the sites they wish to visit. Search engines such as http://www.onekey.com/ and http://www.startup-page.com/ are examples of engines that specialize in blocking out "indecent" content from their search list. The engine http://www.askjeeves.com/ is a popular search engine that has a subsidiary site http://ajkids.com/ for users who prefer a filtering search engine.

47. The popular search engine http://www.yahoo.com/ has stated in its terms of service, "You agree not to use the Service to . . . upload, post, e-mail, transmit or otherwise make available any Content that is unlawful, harmful, threatening, abusive, harassing, tortious, defamatory, vulgar, obscene, libelous, invasive of another's privacy, hateful, or racially, ethnically or otherwise objectionable. . . . See http://docs.yahoo.com/info/terms/ Terms of Service 6(a).

48. At a white supremacist Web site, the warning before entering the site declares, "This site contains content and images, which are considered politically incorrect, if you are a bleeding heart liberal, politician, judge, newsmedia, non-white, homosexual, abortionist or suffer from some other type of delusions, please leave immediately." See [http://home.hiwaay.net/~akc/]. At an anti-Jew site, the warning states, "Before entering this site, please keep in mind that: The following WebPages contain only & only the truth about kafirs (i.e., hindus, jews, etc.) and the hindu country india. If you belong to one of these groups and you cannot stand the truth, we recommend that you don't enter this site." See http://www.brain.net.pk/~nauroze/ killindex.html/.

49. Yochi Benkler, *Part IV: How (If At All) To Regulate the Internet: Net Regulation: Taking Stock and Looking Forward*, 71 U. Colo. L. Rev. 1203, 1238 (2000).

50. Sexually explicit magazines such as *Playboy* or *Hustler* are kept in plastic wrappers on newsstands. Only those who wish to purchase them can view their contents.

51. The U.S. Supreme Court has upheld the zoning of sexually explicit movie theaters into certain areas of town. See *Young* and *City of Renton*, supra. The movie rating system is a voluntary system sponsored by the Motion Picture Association of America and the National Association of Theater Owners. A committee of consumers rate films. Enforcement of the ratings is voluntary for theater owners and consumers. Theme, language, violence, nudity, sex, and drug use are among the criteria considered. See [http://www.filmratings.][com/question.htm/] (visited on June 3, 2001).

52. 1-900 numbers prohibit callers younger than eighteen. This prohibition is enforced by asking the age of callers upon receiving a call.

53. See Thomas B. Nachbar, *Paradox and Structure: Relying on Government Regulation to Preserve the Internet's Unregulated Character*, 85 Minn. L. Rev. 215 (2000).

54. A platform called PICS allows software to recognize ratings on Web sites. PICS does not actually rate the Web site, it is a template that allows multiple independent rating systems to be standardized. John F. McGuire, *When Speech Is Heard Around the World: Internet Content Regulation in the United States and Germany*, 74 N.Y.U. L. Rev. 750, 783 (1999).

55. Internet browsers such as Netscape Navigator or Microsoft Internet Explorer can be easily programmed to read ratings and exclude user specified ratings.

PART THREE
SPECIAL SYMBOLS, SPEAKERS, AND SHOWS

8

WHEN HATE GOES TANGIBLE:
LOGOS, MASCOTS, CONFEDERATE
FLAGS, AND MONUMENTS

When readers think of hate speech, they usually think of words and messages—an epithet, a cutting remark, graffiti defacing a Jewish temple or a black theme house, or flyers or E-mails sent to minority students questioning their intelligence or fitness for university life.

Sometimes, however, the disparaging message finds a tangible, physical form. A group of skinheads burns a cross on a black family's lawn. A Southern state flies the Confederate flag over its statehouse or other official buildings. A college student displays that flag on a dorm wall or hangs it out a window for all to see. A sports team adopts as its logo a fierce-looking Indian. The fans devise a cheer that includes a tomahawk gesture. At halftime, a pseudo-Indian, dressed in war paint, prances up and down the field on a horse, whipping up the fans.

A lawyer at a major law firm interviews a minority candidate. The interviewer wears a watch that plays "Dixie" every hour on the hour. A law school displays portraits of famous professors who have taught there. Every one of them is white and male, even though eminent women and professors of color have taught at the school.

A Southern university features a prominent statue of Robert E. Lee, architect and leader of Southern resistance. An elite Northern university names several buildings after famous slave owners.

All of these practices have drawn challenges. All, arguably, demonstrate insensitivity (if not worse) to the feelings of some minority group. In a few cases, the practice may have been adopted for that very reason.

Imagine that you are a white American and find yourself (perhaps as a Peace Corps volunteer) in a part of the world populated by very few whites. Those who live or work there are not very popular right now because of conflicts that have broken out between your home and host countries. While walking down the street one day, you come across a banner featuring an unflattering likeness of a Caucasian. The figure is cross-eyed, sports a silly grin, and has a piece of hay stuck in his teeth. An accompanying caption says some unflattering and stereotypical things about Americans—for example, that you are ignorant, uncultured, loud, and unable to speak any language but English.

How would you feel? Would you laugh it off? Feel offended? Threatened? Suppose you are the parent of a small child who asks you what the poster means. What would you say?

This chapter examines some of the issues that can arise when hate takes tangible form. As the reader might surmise, most such cases do not present the same degree of immediacy as a hate message that is tailored to one individual ("Jones is a typical black affirmative action baby; he doesn't deserve to teach on this campus") or delivered face to face ("Jones, me and my buddies find you a sad excuse for a professor. You're a typical affirmative action hire and an embarrassment to this university"). Perhaps for that reason, statues, monuments, and the like are rarely the grounds for a lawsuit. On the other hand, perhaps because they are intended to be seen by a large audience, they contribute to a climate of opinion that is injurious to members of the group singled out. They etch a public stereotype a little deeper, at the same time that they attack the self-regard of members of the target group. For this reason, redress has generally taken the form of petitions, requests for administrative rulings, and appeals to the legislature, rather than individual lawsuits seeking money damages or an injunction.

But tangible symbols have a quality that words—at least of the spoken variety—do not: They are enduring. Words disappear as soon as they are spoken. They may resonate in the mind of the victim, causing him or her to recall them over and over again. But a flag, monument, or a sports logo is always there to remind members of the group it spotlights of its unsolicited message.

Moreover, it is hard to "talk back" to a statue. Most tangible expressions of racism are inert. One cannot enter into a dialogue with an inanimate object or initiate a conversation with a horseback-riding mascot in front of 100,000 fans. The usual First Amendment objection to suppression of hate speech (namely, that it is better to "speak back") thus does not apply in the case of flags, monuments, sports mascots, and logos. Theoretically, an Indian tribe that objects to the co-optation of an Indian likeness could respond by selecting a sports logo for its own team that denigrates whites. A black community offended by a statehouse that flies a Confederate flag could fly a banner with Martin Luther King Jr.'s likeness on top of a black community center. But the two displays are not comparable; one does not cancel out the other. What the vilified or offended group really wants is for the offending display to stop.

A further obstacle is that, with tangible tokens and icons, the sponsoring group can often maintain that they are (1) not insulting at all; or (2) intended to convey, not hate, but regional solidarity and pride.

Not Insulting at All

What is insulting is a highly personal, subjective matter, or so it might be argued. Thus, individuals who post, build, erect, or create racialized objects and logos often retreat to the position that what they have done is not insulting at all. Not long ago, a region in Oklahoma sponsored an annual county fair with a degrading logo—a pig with features that looked Mexican—that appeared on banners, posters, and tickets. Minorities immediately challenged the logo. The sponsors, who had already spent a good deal of money printing full-color posters and hanging them around town, pretended surprise. Declaring that they had checked the logo with one of their employees, a Mexican American, and that he had not found it offensive, they resisted the demand to retire the pig. Only when the minorities threatened a boycott did the organizers decide to try a different logo.

Regional Pride

With the Confederate flag controversy, one often encounters a second response. In addition to the first ("there's nothing insulting about the flag; it's all in your head"), defenders counter by asserting a cultural right to fly the flag as a symbol of Southern pride.[1] One person's hate speech is another's beloved regional symbol. One person's mark of exclusion—or badge and incident of servitude—is another's totem of local pride.[2] Although most courts appear to have rejected this argument, at least in school settings one court found that school districts could not ban racially sensitive slogans and symbols, such as the Confederate flag worn on a shirt, if they allowed other symbols such as Malcolm X shirts worn by black students (see Chapter 5).

SPORTS SYMBOLS AND MASCOTS

With sports symbols, another set of considerations comes into play: tradition and the great respect Americans pay sports heroes. Americans love their sports. Many fans identify with a team. When it wins, an entire city is happy; when it loses, everyone is downcast. The same indulgence attends everything associated with a team, ranging from silly-looking uniforms, preposterously overage cheerleaders, and mock-serious sports commentators who learnedly analyze the tactics and strategy of what might otherwise be considered a children's game played by grown-ups.

All this means that when a team adopts a logo, nickname, or mascot, such as Indians, Braves, or Seminoles, or continues one from a former era (such as Rebels),[3] persuading it to change will not be easy. Fans will protest ("Where's your sense of humor?"). Management will insist that the logo or mascot is intended to honor those it depicts. Tradition will weigh heavily on the side of the logo's defenders. ("We've always been the Braves. No one today gives it a second thought.")

Yet many in the group (usually Indians) singled out for the dubious honor may object. The ridiculous painted warriors parading along the sidelines mock the idea of Indian honor and tradition. The term "redskin" is a hated insult.[4] The fierce-looking Seminole whose likeness adorns T-shirts and banners reinforces the image of the bloodthirsty savage.[5] One Indian parent recounted taking his son to a basketball game at the local sports stadium. When a garishly painted Indian look-alike strutted and preened in front of the crowd, the parent had to take his son home in tears.[6] Dozens of accounts like this one reinforce how demoralizing many Indian tribes find it when college or professional teams borrow their histories, dress, or traditions, usually without asking.

Although no court has awarded relief to an Indian plaintiff in a situation like the one mentioned above (or is likely to do so anytime soon), and legislative relief is unlikely because of the public outcry likely to accompany any bill, a recent lawsuit explored an unusual avenue for relief. The federal statute that sets up protection for trademarks provides an exception for items considered scandalous or disparaging.[7] A group of Indians invoked this provision in a challenge to a team logo and name (Washington Redskins) that Native Americans everywhere find offensive. If successful, this strategy would deprive the team of the exclusive right to market sweatshirts, banners, and other paraphernalia bearing the logo and likeness.[8] Anyone could market cheap knock-offs. Deprived of the possibility of financial gain, the team might opt for a new logo, one that could be trademarked. The lawsuit, which had not reached final judgment at the time this book was written, thus harnesses the profit motive in the service of antiracism. Similar actions are said to be pending or contemplated.[9]

Other time-honored means for putting pressure on an organization that sports an offensive logo or symbol include protests, consumer boycotts, and official condemnations. Recently, the NAACP called for an economic boycott of South Carolina because a Confederate flag flies above the state capitol. The boycott posed a problem for Democratic Party presidential hopefuls. If they traveled to South Carolina to campaign, and spent money there, they risked alienating one of the party's most loyal constituencies, African Americans.[10] Recently, the U.S. Commission on Civil Rights and a number of state human rights agencies called for an end to the use of Indian sports mascots, while a few newspapers have adopted a policy of not printing the names of teams that use Indian mascots.

CROSS-BURNING

Another tangible symbol of racial hate is the burning cross. Long associated with the Ku Klux Klan and Southern white supremacy, the burning cross has recently reappeared as a token of white supremacy. During the Klan's heyday in the 1920s and 1930s, Klan meetings would feature hooded figures, speeches touting white virtue, and large

> ### Florida v. T.B.D., 656 So.2d 479, 480 (2001).
>
> The present statute proscribes conduct that falls within the category of "threats of violence." An unauthorized cross-burning by intruders in one's own yard constitutes a direct affront to one's privacy and security and has been inextricably linked in this state's history to sudden and precipitous violence—lynchings, shootings, whippings, mutilations, and home-burnings. The connection between a flaming cross in the yard and forthcoming violence is clear and direct. A more terrifying symbolic threat for many Floridians would be difficult to imagine.
>
> The banned conduct also constitutes "fighting words." A flaming cross erected by intruders on one's property "inflicts [real] injury" on the victim in the form of fear and intimidation and also "tends to incite an immediate breach of the peace" where the victim or intruder may be inclined to take further action. In the lexicon of the United States Supreme Court, it is the extraordinarily threatening *mode* of expression, not the idea expressed, that is intolerable. *See R.A.V.*, 505 U.S. at 391–93, 112 S. Ct. at 2548–49. Again, it is difficult to imagine a scenario more rife with potential for reflexive violence and peace–breaching.

burning crosses. The Klan would also burn crosses, often under cover of darkness, in the yards of their enemies—rebellious Negroes or their white sympathizers.

In 1992, the Supreme Court reversed the conviction of a white teenager who had burned a cross on the lawn of a black family in St. Paul, Minnesota.[11] Finding that the ordinance under which the youth had been charged singled out racial motivation for harsh treatment, the Court declared it unconstitutional. A few years later, however, an African American family living in Texas won a large judgment against five men who trespassed on their property while wearing pillowcases over their heads and carrying a large wooden cross wrapped in sheets. The family awoke to find a smoldering cross in their yard. Less than a year later, they filed suit alleging violation of their civil rights, conspiracy to violate those rights, and various common law torts such as slander, nuisance, and intentional infliction of emotional distress. After a seven-day trial, a jury that included two blacks awarded compensatory damages for the family's claims.[12]

And, as this book went to press, the Supreme Court upheld a Virginia statute that makes it illegal to burn a cross with the intent to intimidate another.[13]

QUESTIONS FOR DISCUSSION, CHAPTER 8

1. Are the song "Dixie" and the Confederate flag drenched in histories of slavery and pain? Or are they neutral regional symbols that take on whatever meaning we choose to give them?
2. Should we be especially vigilant to protect "the speech we hate"—like that of the Ku Klux Klan and white supremacists?
3. Can't those who are offended by a Confederate flag, Indian mascot prancing up and down the field, or a public statue of Robert E. Lee simply avert their eyes?
4. If a high school football team has called itself the Braves (or the Fighting Mohawks) for a long time, so that hardly anyone ever thinks about the symbol (apart from the team) any more, has the label lost its sting?
5. How do you feel about the term *redskin*?
6. The Sambo restaurant recently changed its name in response to criticism that it made many black patrons uncomfortable. If you are white, how would you feel about patronizing a restaurant called Hayseed, Honkie, or Hillbilly?

CLASS EXERCISE

Name as many tangible things—logos, brand names, songs, statues, flags, banners, mascots, and so on—that you personally have seen within a twenty-mile radius of your school and that you strongly suspect are offensive to a small group.

What can be done about such displays?

RECOMMENDED READING, CHAPTER 8

Charles Bernstein, *Sambos: Only a Fraction of the Action: The Inside Story of a Restaurant Empire's Rise and Fall* (1984).

Mark R. Connolly, *What's in a Name? A Historical Look at Native American–Related Nicknames and Symbols at Three U.S. Universities*, 71 J. Higher Ed. 515 (2000).

Debbieann Erickson, *Trampling on Equality—Hate Messages in Public Parades*, 35 Gonzaga L. Rev. 465 (1999/2000).

James Forman Jr., *Driving Dixie Down*, 101 Yale L.J. 505 (1991).

M. M. Manring, *Slave in a Box: The Strange Career of Aunt Jemima* (1998).

J. Michael Martinez et al., eds., *Confederate Symbols in the Contemporary South* (2000).

"Popular Hispanic Figurines Spark Image Controversy," *Denver Post*, May 29, 1999, at A2.

Bruce Stapleton, *Redskins: Racial Slur or Symbol of Success?* (2001).

NOTES

1. See, e.g., "A Change of Mind in Austin," *Economist*, June 3, 2000; Adam Nagourney, "Confederate Flag Boycott Tests Candidates' Resolve," *New York Times*, February 7, 2003, at A16; Alexander Tsesis, *The Problem of Confederate Symbols: A Thirteenth Amendment Approach*, 75 Temple L. Rev. 539 (2002).

2. See Tsesis, ibid.; Mark R. Connolly, *What's In a Name?*, 71 J. Higher Ed. 515, 531 (2000). On the new Southern "heritage" movement, see, e.g., Southern Poverty Law Center, *A March through Dixie Has Onlookers a Bit Bewildered*, Intelligence Report, winter 2002, at 2; Heidi Beirich and Mark Potok, *A War Within*, in id. at 37.

3. See, e.g., "Short Subjects: Endangered Mascot Watch," *Chronicle of Higher Education*, January 5, 2001, at A8.

4. See Jeff Dolley, *The Four Rs: Use of Indian Mascots in Educational Facilities*, 32 J.L. & Ed. 21, 26–30 (2003).

5. Ibid.

6. See Fred Villeux, "Indians Are a People, Not Mascots," in *The Price We Pay: The Case Against Racist Speech, Hate Propaganda, and Pornography* (Laura Lederer and Richard Delgado, eds., 1995).

7. Section 2(a) of the Lanham Trademark Act, 15 U.S.C. § 1052(a) (1997).

8. *Harjo v. Pro-Football, Inc.*, 50 U.S.P.Q.2d (BNA) (Trademark Trial and Appeal Board, 1999). At the time we went to press, the case was still under appeal. See Carol D. Leonnig, "Judge Rules Redskins Trademark Valid," *San Francisco Chronicle,* Oct. 2, 2003, at A2 (reporting that a U.S. District Court reversed the federal trademark panel's 1999 decision to cancel six federal trademarks for Washington Redskin products).

9. See also Sue Ann Presley, "Justice Department Looks into Indian Mascot Use," Boulder (Colorado) *Daily Camera,* February 18, 1999, at 2A.

10. See "Candidates' Resolve," supra.

11. See *R.A.V. v. St. Paul,* 505 U.S. 377 (1992).

12. See Nick Upmeyer, "Texas Family Wins Cross-Burning Trial," *National Law Journal,* March 10, 2003, at B1.

13. See "A Decision on Cross-Burning" (editorial), *New York Times,* April 8, 2003, at A30.

9

LAWYER DISCIPLINE:
WHEN THE SYSTEM
SETS OUT TO PURGE HATE

Sometimes, lawyers are not the ones debating hate speech. Sometimes, lawyers and judges are the very ones uttering it. What should be done about a lawyer or judge who espouses white-supremacist views or persists in browbeating clients or litigants of color?

A number of cases have brought such issues to the fore. In one, Matthew Hale, a white supremacist, established a racist congregation called the World Church of the Creator. Hale's Web site explained his philosophy, which included white solidarity in the face of imminent engulfment by ethnic hordes; holy war, if necessary, to preserve white civilization; and denunciation of the "mud races." Hale preached a strange theology featuring sixteen commandments, rejection of standard Christianity, and biological theories of racial difference and hierarchy. His site contained links to the Ku Klux Klan, the Nazi Party, the White Aryan Resistance, and kindred groups. Hale aimed a portion of his outreach efforts at white children, marketing a line of puzzles and games designed to teach them about their own racial superiority.[1]

The controversy came to a head when Hale, a graduate of Southern Illinois University law school, applied for membership in the Illinois bar. Like most state licensing procedures, Illinois's required that Hale demonstrate his character and fitness to practice law.[2] When the state bar refused to certify him fit to practice law, even though he had passed the state's bar examination, Hale petitioned for review by the Illinois Supreme Court, which rejected it. He then applied for certiorari (discretionary review) by the U. S. Supreme Court, which also declined to hear his case.

The Illinois bar committee turned Hale down on the ground that his published statements demonstrated disdain for constitutional values of equal citizenship that all lawyers are sworn to defend. (Indeed, Hale advocated abolishing the Fourteenth Amendment's Equal Protection Clause.) They also showed that he supported violence, if necessary, to rid the country of the "mud races."[3] His supporters complained that Hale was being punished, in effect, for speech. (Hale freely bandied about racial slurs and epithets.) They also pointed out that his exclusion from the practice of law discouraged the development of cyberspace, since Hale's views would not have attained such notoriety if he had not broadcast them via his Web site, thus bringing them to the attention of many watchful eyes.[4] If he had not made known his views as he did, he would be a practicing lawyer today.

His detractors pointed out that courts in every state permit bar associations to screen candidates for moral fitness, and that they routinely deny admission to would-be lawyers who are felons, chronic alcoholics, or deadbeats who skip out on their debts.[5] To the charge that these criteria concern acts, not attitudes, and that Hale was disciplined for having a bad attitude, Hale's opponents replied that bar associations are well within their rights to assume that attitudes predict future behavior and that Hale had been convicted of a number of offenses.[6] An applicant who shows contempt for persons of color and Jews—and even urged that they be deported from the United States—will likely treat them that way when encountering them in the course of legal work. Because Hale rejected a fundamental tenet of our legal system—racial equality—he could be excluded from practicing within that system. An ordinary citizen is free to believe that the world is flat, they argued. But if a science or geography teacher holds that view, a school system is not required to give him a classroom in which to promulgate it.[7]

Hate Speech in Court

Hate speech has not just played a role in determining whether a law graduate is fit to practice law. It has also played a role in court. Sometimes lawyers use hate speech toward a participant in the courtroom drama—usually someone connected to the other side. At other times a judge regales a lawyer or witness with racist or sexist invective (see Chapter 4). In one case, a lawyer characterized the opposing counsel as employing "little sheeny Hebrew tricks." In another a prosecutor described some defendants as prevaricating "little child-eating bastards." A state court judge told a woman lawyer who had exasperated him that he did not believe ladies should be lawyers, but should be at home raising families. Needless to say, all these cases merited—and received—sanction.

THE BAR'S POSITION

The American Bar Association may one day be called upon to decide whether to incorporate rules against lawyers who utter hate speech in its official Model Rules of Professional Conduct. In 1997, the Young Lawyers Division passed a resolution condemning bias by lawyers in the course of their professional activities. The division moved that the association at large adopt it, and the House of Delegates did.[8] Whether the resolution will one day be incorporated into the official rules of professional conduct is an open question. If it is, the Matthew Hale case will become a national precedent.

Meanwhile, Hale did little to indicate that he had reformed. In a 2002 interview with a *New York Times* columnist, Hale recalled how he first came to believe that nonwhites were inferior: At a dance, he saw white girls "betraying their race" by kissing black boys. He felt nauseated; as he told the interviewer, "Interracial marriage is against nature. It's a form of bestiality." When the columnist, a white man, informed Hale that he was married to a Chinese woman, "It was . . . an awkward moment."[9]

When the columnist asked him whether he encouraged killing members of nonwhite races, he shrugged. "Suppose someone goes out and kills ten blacks tonight. Well, there are millions more."[10] Hale's words might carry more weight than one might think. He built his World Church of the Creator into an international organization with members in forty-nine states and twenty-eight countries. It boasted 70,000 to 80,000 fellow travelers and considered itself the fastest-growing white racist and antisemitic church in the country.[11] Hale felt that he has helped the white supremacist upgrade its image. "People used to think of a guy with a beer belly, spitting out tobacco. . . . Now they think of . . . determined, energetic leaders, educated, and idealistic. We're the best."[12]

We close this chapter on lawyer standards and disciplines with an invitation to a simple thought exercise. Will free speech law some day compel the admission of lawyers like Hale to the bar? If not, why not?

QUESTIONS FOR DISCUSSION, CHAPTER 9

1. Should bar associations hold lawyers and would-be lawyers to a higher standard of racial behavior, or treat them like anybody else?
2. Racists and skinheads from time to time need lawyers. So, what is wrong with tolerating the occasional lawyer who shares their attitudes and lets it show?
3. Suppose a judge frequently lectures black defendants using the term "you people." Given that African Americans do, in fact, commit a disproportionate amount of the nation's crime, what's so bad about that?
4. If an applicant to the bar believes that black women are animals and white girls who dance with black boys are betraying their race, isn't he within his right to hold these beliefs?
5. If, for the sake of argument, bar associations are within their rights in expecting lawyers to exemplify higher standards of race-based behavior than the average citizen, what *other* professional groups might be entitled to do so as well?

CLASS EXERCISE

A black candidate to the bar believes as strongly as Mr. Hale did that whites are Satanic and that the legal system relentlessly disadvantages people of color. He is outspoken about his views and plans to urge black jurors to engage in "jury nullification"—acquitting black defendants charged with nonviolent crimes, even if the evidence shows they are guilty—if he is admitted to practice.

If you believe Hale has no business practicing law, what about the outspoken black would-be lawyer?

Recommended Reading, Chapter 9

American Bar Association, Center for Professional Responsibility, Annotated Model Rules of Professional Conduct (fifth edition, 2002).

Nicholas Kristoff, "Hate, American Style," *New York Times*, August 30, 2002, at A19.

Andrew Taslitz and Sharon Stiles-Anderson, *Still Officers of the Court: Why the First Amendment Is No Bar to Challenging Racism, Sexism, and Ethnic Bias in the Legal Profession*, 1 Geo. J. Legal Ethics 787 (1996).

Notes

1. See W. Bradley Wendel, *"Certain Fundamental Truths": A Dialectic on Negative and Positive Liberty in Hate-Speech Cases*, 65 L. & Contemp. Probs. 35, 35–37 (2002); Nicholas Kristoff, "Hate, American Style," *New York Times*, August 30, 2002, at A19.

2. See Wendel, *Truths*, supra; Andrew E. Taslitz and Sharon Styles-Anderson, *Still Officers of the Court: Why the First Amendment Is No Bar to Challenging Racism, Sexism, and Ethnic Bias in the Legal Profession*, 9 Geo. J. Legal Ethics 781 (1996).

3. Wendel, *Truths*, supra.

4. See *Comment, Hate Speech Hypocrisy: Matt Holcomb, the New Politics of Bar Admission*, 63 Mont. L. Rev. 419 (2002).

5. Taslitz and Styles-Anderson, *Still Officers*, supra; Wendel, *Truths*, supra, at 39.

6. Wendel, *Truths*, supra, at 35–48.

7. Ibid. at 43.

8. See Nat Hentoff, "Lawyers Unleash the Thought Police," *Rocky Mountain News*, August 25, 1997, at A14.

9. Kristoff, "American Style," supra.

10. Ibid.

11. Ibid.

12. Ibid.

Part Four
Hate in Broader Focus

10

TALK SHOWS:
HATE ON THE AIRWAVES

A pervasive and disturbing brand of hate speech has found a place on the nation's AM and FM airwaves. While most radio programs do not sanction hate speech, a significant fraction of talk shows are hosted by right-wing conservatives who provoke listeners with inflammatory rhetoric and goad callers to direct their wrath at minorities, environmentalists, liberal politicians, and government social programs. "Hate radio," as it is sometimes called, reaches millions of listeners daily and indirectly affects the lives of countless others. It is also safely tucked under the arm of First Amendment protection. What is the nature of hate radio and why did it proliferate so rapidly over the past two decades? Who supports these shows and why? And, what are the harms of and available remedies to combat hate speech on talk radio?

THE RISE OF HATE SPEECH ON TALK RADIO

Between 1980 and 1998, the number of talk radio shows increased from 75 to 1,350.[1] The most popular show, Rush Limbaugh, in a recent year aired on over 600 radio stations, five days a week, three hours per day, and attracted an audience of more than 20 million listeners per week.[2] One survey showed that 18 percent of the adult population listens to at least one call-in political talk radio show at least twice a week,[3] while another found that 15 million people per day listen to at least a portion of a talk show.[4] Three primary reasons have been advanced to explain this seemingly explosive trend—technology, demographics, and the demise of the Fairness Doctrine.

Starting in the 1960s, AM stations began losing listeners due to the rising popularity of FM stations, which were capable of providing stereophonic music. Over the next few decades, AM stations began switching from their "Top 40" music formats to talk shows in search of greater profits. Technological advances such as the tape delay (available since the 1950s), inexpensive 800 numbers, cellular phones, and satellite communications all contributed to the popularity of the call-in format and the nationwide syndication of programs at a relatively low cost.[5] The aging baby boomers provided a growing audience base, since listeners tend to prefer talk to music as they get older.[6]

While call-in radio shows have been on the air since the early 1950s, the dramatic rise in the number of so-called "hate jocks" began with the repeal of the Fairness Doctrine in 1987. Adopted in 1949 by the Federal Communications Commission (FCC), this doctrine essentially required radio stations to provide a forum for opposing views on controversial issues. After a number of legal challenges, the doctrine was ultimately repealed. In justifying its decision, the FCC reversed policy dating to the 1920s which had held that control of the airwaves belonged to the listeners, not the speakers.[7] The elimination of the Fairness Doctrine thus accorded full First Amendment rights to talk show hosts without any requirement that they offer other views.

Since the abolition of the Fairness Doctrine, Congress has twice made serious attempts to reinstate it as federal law, in 1987 and 1993. The doctrine's supporters point to numerous public interest benefits, which include ensuring that the wealthy do not control the time reserved for editorial advertisements, preventing private censorship by broadcasters, promoting the public's access to the airwaves, and recognizing the doctrine as an effective tool in responding to personal attacks and antisemitic or racist messages.[8] Opponents counter that the doctrine inhibits rather than promotes the flow of news and information, because broadcasters will refuse advertisements and avoid controversial issues rather than face fairness challenges.[9] President Reagan vetoed the 1987 legislation, while the 1993 bill fell just short of enactment.

For his part, Rush Limbaugh, a popular conservative talk show host, saw to it that his listeners would forever oppose the resurrection of the Fairness Doctrine by mischaracterizing the 1993 bill as the "Hush Rush Bill."[10] To the contrary, the bill was not directed at talk radio hosts, nor did it require stations to provide equal time; it simply would have prohibited stations from constantly airing programs with the same perspective, without *any* opposing views.[11] In 1993, the conservative Heritage Foundation convened a panel of talk show hosts to discuss the merits of the Fairness Doctrine. Not surprisingly, the panel concurred that the proliferation of talk shows since 1987 demonstrates the benefits of the "unfettered exchange of information" that has resulted in "millions of Americans [achieving] a level of political sophistication the country hasn't known before."[12] Any attempt to reinstate the doctrine was simply an effort by the government to "impos[e] political censorship under the guise of protecting free speech."[13] Limbaugh's followers on the talk show scene, who include G. Gordon Liddy, Oliver North, Neal Boortz, Ann Coulter, Mike Gallagher, and Michael Savage, all fell into line.[14]

One liberal media watch group, Fairness and Accuracy in Reporting (FAIR), suggests a more ominous reason for the increase in the number of hate radio shows. The recent proliferation, says FAIR, is a result of "a deliberate process in which major broadcasters like ABC/Cap Cities [now Disney/ABC] have chosen to narrowcast to conservative audiences by stoking prejudice and fear."[15] To the extent that this allegation is true, it does not bode well for the forces opposing hate radio in this country.

THE NATURE OF HATE SPEECH ON TALK RADIO

As with other types of hate speech, hate radio runs the gamut from subtle references to "those people" or "foreigners" to calling blacks "savages"[16] and feminists "femi-nazis."[17] One writer characterized a typical hate radio program as consisting of "long solo talk spiels, generally without guests, using screened callers who will spout the party line, and/or are easy debate subjects."[18] Another was struck not so much by abrasive treatment of race and gender, but by overall scorn for anything "different" in the world.[19] Examples of hate speech from some of the more widely listened to shows[20] include the following:

Rush Limbaugh to a black caller: "Take that bone out of your nose and call me back."[21]

Rush Limbaugh on immigrants: "Taxpaying citizens are not being given the access to these welfare and health services that they deserve and desire, but if you're an illegal immigrant and cross the border, you get everything you want."[22]

Bob Grant following a gay pride march: "Ideally, it would have been nice to have a few phalanxes of policemen with machine guns and mow them down."[23]

Bob Grant on environmentalists: "I'd like to get every environmentalist, put 'em up against a wall, and shoot 'em."[24]

Michael Savage in response to protesters: "I wonder how many of those people outside the radio station are American citizens? I wonder how many of them are front groups for the very terrorists that John Ashcroft is looking for."[25]

In addition to the statements of the hosts themselves, the callers to these shows are often encouraged to vent their prejudices and hatred of disfavored groups. The Bob Grant show has taken this feature to another level by allowing callers to promote white supremacist groups such as the National Alliance and the National Association for the Advancement of White People. Grant not only professes his support for these groups, but routinely encourages callers to give out the groups' addresses and phone numbers.[26]

Supporters of talk radio downplay the incidence of hate speech on their favorite shows, citing one study that found that the controversial statements reported by the mainstream media are not typical of the hosts quoted nor of the shows with the largest audiences.[27] This begs the question, however, because the frequency of blatantly inflammatory hate speech is not the issue. What is more telling are the numerous subtle statements that reinforce general bias against minorities, women, and the politically powerless, statements that are not egregious enough to make the nightly news, but are perhaps more harmful than the occasional brazen outburst.

Another disturbing characteristic of hate radio shows is the lack of any accountability. One writer noted that "[i]nside his bubble, Rush can make wild, unfounded assertions that would doom any politician."[28] Another writer observed that "[w]hat passes for political debate on many talk shows is often a cacophony of inflammatory rhetoric and half-truths."[29] As discussed above, the demise of the Fairness Doctrine ensured that nothing the host says will be subsequently corrected or challenged by an opposing viewpoint unless the station so chooses, an unlikely prospect at best. The danger is that the listeners to these programs will accept fantasy and myth for fact and truth, and act accordingly.

Who Supports Talk Radio and Why?

Supporters of talk radio include listeners, advertising sponsors, station managers, and public figures who either implicitly or explicitly embrace the host's message of hate.

Listeners

A number of studies have sought to identify the demographics of talk radio fans. In general, these studies have found that the majority of listeners are college-educated white males over the age of thirty who fall in middle- to upper-income brackets.[30] Furthermore, "political talk radio listeners are more likely than non-listeners to consume all types of news media (except T.V. news), to be more knowledgeable about politics and social issues, and to be involved in political activities . . . regardless of the ideology of the hosts of the programs to which they listen."[31] One study suggested that it would be incorrect to assume that the viewpoints of callers are identical to those of the average listener.[32] Another found that talk radio listeners across the spectrum harbor strong anti-government sentiments.[33] This trend may be explained, in part, by feelings of lower "political efficacy" reported by listeners compared with non-listeners, in spite of greater political engagement.[34]

What explains the popularity of talk radio programs, especially those that disseminate hate speech? Studies indicate that people listen to talk radio for a variety of reasons, including to keep up on issues, to learn what others feel about issues, to learn more about information picked up elsewhere, and for entertainment.[35] Listeners also tune in to hear a reflection and affirmation of their own views.[36] Interestingly, a poll conducted by a popular women's magazine indicated that a majority of regular female listeners tune in because "they like what they hear," in spite of one-half of the respondents agreeing that talk radio is generally disrespectful toward both minorities and women and one-third believing that it encourages violence.[37] Perhaps this result reflects society's seeming obsession with all that is dysfunctional, from talk show hosts who flout standards of decency to scandals and tragedies to disturbed relationships, and talk radio's willingness to provide these elements to an avid audience. Talk shows are adept at creating large-scale dramas designed to draw people in when the host stakes out a controversial position. In the words of one commentator, "[t]he more interesting or infuriating the chat, the more audiences love to love or love to hate the show and its host."[38]

For the portion of the audience that does not tune in solely for entertainment purposes, other explanations have been proposed for the attraction of hate radio. One researcher posits that people tune in "to release and express their feelings of anger and pain."[39] These feelings are a result of two coinciding phenomena. The first is the increasing complexity of society and the attendant loss of control over one's life, resulting in strong feelings of victimization. The second is the absence of the views of these disaffected individuals from the mainstream media.[40] Talk radio hosts recognize these sentiments and tailor their routines to identify scapegoats for all that has seemingly gone wrong in their listeners' worlds. One way they do this is by reinforcing the idea that this country is deteriorating because of the influx of nonwhites. Instead of a friendly admonition not to blame others for one's lot in life, callers and listeners can generally expect to receive sympathy and validation of their anger and resentment toward people of different groups.[41] This, in turn, creates a sense of belonging to a community of like-minded sufferers, but further polarizes individuals along racial, class, and gender lines. While the venting that occurs on talk shows may have some minor therapeutic value, it does little to address the underlying problems, leaving the callers and listeners anxious, angry, and alienated from the larger community.[42]

Listeners include those who obtain their daily news and political information from a variety of sources, as well as those who exclusively listen to one or two talk shows with a specific ideological bent. One study found that talk shows were the sole source of political information for 44 percent of their listeners.[43] The danger with the latter group is that the talk show host wields an almost cult-like influence over their attitudes and beliefs. For example, Rush Limbaugh regularly tells his listeners to forgo reading the newspaper because he will digest the news for them and tell them what to think.[44] That hate jocks are in many cases articulate, sincere, and seemingly empathic individuals only adds to their ability to indoctrinate their listeners. To these listeners, hearing is believing, and believing can only result in more hate, both on and off the air.

COMPANY SPONSORS

Why do companies support hate radio shows with their advertising dollars? And why do corporate owners of radio stations carry these shows? In most cases, the answer is the power of the dollar. As long as the show generates revenue for the owners and the advertisers, decisionmakers find it easy to turn a deaf ear to anything but the most egregious offenses. As one ABC producer put it, "If the person has good ratings, a station has to overlook the garbage that he spews out. A radio station always fights for a host's constitutional rights if the show is profitable enough, and Grant had high ratings because he kept beating up on minorities. If his audience had been small, the managers would forget the Constitution and declare him a bigot. . . . Our advertisers are aware that hate sells their products."[45] In rare cases, the host may be fired or forced to apologize for crossing the owner's own line of tolerance, or listener outrage alone may induce a company to pull its ads. For example, in 1996 Disney/ABC fired Bob Grant for expressing his disappointment that Ron Brown, the secretary of commerce under President Clinton and a black man, might be the only survivor in a fatal plane crash (he was not). Two weeks later another station in the same city picked up his show.[46] Grant, who had spent more than twenty years vilifying blacks, immigrants, and other minorities, described David Dinkins, the former mayor of New York, as a "men's room attendant," called Harlem churchgoers "screaming savages," and advocated drowning Haitian boat people.[47] As discussed later, in less egregious cases, opponents of hate radio are occasionally successful in making their voices heard through boycotts of advertisers' products.

Another reason companies are attracted to certain hosts is that the hosts rarely, if ever, criticize the corporate culture. This, too, reflects a desire to protect the company's bottom line. To underscore this point, consider the following example. Disney/ABC has repeatedly been criticized for carrying hate radio shows on its stations. In 1995, as Disney was in the process of acquiring the ABC radio networks, ABC carried a radio program by Jim Hightower.[48] Unlike hate radio programs, Hightower's show advocated for the rights of blue-collar workers, pensioners, and middle-class consumers by pointing out examples of the greed and misdeeds of corporations. On one show, Hightower criticized Disney for paying homeless workers minimum wage and making them pay for their uniforms and tools out of their salaries. He also took ABC to task for not confronting big tobacco companies.[49] Shortly after the takeover, he was dropped from the network. In stark contrast, Disney-owned stations carry Michael Savage, Rush Limbaugh, and Dr. Laura Schlessinger, among others, in spite of Disney's desire to maintain its family-friendly image. It defends its decision to carry these shows as promoting a "diversity of voices."[50] As summed up by one victim of Savage-inspired hate speech, "Disney family values are really making-a-profit values. It's all about money, and it's all about not caring about people's lives and not caring that a lot of this can feed into violence."[51]

PUBLIC FIGURES

Opponents of hate radio also decry the "aura of respectability" bestowed on these shows by conservative politicians.[52] If hate radio is antithetical to family values—not to mention ordinary civility—why do these public figures go out of their way to cozy up to prominent hate jocks? A look at the results of recent elections provides the likely answer. While company sponsors focus on the bottom line, politicians focus on who can deliver the vote. Studies have shown that talk radio listeners are not only more likely to vote than non-listeners, they are much more likely to vote Republican. This is not surprising, since conservative talk show hosts essentially serve as precinct captains for the Republican Party at election time. In 1994, newly elected Republicans were so grateful for the role that Rush Limbaugh played in the elections that they made him an honorary member of Congress.[53]

Conservative politicians who curry favor with talk radio hosts are often accused of applying a double standard when charged with pandering to hate speech. If the politician decides that invoking the wrath of a few liberals is worth it, he will defend the host's conduct by saying it is not his place to censor what is said on the air. If, on the other hand, a particular minority group has been insulted, say Puerto Ricans in New York, the politician will inevitably condemn the host's statements if the votes of this group are more important than the votes the host can deliver.[54]

The Harms of Hate Speech on Talk Radio

As with hate speech generally, hate speech on talk radio harms all who lie in its path. The specific types of harms are no different from those discussed in Chapter 1. However, the hate radio format is unique in that it reaches a large daily audience, which amplifies its impact. As one author pointed out, if the famous Orson Wells Martian landing hoax was capable of causing widespread panic, what does that say about the power of a Rush Limbaugh to convince his mainly white, male audience that they and their way of life are in need of protection?[55] Ultimately, it may not matter whether the talk show host persuades his audience to accept his view of reality or whether listeners tune in to hear their preexisting beliefs reinforced. The overall result is a synergy in which the audience embraces the host's rhetoric as the truth, while the size of the audience empowers individuals to act on what they have heard. This may include inculcating hate-based viewpoints in one's children, engaging in hate speech against individuals and groups targeted by the host, and even committing violent hate crimes.

Specific acts of violence perpetrated on targets of hate radio are surely one of the more serious harms. That physical harms occur at all attests to the power of talk radio hosts to influence the actions of a small minority of angry, resentful listeners who are willing to carry out the host's directives. In general, both supporters and opponents agree that the proliferation of right-wing radio programs directly correlates with an increase in hate crimes.[56] For example, the day after one host spoke disparagingly of a town with a large immigrant population, "two businesses and a house belonging to Indian immigrants were spray-painted with swastikas and ethnic slurs, and one of the businesses was hit with gunfire."[57] Numerous targets of hate jocks report receiving hate-filled calls and letters, including threats of violence and death.[58] Right-wing hosts who advance preposterous conspiracy theories encourage listeners to arm themselves against the government. One avid fan proceeded to Washington and fired thirty rounds at the White House.[59] Fortunately, no one was injured.

A related danger is that hate radio listeners will become hardened to human tragedy and suffering. Shockingly, many hosts cannot contain their glee at the death of anyone who disagrees with their ideology. For example, Rush Limbaugh had a field day after the deaths of environmentalist Judi Bari and homeless advocate Mitch Snyder.[60] Ironically, these same hosts, along with most Americans, professed shock and dismay when Islamic fundamentalists celebrated after the 2001 terrorist attacks.[61] Such uncompassionate sentiments only promote widespread indifference to the plights of others, if not outright sociopathy.

The silence of the mainstream media in exposing the harms of hate radio is a factor in its growing power. One author charged that "the mainstream media have made far right and extremist hate in the media acceptable by pretending that more moderate hatemongers essentially reflect mainstream America . . . . By pandering to such hatemongers the mainstream media are acting as enablers for the violence-producing rhetoric."[62] Perhaps the media's lack of attention reflects the corporate owners' agreement with the opinions espoused by the hosts. At the very least, it reflects the decisions of some media owners not to criticize their major moneymakers. Whatever the cause of the silence, the result has been the implicit bestowing of legitimacy on the words of the hate jocks.

Some maintain that the harms of talk radio pale by comparison to its contribution to national dialogue. But hate radio does little to foster dialogue or bring adversaries closer together. As one author noted, "the talk show demagogues are adept at manipulating anger and turning righteous resentment into fearful hatred of the oppressed."[63] Even suggesting that hate radio furthers the search for the truth provides right-wing hate jocks with an aura of legitimacy. As long as hate radio is on the air, right-wing groups will use it to promote social division. Although some might hail hate jocks as champions of free speech, the reality is that this form of speech does little to advance the purposes of that liberty.

REMEDIES

Responses by opponents to hate radio include calls for censorship, concerted action such as boycotts and protests, legal action, and calls for regulatory intervention. A number of formal organizations monitor right-wing hate groups as well as hate speech in the media.[64] With the advent of the Internet, these groups have been able to reach a larger audience and coordinate campaigns via E-mail. Local boycotts by community groups have achieved some success in smaller cities.[65] Demonstrations, calls, and letter-writing campaigns have also pressured sponsors to withdraw support and pressured stations to fire or reprimand hate jocks.

Legal action is an option for opponents of hate radio who feel they have been personally targeted or harmed. In one case, two radio station employees sued a station owner (Disney) for racial discrimination and sexual harassment after two hate jocks gave away black plastic gardening tools, referring to them as free "black hoes." Disney paid $2 million to settle the suit.[66] In another case, an outspoken critic of Bob Grant sued him for libel, intentional infliction of emotional distress, and invasion of privacy after Grant called him a wife-beater on the air and revealed that he had been treated at a psychiatric facility.[67] The court held that the plaintiff's allegations did not meet the required legal standard and granted summary judgment to the defendant. This case illustrates the limitations of traditional remedies in situations like these. As one minority critic lamented, "Did the civil rights movement guarantee us nothing more than the freedom to use public accommodations while surrounded by raving bigots?"[68]

To opponents of hate speech, it is no small irony that the FCC (and the courts) draw a distinction between "indecent" and hate speech. Whereas Howard Stern has been fined thousands of dollars for graphic on-air descriptions of sex organs and bodily functions, Bob Grant is simply exercising his First Amendment rights when he tells a distraught caller to "get a gun and go do something."[69] Instead of outright censorship, which has little chance of passing constitutional muster, some critics continue to call for the reinstatement of the Fairness Doctrine. This, too, is an unlikely prospect in light of the prior failed attempts by Congress to reinstate it.

Another suggestion has been to include more progressive voices on the air providing alternative points of view.[70] This approach follows the accepted line of reasoning that the best answer to hate speech is more speech. While a few stations feature liberal talk show hosts, their numbers are dwarfed by right-wing shows. One explanation for the shortage is that liberal hosts are not as entertaining as conservative hosts. One writer noted that "[t]he low guffaw and gutter humor of throwing feces at liberals is part and parcel to the spectacle" that attracts listeners to hate radio.[71] The conservative bent of media owners and corporate sponsors also prevents more liberal voices from being heard. For example, after dropping Jim Hightower, Disney/ABC did not carry any liberal or progressive talk show hosts.[72]

In sum, in spite of the efforts of opposition groups, the reality is that until millions of listeners, the mainstream media, conservative politicians, and corporate sponsors denounce and refuse to support hate radio, this potent form of hate speech will continue unabated.

QUESTIONS FOR DISCUSSION, CHAPTER 10

1. Why has conservative talk radio caught on as it has?
2. Why is there no liberal counterpart to Rush Limbaugh?
3. If a radio station caters to a white supremacist audience with tirades against blacks, gays, and immigrants, what should be done? Nothing? Should the FCC suspend its license? Should listeners boycott the station? Its advertisers?
4. Listeners have to tune in to a hate program on the radio. Hardly ever is anyone an involuntary listener. Is this an argument for (or against) non-regulation?
5. Society's racial attitudes have been greatly improving—or so we like to think. Why, then, are conservative radio programs laced with anti-minority sentiment so popular?

CLASS EXERCISE

The class has just received the news that a liberal foundation is prepared to give it $500,000 to start up a progressive talk show aimed at countering the host of conservative or white supremacist shows that now dominate the airwaves.

How would you run such a show? And what will you do when your grant runs out?

Recommended Reading, Chapter 10

Maria L. Marcus, *Policing Speech on the Airwaves: Granting Rights, Preventing Wrongs*, 15 Yale L. & Pol'y Rev. 447 (1997).

Steven Rendell et al., *The Way Things Aren't: Rush Limbaugh's Reign of Error* (1995).

Gini Scott, *Can We Talk? The Power and Influence of Talk Shows* (1996).

David Shaw, "Are Liberals Ready for Their Own Rush Limbaugh?," Boulder (Colorado) *Daily Camera*, March 9, 2003, at E6.

Nadine Strossen, *Incitement to Hatred: Should There Be a Limit?* 25 S. Ill. U. L.J. 243 (2001).

Donald J. Warren, *Radio Priest: Charles Coughlin, Father of Hate Radio* (1996).

Notes

1. *The Talk Radio Research Project*, Talkers Magazine Online, [http://www.talkers.com/talkaud.html] (fall 2002).

2. Joseph N. Cappella, Joseph Turow, and Kathleen Hall Jamieson, *Call-In Political Talk Radio: Background, Content, Audiences, Portrayal in Mainstream Media*, a report from the Annenberg Public Policy Center, University of Pennsylvania, August 7, 1996, at 10.

3. Ibid. at 12.

4. Diana Owen, "Who's Talking? Who's Listening? The New Politics of Radio Talk Shows," in *Broken Contract? Changing Relationships Between Americans and Their Government*, 127, 130 (Stephen C. Craig, ed., 1996).

5. Cappella et al., supra, at 6.

6. Ibid.

7. Hugh Carter Donahue, *The Battle to Control Broadcast News: Who Owns the First Amendment?* 145 (1989).

8. Ibid. at 140–141.

9. Ibid.

10. Jeff Cohen, *The "Hush Rush" Hoax: Limbaugh on the Fairness Doctrine* [http://www.fair.org/extra/9411/limbaugh-fcc.html] (Nov./Dec. 1994).

11. Ibid.

12. *The "Fairness Doctrine": Pulling the Plug on Talk Radio*, a Heritage Foundation Panel Discussion, Oct. 7, 1993, at 3.

13. Ibid. at 4.

14. See Peter Carlson, "The Breathless Harangue: It's All the Rage," Boulder (Colorado) *Daily Camera*, March 20, 2003, at E1.

15. Jeff Cohen and Norman Solomon, *Spotlight Finally Shines on White Hate Radio* [http://www.fair.org/media-beat/941103.html] (Nov. 3, 1994).

16. Ibid.

17. Steven Rendall, Jim Naureckas, and Jeff Cohen, *The Way Things Aren't: Rush Limbaugh's Reign of Error* 33, (1995).

18. Hart Williams, *Stop Hate Radio* [http://www.hartwilliams.com/ stophate/] (Dec. 18, 2000).

19. Patricia J. Williams, *The Rooster's Egg*, 47 (1995).

20. The content of *shortwave* talk radio is, if anything, even worse. See James Latham, *In Hate's Pay*, Intelligence Rep. (Southern Poverty Law Center), summer 2002, at 23; James Latham, *From America with Hate*, Intelligence Rep. (Southern Poverty Law Center), fall 2001, at 56. Internet-based "radio" and music shows are worse still. See *White Pride, World Wide*, Intelligence Rep. (Southern Poverty Law Center), fall 2001, at 24.

21. Rendall et al., supra, at 49.

22. Ibid. at 47.

23. Jim Naureckas, *50,000 Watts of Hate: Bigotry is Broadcast on ABC Radio's Flagship* [http://www.fair.orgextra/9601/bob-grant.html] (Jan./Feb. 1995).

24. Cohen and Solomon, supra.

25. Northwest Cable News, *Show Responds to "Hate Radio" Accusations* [http://www.nwcn.com/cgi-bin/gold_print.cgi] (April 25, 2002).

26. Fairness and Accuracy in Reporting (FAIR), *Dial H for Hate: Neo-Nazi Recruitment on ABC's Flagship* [http://www.fair.orgextra/9506 /grant.html] (June 1995).

27. L. Brent Bozell III, *Talk Radio: Media Hate "Democracy in Action,"* [http://secure.mediaresearch.orgcolumns/news/col19960919.html] (September 19, 1996). *See* Capella et al., supra (Annenberg Center report).

28. Stephen Talbot, "Wizard of Ooze," *Mother Jones*, May/June 1995, at 43.

29. Cappella et al., supra, at 41.

30. Ibid. at 14; Talkers Magazine Online, supra; Owen, supra, at 132–133.

31. Capella et al., supra, at 14. (It is worth noting that the political knowledge factor measured in some of these surveys is based on listener self-assessments.)

32. Ibid. at 11.

33. Owen, supra, at 134.

34. Ibid. at 135.

35. Ibid. at 143.

36. Ann Hornaday, "Talk Radio! Why Women Are Tuning in to America's Biggest Baddest Boy's Club," *McCall's*, June 1995, at 82.

37. Ibid. at 84.

38. Gini Scott, *Can We Talk? The Power and Influence of Talk Shows*, 87–88 (1996).

39. Ibid. at 8.

40. Ibid. at 9.

41. Ibid. at 15.

42. Ibid. at 12.

43. Hornaday, supra, at 85.

44. Rendall et al., supra, at 58.

45. Ursula Owen, *The Speech that Kills* (Iain Walker Mem. Lecture), Amer. Online, [www.oneworld.org], June 7, 2001, at 1.

46. FAIR, *FAIR's Bob Grant Success* [http://www.fair.org/extra/9606/grantsuc.html] (June 1996).

47. U. Owen, supra.

48. FAIR, *Hightower Gets the Mickey Mouse Treatment* [http://www.fair.org/extra/9512/hightower.html] (Dec. 1995).

49. Ibid.

50. Daniel Zoll, *Radio Rat Poison, The Dark Side of Disney: Nasty, Vicious Hate Radio in one of the Nation's Most Tolerant Progressive Markets* [http://sfbg.com/News/34/51/51disney.html] (September 20, 2000).

51. Ibid.

52. H. Williams, supra.

53. Talbot, supra, at 41. In a speech he delivered to the freshman Republican legislators Limbaugh stated, "I'm sick and tired of playing the phony game I've had to play and that is this so-called compassion for the poor. I don't have compassion for the poor." Olshaker, *A Media Establishment in Denial Over Hate Speech-Hate Crime Link* [http://www.onlinejournal.com/ Media/Olshaker121202/olshaker 121202.html] (December 12, 2002).

54. FAIR, *Hate Talk and Politics* [http://www.fair.orgextra/9708/grant-giuliani.html] (August 1997).

55. P. Williams, supra, at 45.

56. Robert L. Hilliard and Michael C. Keith, *Waves of Rancor, Tuning in the Radical Right*, 9 (1999).

57. FAIR, *Hate Talk and Politics*, supra.

58. Rendall et al., supra, at 76–77.

59. Hornaday, supra, at 85.

60. Olshaker, supra.

61. Ibid.

62. Hilliard and Keith, supra, at 222.

63. Ibid. at 5.

64. E.g., Radio for Peace International, the Anti-Defamation League of B'nai B'rith, the Southern Poverty Law Center, Fairness and Accuracy in Reporting, Political Research Associates, and StopHateRadio.org.

65. For example, Michael Savage was finally driven off the air in Eugene, Oregon, after a long boycott campaign.

66. Zoll, supra.

67. *Wilson v. Grant*, 297 N.J. Super. 128, 135 (1996).

68. P. Williams, supra, at 52.

69. Naureckas, supra.

70. David Shaw, "Are Liberals Ready for Their Own Rush Limbaugh?," Boulder (Colorado) *Daily Camera*, March 9, 2003, at E6. See also Orville Schell, "Sending 'Liberal Media' Truism to the Fact-Checker," *New York Times*, March 20, 2003, at B6.

71. H. Williams, supra.

72. Zoll, supra.

II

STRETCHING TO MAKE A POINT: THE CASE OF HATE SPEECH AGAINST WHITES

If hate speech against minorities is insidious and harmful (Chapter 1), what about hate speech against whites? How damaging are words like *honky*, *cracker*, and *whitey*? And what of black and brown nationalists who express contempt for white people and preach racial separation and division? This chapter addresses these and similar issues, including antisemitic speech by minorities against Jews, who could be seen as a subgroup of whites, even though they are clearly an ethnic and religious minority.

An intriguing related development is the recent effort by certain conservatives to banish the word *racist* to a distant circle of purgatory. According to some, the word *racist* is itself the new form of racist hate speech—damaging, wounding, and unfair. A black or brown person who hurls the term casually can do real harm to an innocent white. The accusation is easily made but hard to refute. Thus, we should retire it from our vocabulary or reserve it for the rarest examples.

A final issue is the matter of hoax crimes and hate speech. Every now and then people of color are charged with fabricating a hate offense against themselves, presumably to gain sympathy. Opponents of hate speech regulation often seize on these rare events to discredit the movement to take hate seriously. The final section of this chapter considers various celebrated hoaxes such as the Tawanna Brawley case, various university cases in which minority students were accused of perpetrating their own hate crimes, and the alleged black church-burnings hoax.

THE NATURE OF HATE SPEECH AGAINST WHITES

As a threshold question, one might ask whether it is even conceptually meaningful to speak of hate speech against whites. According to one common view, it is not. Racism is not just an attitude, but a matter of power; and since most power today resides in the hands of the white majority, minorities cannot be racists.[1] By the same token, nothing that minorities say can be considered hate speech, except, perhaps, in those relatively rare situations (a prison, an inner-city classroom) where blacks are in the majority and whites have something to fear from them. A broader definition of racism would identify it with racial or ethnic antipathy directed at the members of a different race or ethnic group, regardless of the race of the perpetrator or the power relationship between victim and offender. Thus, blacks and other minorities would be guilty of hate speech when they lash out at the white majority simply for being white, either one-on-one or in more general attacks by those in a position to reach a large audience such as politicians, black nationalists, rap artists, or writers.

Definitions aside, one needs to know whether hate speech against minorities and that against whites are comparable in gravity. In a recent article, a federal district court judge stated that after the terrorist attacks of 9/11, all Americans "know now what it feels like to be detested because of a generic characteristic—[being] American."[2] She compared this feeling to those of minorities targeted by racism. But how well does this analogy hold? In *The Rage of a Privileged Class*, Ellis Cose contended that while white racism, black racism, and antisemitism are all harmful, they "do not lead to the same place or spring from the same stream."[3] So what accounts for the difference?

One factor is historical context. Purely racial insults and name-calling (*honky, cracker, whitey*) directed against whites do not evoke and call up a specific oppressive history for the white majority. (see Chapter 1). On the other hand, words such as *nigger, wop, spic, chink*, or *kike* (see Chapter 4) do carry a historical message that often multiplies their impact.[4] Not only does hate speech against whites not reflect long-standing stereotypes, but only in the last few decades have

Judge Richard Posner, Wittmer v. Peters, 87 F.3d 916 (7th Cir. 1996).

We are mindful that the Supreme Court has rejected the "role model" argument for reverse discrimination. . . . The argument for the black lieutenant is not of that character. We doubt that many inmates of boot camps aspire to become correctional officers, though doubtless some do. . . . The black lieutenant is needed because the black inmates are believed unlikely to play the correctional game of brutal drill sergeant and brutalized recruit unless there are some blacks in authority in the camp. This is not just speculation, but is backed up by expert evidence that the plaintiffs did not rebut. The defendants' experts . . . did not rely on generalities about racial balance or diversity; did not, for that matter, defend a goal of racial balance. They opined that the boot camp in Greene County would not succeed in its mission of pacification and reformation with as white a staff as it would have had if a black male had not been appointed to one of the lieutenant slots. For then a security staff less than 6 percent black (4 out of 71), with no male black supervisor, would be administering a program for a prison population almost 70 percent black. . . .

We hold . . . that . . . the preference that the administration of the Greene County boot camp gave a black male applicant for a lieutenant's job on the ground of his race was not unconstitutional.

whites actually been subjected to one of the more dramatic forms of minority hate speech, that of black nationalists, while some minority groups have been publicly and privately castigated for centuries.[5]

Another difference lies in the nature of the stereotypes associated with whites and minorities. Whites are not a stigmatized group in this country. Negative minority stereotypes, on the other hand, serve the dual purpose of generating feelings of contempt for the minority group while enhancing the superior stature of the majority. One consequence of this duality is that any minority with redeeming qualities is thought to be an exception to an otherwise accurate negative stereotype,[6] whereas whites as a rule are not collectively implicated by negative stereotypes such as *trailer park trash, Southern cracker*, or *angry white male*. That both superior and inferior stereotypes are ingrained in our culture is reflected in the results of a survey that showed that blacks, including those with racist and anti-semitic tendencies, rated Jews higher in intelligence than blacks, while most whites (including Jews) tended to see blacks as significantly less intelligent and less motivated than whites.[7] This survey suggests that unlike white racists, most black racists do not believe that whites are unintelligent, lazy, or incompetent because of their whiteness.[8] The hate speech that arises from these very different sources exhibits a dual nature as well. Simply put, the hate speech of minorities is born of envy, anger, and resentment toward whites, whereas hate speech directed at minorities derives from a sense of moral, intellectual, and biological superiority.[9]

Furthermore, unlike the majority, minorities (especially recent immigrants) often serve as scapegoats for economic downturns and unemployment.[10] Minorities are made to feel that their ethnic group hinders the well-being of society.[11] Often hate speech directed at minorities reflects this "angry white male" mentality. In contrast, hate speech directed at whites often reflects the attitude that the majority has hindered minorities' progress and kept them from achieving their rightful place in society. Bad press for minorities, then, accuses them of being a drag on the economy—were it not for them, whites would be even richer than they now are. The black version accuses whites of unfairly denying blacks a chance at advancement—of keeping the gap between whites and blacks larger than it should be.

A final difference lies in the size of the majority compared to any given minority group. As that same district court judge noted, "Dominant views have no difficulty setting up shop on the main street of public opinion. Minorities are fewer in number, and those subject to historic discrimination have significantly less political or economic leverage to be heard."[12] While hate speech "silences all but the more stalwart of the minority members," the majority benefits from its dominance of "the marketplace of ideas" to counter the harms of hate speech directed its way.[13]

Types and Frequency of Hate Speech Against Whites

As discussed in Chapter 1, hate speech can take numerous forms, from vitriolic attacks on individuals to sophisticated denunciations of entire groups. The following sections discuss the common types of hate speech against whites and their relative frequencies. Interestingly, the literature suggests that hate speech against whites is typically perpetrated by black males, whereas hate speech by white racists is not confined to black male victims, but extends to all minorities, black and nonblack, male and female, alike. Whether this indicates that other minority groups do not harbor as much anger and resentment toward whites as blacks, or merely suppress it (for example, to avoid being deported), or whether the incidence of hate speech by these other minority groups is underreported is not known.

Speech Directed at Individuals

Hate speech directed at individual whites typically arises in situations where an angry speaker of color victimizes an "innocent" white or challenges a white person he or she believes guilty of disrespect or racism. The typical response is to call the white person names (*honky* or *cracker*) or to hurl words aimed at humiliating or humbling the white person ("You racist m_____f_____. You going to meet with your KKK friends now?"[14]).

A computerized search of case law suggests that hate speech directed at individual whites occurs much less frequently than that directed at individual blacks. When the words *honky* and *white cracker* were used as search terms, the search yielded 187 hits. When the word *nigger* was used, the results exceeded 3,000 hits. Moreover, the latter search yielded a significant number of civil actions based on racial discrimination, while the former yielded only a handful of such cases. Might it be that the incidence of black and white hate speech is roughly the same, but the extent of the harm experienced by the individual is much greater when the victim is a minority, and this results in the greater number of lawsuits?

If the reported decisions are any guide, whites are simply not suing very often for individual, in-your-face hate speech. In *Conrad v. P.T.O. Services*, a white truck driver sued his employer for workplace discrimination of several kinds, including calling him a "f___ing honky" three or four times during the thirteen months he worked there.[15] A federal trial court found that the language of the supervisor, who was black, was not sufficiently closely tied to the forms of discrimination Conrad suffered to prove discrimination directly. But, in connection with other evidence, the name-calling gave rise to a circumstantial case so that the white worker was entitled to a jury trial on some of his claims.

In *Hancock v. Cracker Barrel Old Country Store*, another federal district court considered the case of a white worker who had sued for wrongful termination and a racially hostile work environment, citing evidence that a black co-worker frequently cursed her, sometimes preceding his imprecations with the word *white*.[16] The court entered summary judgment against the white woman, finding that the co-worker was undoubtedly unpleasant, but that his conduct was not so severe or pervasive as to create a racially hostile workplace.

Whites are suing—or complaining—however, for being called a *racist*. In one case, *Goetz v. Kunstler*, a famous radical lawyer, William Kunstler, was unsuccessfully sued for defamation by Bernhard Goetz when the lawyer called Goetz, who had shot four black youths on a New York subway, a racist.[17] In another, a Jewish family living near Denver became alarmed when their neighbors, who were white, feuded with them over a dog's behavior, then tried to run one of them over with an automobile. When the Jewish family intercepted a number of cell phone calls from the neighbors suggesting that they might be contemplating further violence, the Jewish family sought help from a Jewish organization and complained to the press about the racism and antisemitism of their neighbors. The police decided not to press charges against the neighbors, finding that they had not yet committed a violent act, and the neighbors countersued the Jewish family and the Jewish organization for defamation, winning a large settlement.[18]

As mentioned earlier, an all-white fraternity staged a party with a Fiji Islander theme that minority groups found offensive. After a public outcry, the fraternity president complained that the minorities were insensitive and humorless, and that he found their accusations of racism tiresome and provocative.[19]

Whites are also lodging complaints for overhearing offensive language casting aspersions on their group. In *Simmons v. American Airlines*, a female passenger complained to a flight attendant that a black male passenger (Simmons) sitting near her had used the terms, "damn white bitch" and "honky bitches" during a cell phone conversation. [20] When the crew, without warning, removed him from the flight, he sued for racial discrimination. When the airline failed to give a satisfactory, nondiscriminatory reason for acting as it did, a federal appeals court allowed the suit to go forward, mentioning that the facts Simmons alleged strongly suggested that his race played a part in his ejection.

And in an extraordinary example of turnabout, the author of a comment in *Case Western Law Review* argued that hate-speech codes, under which minorities may obtain redress for insult and invective, violate the Thirteenth Amendment rights of whites and constitute a kind of white slavery.[21]

In conclusion, it appears that the law punishes minority speakers of hate speech, and protects those who are wrongfully accused of it, to much the same extent as whites, although the number of cases presenting such issues is relatively small.

Black Nationalists

This does not mean that white people do not complain of *general* hate speech and vituperation aimed at them. Much of this takes the form of assertive, rude, or scathing words spoken by black nationalist leaders. In 2001, the Southern Poverty Law Center (SPLC) counted fifty-one active chapters of black nationalist or separatist groups across the United States.[22] While the Nation of Islam is the best known group, two others—the House of David and the New Black Panther Party[23]—boast numerous chapters as well. No brown separatist group was listed. By contrast, 625 hate groups were listed under the headings racist skinhead, Christian Identity, neo-Confederate, Klan, neo-Nazi, and "other"—for example, the Council of Conservative Citizens and the National Association for the Advancement of White People.[24]

The Southern Poverty Law Center (whose national leader, Morris Dees, is white) describes black separatists as anti-white and antisemitic, opposed to integration and intermarriage, and desirous of separate institutions—even a separate nation—for blacks.[25] The leader of the Nation of Islam, Louis Farrakhan, for example, has accused whites of perpetrating cruelty toward blacks and behaving like devils and agents of Satan.[26] Many of his remarks single out Jews for their supposed role in the slave trade. One author suggested that black separatists target Jews, a relatively weak and small group, as representatives of the broader white society.[27] Another likened the ideology of Louis Farrakhan to that of white supremacists, in that it promotes separatist, non-democratic ideals that are not confined to prejudice against Jews but against all people who are not descendants of Africans brought to America as slaves.[28] Yet another faulted Farrakhan for not appreciating the advances this country has made toward eliminating racism, accusing him instead of seeking racial revenge and blaming whites for every failure of the black community.[29]

Speakers representing the Nation of Islam have publicly castigated whites on numerous occasions; starting in the 1980s, these speakers increasingly appeared on college campuses. Perhaps the most publicized event occurred when Khalid Abdul Muhammad spoke at Kean College in New Jersey in 1993.[30] His three-hour tirade targeted not only Jews ("bloodsuckers") and the Pope ("white cracker") but even other blacks ("Spook Lee") with whom he disagreed.[31] The event drew widespread attention not only for what Muhammad said, but also for the positive reaction of the largely black audience.[32]

If black separatists are little different—in motivation, if not in impact—from their white counterparts, what explains the level of support and encouragement from blacks who may not otherwise display race-conscious behavior in their daily lives? While some supporters may actually endorse the separatist rhetoric, it is more likely that a majority support it because of anger and resentment at injustices suffered over the years as well as frustration with the glacial pace of social change. It may also be that hate speech inevitably begets more of the same, so that unless stricter controls are put in place, this will be the continuing legacy of First Amendment protection.

RAP MUSIC

"From black rap music to black poetry, we are seeing more and more outright racism passing as legitimate cultural expression."[33]

Some rap musicians and groups are notorious for lyrics that disparage women (*hos* and *bitches*), police, and white people generally. At times, misogyny and race-baiting come mixed up with what most would regard as legitimate social commentary. A few radio stations refuse to broadcast the most offensive recordings, just as some music stores either refuse to stock them or label them to alert the unwary. Whether such artistic forms are a good or bad thing may be debated, but one criticism seems particularly inapt—the neutralist or parallel-position one. This criticism points out that a white group that sang lyrics disparaging of blacks would never get away with it. But the positions are not parallel. The black groups sing harsh words about whites (perhaps too harsh) as part of an effort to protest injustice and racism. The average white has never experienced injustice or racism at the hands of blacks.

The Harms of Hate Speech Against Whites

As discussed in Chapter 1, hate speech has adverse impacts on the victim, the speaker, and society at large. To what extent are those harms present when the victim is white?

Harms to the Victim

Not surprisingly, the factors that distinguish black from white racism also tend to reduce the harms of minority hate speech. [34] As previously discussed, historical context is one important factor. Racial and ethnic insults evoke memories of catastrophic events for most minorities (such as slavery or the Holocaust), which is somewhat akin to rubbing salt in a wound that is slow to heal. Every African American knows the cultural meaning of the term *nigger*. By comparison, most whites have little or no historical understanding of the terms *honky* or *cracker*,[35] much less associate them with lynching or signs excluding members of their race, and are likely to be equally insulted by being called a jerk, a slob, or even a racist.

The association of whiteness with superiority, purity, and other favorable stereotypes also influences white victims' ability to cope with hate speech. Because whites have not been exposed to negative stereotypes throughout their lives, they are not at high risk of internalizing social stigmas expressed through hate speech and making them a part of their self-identity. In addition, one author suggests that the longer a negative stereotype persists in a culture, the more readily it is used to justify violent action against the targeted group.[36]

The size of the majority relative to other groups reduces the magnitude of the harm as well. "Safety in numbers" insulates white victims of hate speech from feeling isolated and insecure. Being in the majority also ensures that the frequency of hate speech attacks will be much lower than that of those directed at minorities. Whites simply do not live in daily fear of being insulted by a minority person. Finally, the cumulative effect of numerous incidents of hate speech from a variety of sources does far greater damage to an individual or minority group than a small number of relatively isolated incidents would.

The subtleties of white privilege also factor into the harms of minority hate speech.[37] According to this theory, whites live in a world where their race has rarely hindered their professional or social progress (unless, of course, they consider themselves victims of affirmative action). Moreover, whites are raised to ignore or shrug off anything that a minority might say to or about a white person.[38] As this type of armor is effective mainly for whites, minorities necessarily suffer greater harms from hate speech.

PERPETRATOR, GROUP, AND SOCIETAL HARMS

No one can dispute that hate speech offends, degrades, and demoralizes the intended victim, no matter the race of the perpetrator or target. However, as discussed earlier (see Chapter 1), some of the most long-lasting effects of hate speech redound to the perpetrator, his or her group, and society as a whole.

In addition to the harms discussed in Chapter 1, perpetrators who combine hate speech with criminal activity are likely to be subjected to penalty-enhancing statutes. The constitutionality of such statutes was upheld in the case of *Wisconsin v. Mitchell*.[39] In this case, a black defendant received a longer prison term for selecting his white victim based on race. Sentence-enhancement statutes are passed, in part, because of the recognition that biased action is harmful to society at large and evidence a higher degree of depravity than a similar offense committed without racial motivation.

Another potential harm to minority perpetrators of hate speech is the very real threat of physical violence. For example, in 1994 Khalid

Muhammad was shot and wounded at a California rally.[40] The assassination of Malcolm X is a prime example. While violent retaliation for hate speech is certainly always possible regardless of the race of the speaker, once again, the larger size of the majority, and the greater number of hate groups within the majority, make this a greater threat for minority perpetrators.

Minority communities also pay a toll for hate speech uttered by their members. One commentator noted that "an African-American leadership that speaks only to the rage that burns in the souls of so many blacks at the sins of the past and continuing (although much diminished) sins of the present does itself and its constituents no good. Such leadership burns bridges to the vast majority of Americans who want to build a just society."[41] With minority hate speech, the words of a relatively small faction can easily fuel a backlash against affirmative action and other programs aimed at benefiting minorities. The same writer speaks of "race fatigue" which besets many whites who feel that society's efforts to eliminate racism are unappreciated and therefore worthless. A financial toll also comes due when corporate donors decide to stop contributing to universities that provide a forum for black separatist speakers, such as occurred in the aftermath of a speech given by Khalid Muhammad at Howard University, a historically black school.[42] The United Negro College Fund also sustained adverse financial consequences.[43] In sum, hate speech by minorities, even if not particularly injurious to individual white victims, can nevertheless harm the minority community.

Society at large suffers from minority hate speech as well. In addition to the harms discussed in Chapter 1, minority hate speech may do as much to reverse the progress made toward eliminating racism as white hate speech does. This is because the reduction of white racism is measured, in part, by the lessening frequency of white hate speech. The growing phenomenon of hate speech against whites, which was not previously widespread, gives some whites permission to throw up their hands and stop supporting civil rights.

SPECIAL FORMS OF HATE SPEECH AGAINST WHITES

Now consider three nontraditional forms of hate speech against whites—calling a white a racist, invoking a double standard, and perpetrating a minority-on-white racial hoax. In each case, whether this activity constitutes hate speech is addressed along with the potential harms to the victim, the perpetrator, and society.

PLAYING THE RACE CARD: IS CALLING SOMEONE A "RACIST" HATE SPEECH?

Increasingly, conservatives are accusing their critics of using charges of racism as a means of putting whites on the defensive while painting themselves as victims. One headline declared: "'Conservative' and 'Racist': The Ashcroft Nomination and the Left's Foulest Card."[44] The writer posited that liberals, led by black-activist groups, are determined to implement a "new racial McCarthyism" whereby those accused of racism will suffer disqualification from public office, and conservatism will become a form of racism. Further, charging someone with racism serves to avoid substantive argument on legitimate social issues. The message is that any opposition to pro-black policies renders that person a pariah. According to a second writer: "[E]fforts to smear and stereotype [one's] adversaries as racists have become so routine as to seem unremarkable, and so common as to suggest a strategy of spreading fear and loathing among black voters."[45] For another, "Crying 'racism!' over and over is a strategy to keep blacks angry and whites guilty."[46] And when Democrats on the Senate Judiciary Committee raised questions about a certain judicial nominee's history of racial insensitivity, a Republican senator accused them of describing the nominee, a Southerner, with the worst possible epithet for a Southern man, "by calling him a racist."[47]

What those accusations ignore is that the person charged with racism may in fact deserve it. If the allegation is true, the victim can hardly cry foul. No doubt the more the victim feels innocent of the charge, the greater the outrage he will feel. For example, under the headline "How I Was Smeared," one journalist described the "gruesome" experience of being unjustly accused of racism following a speech he made to the National Center for Policy Analysis.[48] The difficulty with analyzing this as hate speech is that the critic may in fact have believed that aspects of the victim's speech were indeed racist. If so, one who speaks out in public on sensitive subjects must expect to receive criticism.

Even when criticism of a speaker as racially insensitive (or worse) contains an element of truth, some decry such charges because they inflame tensions and enlarge the ever-widening gap between racial groups. Conservatives see their accusers as "silencing those who question liberal orthodoxy and otherwise cutting off meaningful dialog."[49] Others note that accusing a prominent white of racism, whether deserved or not, can backfire. "[S]ophisticated blacks have learned that to suggest that whites are racist is not a useful exercise in the current climate—at least when talking to whites . . . . In the eyes of most whites, affluent blacks seem to have no real cause for complaint . . . . To the extent that racism is perceived as a problem by whites, it is increasingly seen as an evil perpetrated by blacks—with whites (particularly Jews) serving principally as victims."[50] In sum, deciding whether or not to speak out against what one perceives as racist views is a double-edged sword—to do so may risk a white backlash and charges of hate speech; yet, to keep silent may signal acceptance of racist ideology and policies.

THE DOUBLE STANDARD

How does the application of double standards factor into the hate speech debate? Is it hate speech when Black Muslims accuse prison officials of denying their freedom of religion while protecting the rights of inmates who belong to the Aryan Nation (and vice versa)? Is accusing a person or an entity of applying a double standard just a different way of labeling them a racist? Is pointing out a double standard an act of racism itself?

The unique quality of the double standard is that members of both the majority and the minority are adept at pointing out instances of it and professing righteous indignation. Recent examples include accusations that in 2002 the Washington, D.C., police used racial profiling to try to find the "beltway sniper" by looking for "a white car with white people."[51] Another writer chastised the *Washington Post* for running an article by a black journalist who described her crusade to prevent white people from purchasing homes in inner-city Washington, D.C., neighborhoods.[52]

Zealous extremists at both ends of the spectrum derive great satisfaction from pointing out the injustice of double standards to which they are unfairly subjected. Such charges serve as a potent tool for stirring up controversy and intensifying hostilities between groups. A brief tour through the Web pages of white or black hate groups provides more than a taste of this type of lament. One article on the National Association for the Advancement of White People's Web site expressed outrage at a black university official who joked that "white men are the root of all evil" and went unpunished.[53] The article pointed out the harsh discipline received by John Rocker, the baseball player who was fined and suspended for making disparaging remarks about gays and racial minorities. Likewise, the Nation of Islam's Web site charged the Southern Poverty Law Center with following a double standard for listing the Nation of Islam as a hate group, while not listing Elie Wiesel, a death camp survivor, for advising Jews to "set apart a zone of hate, healthy, virile hate for what the German personifies and for what persists in the German."[54]

In sum, double standards play into the hate speech debate by providing antagonists with ammunition to charge that the other side "got away with" hateful speech or behavior when their side would not. Racists within the offended party are able to use the resulting indignation as a bonding mechanism to reinforce sentiments felt by members of the group. Even those who are not racists are likely to feel less conciliatory toward those who appear to gain a free pass from double standards.

RACIAL HOAXES

Racial hoaxes occur when a person wrongfully accuses someone of another race of committing an actual or fabricated crime.[55] When minorities perpetrate hoaxes against whites are they guilty of a form of hate speech? If so, what are the consequences of these "minority-on-white" hoaxes?

Perhaps the most famous (alleged) minority-on-white hoax was the 1987 Tawanna Brawley case. A black teenager was found in a garbage bag covered in feces with racial slurs written on her torso. She accused white racists, including a prominent law enforcement officer, of the attack. Although the victim's family never admitted the crime was a hoax, public opinion swung against her when a grand jury declined to indict the suspects for lack of evidence. Other celebrated hoaxes include a gay residential assistant at the University of

Georgia who admitted to setting his own door on fire, a lesbian student at St. Cloud State University in Minnesota who slashed her own face, and a black dental student at the University of Iowa's College of Dentistry who fabricated E-mail and bomb threats to herself.[56] Cries of hoax also accompanied a series of black church burnings in the South in the 1990s. Critics pointed to a lack of evidence showing racist motives in many of the fires and even suggested that black parishioners may have burned down their own churches for the insurance money. More recently, some conservatives labeled the alleged disenfranchisement of black voters in the 2000 Florida elections a hoax designed to smear Republicans.[57] And, as discussed elsewhere in the book (see Chapter 6), college conservatives have vociferously accused minorities of crying victim and using their minority status to silence conservatives. Recently, a liberal feminist echoed these complaints in an article in *Academe,* the journal of the American Association of University Professors.[58]

Those who take offense at minority-on-white hoaxes charge their perpetrators with deliberately inflaming racial tensions for their own purposes, such as coercing a school administration to provide more minority jobs, titles, or programs. The Center for Democratic Renewal and the National Council of Churches were accused of creating the black church-burning hysteria to solicit contributions to their "Burned Church Fund" that were then largely used for other purposes.[59] Likewise, the Southern Poverty Law Center has been accused of exaggerating the threat of racial terrorism to increase its revenues and public support.

Even those sympathetic to minority causes warn of the "cry wolf" syndrome—allegations of real hate crimes will be taken less seriously—and of a backlash—whites are offended by being made to look like racists, and as a result feel less sympathy toward minority causes. Finally, media coverage may spark a series of copycat crimes, as was alleged to have happened with the black church-burnings story.[60]

QUESTIONS FOR DISCUSSION, CHAPTER 11

1. How damaging *are* words like *honky, cracker,* and *whitey?* If you are white, how does hearing or reading these words make you feel? Irritated? Insulted? Scared? Bored?

2. When you hear a black nationalist railing against white devils, do you have a sinking feeling like it might be true—that
   you (if you are white) might indeed be a devil? Do you feel
   angry? Or that the whole idea is vaguely ludicrous?
3. Again, if you are white, which would bother you more—being called a *racist*, or a *honky*?
4. If a person of color angrily calls a white person a *cracker* or a
   honky, but lacks the power to do anything about whatever
   ticked him off—is that hate speech?
5. The stereotype of the African American is easy to state—stupid, lazy, sexually lascivious, and a welfare cheat. What
   stereotype is called up by the term *honky*? By *cracker*?
6. Is rap music the new vehicle for black expression? For black
   liberation? If so, how shall we see the misogynist, anti-white,
   and homophobic quality of some of it?

CLASS EXERCISE

You are an intern in the office of the dean of students. One day, your
boss asks you (because she knows you have taken a course on hate
speech) for your thoughts on an interesting case over which she must
soon preside. A member of the campus conservative organization has
filed charges, under the university's hate speech code, against the president of the Students of Color organization stemming from a shouting
match that broke out after a recent speech by antiracist lawyer Morris
Dees.

The Students of Color president, who is black, evidently told the
conservative leader, "Why can't more of you honkies be like him?"
The conservative leader found this offensive on several levels.

Was the black guilty of hate speech against the white? One-half of
the class should argue that he was; the other, that he was not.

RECOMMENDED READING, CHAPTER 11

Tomás Almaguer, *Racial Fault Lines: The Historical Origins of White
Supremacy in California* (1994).

Leslie G. Carr, *"Color-Blind" Racism* (1997).

Richard Delgado and Jean Stefancic, eds., *Critical White Studies: Looking Behind the Mirror* (1998).

Ian F. Haney Lopez, *White by Law: The Legal Construction of Race* (1996).

Peggy McIntosh, *White Privilege and Male Privilege: A Personal Account of Coming to See Correspondence Through Work in Women's Studies* (1988).

Kenneth B. Nunn, *Law as a Eurocentric Enterprise*, 15 L. & Inequal. J. 323 (1997).

Stephanie Wildman, *Privilege Revealed: How Invisible Preference Undermines America* (1996).

Notes

1. John Hood, "End Games," *Reason*, February 1996, at 54 (reviewing Dinesh D'Souza, *The End of Racism: Principles for a Multiracial Society*).

2. Ginger Berrigan, *"Speaking Out" About Hate Speech*, 48 Loy. L. Rev. 1, 5 (2002).

3. Ellis Cose, *The Rage of a Privileged Class*, 157 (1993).

4. Richard Delgado, *Toward a Legal Realist View of the First Amendment*, 113 Harv. L. Rev. 778, 797 (2000) (reviewing Steven Shiffrin, *Dissent, Injustice, and the Meanings of America*).

5. Prior to the civil rights movement of the 1960s, the potentially severe consequences faced by minorities who spoke disparagingly of whites were doubtless a potent tool of suppression of minority hate speech.

6. Alexander Tsesis, *Destructive Messages: How Hate Speech Paves the Way for Harmful Social Movements*, 86 (2002).

7. Cose, supra, at 156.

8. Ibid. at 157.

9. Ibid.

10. Tsesis, supra, at 93–94.

11. Ibid. at 96.

12. Berrigan, supra, at 9.

13. Ibid.

14. See *Bynoe v. City of San Jose*, 2002 Cal. App. LEXIS 6972 (July 25, 2002) (trial court denied challenge to disciplinary action by a black firefighter who argued, among other things, that his First Amendment rights were violated because the discipline was based on his speech).

15. 1996 U.S. Dist. LEXIS 14417 at *7 (N.D. Ill. April 4, 1996).

16. 1999 U.S. Dist LEXIS 20417 at **1–2 (S.D. Ala. Dec. 29, 1999).

17. 25 N.Y.S. 2d 447 (1995).

18. See *Quigley v. Rosenthal*, 43 F. Supp. 2d 1163 (D. Colo. 1999); John C. Ensslin, "Neighbors to be Charged with Ethnic Intimidation," *Rocky Mountain News*, December 10, 1994, at 5A; Peter G. Chronis, "Quigleys Sue for Millions," *Denver Post*, January 19, 1995, at B1.

19. See Chapter 4 at note 126.

20. 34 Fed. App. 573, 574, 2002 WL 869930 at * (9th Cir. May 3, 2002).

21. Michael A. Cullers, *Comment, Limits on Speech and Mental Slavery: A Thirteenth Amendment Defense Against Hate Speech Codes*, 45 Case W. Res. L. Rev. 641 (1995).

22. Southern Poverty Law Center, *U.S. Map of Hate Groups, Black Separatist Chapters, 2001* [http://www.tolerance.org/maps/hate/group.jsp? map_data_type_id=1] (accessed April 5, 2003).

23. The original Black Panther Party, formed in 1966 by Bobby Seale and Huey Newton, disavows any connection with this group. *There Is No New Black Panther Party: An Open Letter From the Dr. Huey P. Newton Foundation* [http://www.blackpanther.org/newsalert.htm] (accessed April 5, 2003). Furthermore, the Black Panther Party successfully sued the New Black Panther Party to prevent them from using the Black Panther name. *McCarthy v. The Black Panther Party, Inc.*, 1997 WL 5842729 (Tex. App. Sept. 23, 1997).

24. See supra, note 22.

25. Ibid.

26. Martin A. Lee, *Strange Bedfellows: Some American Black Muslims Make Common Cause with Domestic Neo-Nazis and Foreign Muslim Extremists*, Intelligence Report (Southern Poverty Law Center), spring 2002, at 22.

27. Lawrence R. Marcus, *Fighting Words, The Politics of Hateful Speech*, 59–60 (1996) ("For such people, the 'Jew' is shorthand for the white devil . . . the scapegoat.").

28. Tsesis, supra, at 77.

29. Mortimer B. Zuckerman, "Build Bridges, Don't Burn Them," *U.S. News & World Report*, April 25, 1994, at 104.

30. Muhammad died of a stroke in February 2001 at the age of fifty-three.

31. Marcus, supra, at xvii.

32. Ibid. at xviii.

33. Zuckerman, supra.

34. This is not to quantify the magnitude of harm suffered by different individuals on some kind of sliding scale. That harm will undoubtedly be a function of the type of hate speech at issue and the victims' own unique backgrounds and experiences with discrimination. Still, as a generalization, it will appear that whites, on average, are less affected by all forms of hate speech than minorities.

35. See, e.g., J. E. Lighter, *Random House Dictionary of American Slang*, 503; II, at 136 (1994).

36. Tsesis, supra, at 90.

37. See Stephanie Wildman, *Privilege Revealed: How Invisible Preference Undermines America* (1996).

38. Peggy McIntosh, "White Privilege and Male Privilege: A Personal Account of Coming to See Correspondences Through Work in Women's Studies," in *Critical White Studies: Looking Behind the Mirror*, 291, 295–296 (Richard Delgado and Jean Stefancic, eds., 1997).

39. 508 U.S. 476 (1993) (The Wisconsin Supreme Court deemed the statute violative of the First Amendment for punishing offensive thought. In reversing, the U.S. Supreme Court reiterated its previous pronouncement that "the Constitution does not erect a *per se* barrier to the admission of evidence concerning one's beliefs and associations at sentencing simply because those beliefs and associations are protected by the First Amendment." The statute at issue was not directed at expression but at conduct unprotected by the First Amendment).

40. Kenneth Lasson, *Controversial Speakers on Campus: Liberties, Limitations, and Common-Sense Guidelines*, 12 St. Thomas L. Rev. 39, 52 (1999).

41. Zuckerman, supra.

42. Lasson, supra, at 51.

43. Ibid.

44. Richard Lowry, "'Conservative' and 'Racist': The Ashcroft Nomination and the Left's Foulest Card," *National Review*, Feb. 5, 2001, at 30.

45. Stuart Taylor Jr., "Who's Exploiting Racial Divisions Now?," *National Journal*, December 4, 1999, at 3445.

46. John Leo, *So Which Party Is Now Exploiting Race?* [http://www.townhall.com/columnists/johnleo/jl20021230.shtml] (Dec. 30, 2002).

47. Neil A. Lewis, "Senate Panel Approves Judge's Nomination," *New York Times*, Oct. 3, 2003, at A18.

48. Harry Stein, "How I Was Smeared," *City Journal*, autumn 2002, at 44. ("It is truly a sickening feeling being slandered in this way, the outrage mixing with a profound sense of helplessness.")

49. Ibid.

50. Cose, *Rage*, supra, note 3, at 153.

51. John Leo, "Deadly Political Correctness," *Chattanooga Times/Chattanooga Free Press*, November 6, 2002, at B9.

52. Andrew Sullivan, "Home Base," *New Republic*, July 2, 2001, at 6.

53. Scott Hogenson, *College Takes No Action on White Men as "Root of Most Evil" Comment* [http://www.naawp.com/news/root_of_all_evil.htm] (April 27, 2000).

54. *"Hate" List or Hit List? Morris Dees Persecution of the Nation of Islam* [http://www.blacksandjews.com/dees.html] (accessed Mar. 19, 2003) ("If this statement were uttered from the mouth of someone of the *wrong* religion, that one might end up on the hit-list of the SPLC. But Mr. Wiesel is safely on the white end of this uniquely American double standard.").

55. Katheryn K. Russell, *The Color of Crime: Racial Hoaxes, White Fear, Black Protectionism, Police Harassment, and Other Macroaggressions*, 70 (1998)

(Russell analyzed sixty-seven racial hoaxes reported in the media between 1987 and 1996, of which eleven were black-on-white hoaxes. Ibid. at 80).

56. John Leo, *In Campus Race and Gender Crimes, Principal Victim is Truth* [http://www.townhall.com/columnistsjohnleo/jl000531.shtml] (May 31, 2000).

57. John Leo, "'Disenfranchised?' Dishonest Commentary Overlooks Fact That Voting Investigations Cleared Florida," *Dallas Morning News*, June 17, 2001, at 4J.

58. See Academe (J. of Amer. Ass'n. of University Professors), winter/spring 2002/2003.

59. Michael Fumento, "Politics and Church Burnings: Racist Conspiracy Not Evident in Recent Rash of Church Burnings," American Jewish Committee, *Commentary*, October 1996, at 57.

60. Michael Fumento, "Sharp Rise in Black Church Arsons Is a Myth," *Times Union* (Albany, N.Y.), July 12, 1996, at A11.

12

INTERNATIONAL AND
COMPARATIVE PERSPECTIVES

Despite our nation's checkered history of racial injustice, American courts have been slow to recognize the harm of hate speech and incitement to racial hatred. As earlier chapters have shown, victims are unlikely to obtain judicial relief unless their injuries are clear-cut and dramatic, and the speech that injured them beyond all bounds of decency. Campus speech codes, too, have come in for harsh treatment under the law.

As America becomes more diverse, minorities' political power will increase, at the same time that the country's need for tolerance heightens. The advent of "First Amendment legal realism"—discussed in Chapter 14—promises as much. That development suggests that courts will rely less on mechanical tests and thought-ending clichés (no content regulation, the cure for bad speech is more speech, and so forth). Instead they will examine individual cases in light of the circumstances this book has been considering—Who is the speaker? Who the victim? Is the speech concerted? Face to face? Backed by power or threat? One of many such utterances? With what opportunity to respond?—and also in light of social science knowledge, communication theory, and knowledge of the rhetoric of hate.

Faced with the prospect of a less sympathetic judiciary and a more nuanced First Amendment, some of those who defend hate speech, such as the American Civil Liberties Union, have been arguing that, even if that form of speech could be regulated, that would be a bad idea. Some of their arguments are analyzed in a later chapter, but a few of them are appropriate for consideration now. One is that regulation doesn't work. It inevitably backfires against minorities. Or, it starts society on a "slippery slope" so that the next limitation on free speech becomes that much easier to enact, and soon we will have no free speech at all.

What does the experience of other Western industrialized society show? According to Frederick Schauer, professor of government at Harvard University,[1] and Kevin Boyle, one of Great Britain's most prominent international human rights experts, the United States is unique among Western democracies in its toleration of hate speech.[2] Most other countries provide some form of regulation, believing that human rights and freedoms contain a collective, as well as an individual, dimension and that a citizen's right to promote racist views must be weighed against the interests of society at large.[3] Other countries regulate hate speech because they wish to deter the violence and fighting they believe it encourages, or because it goes against the human dignity and equality on which their societies are premised.[4]

In Canada, for example, both federal and provincial laws criminalize hate speech and crime. One such law came before the Canadian Supreme Court in the famous 1990 opinion in *Regina v. Keegstra*,[5] which upheld it in the face of a challenge that it violated the guarantee of free speech contained in the Canadian Charter, which is patterned after the U.S. Constitution. A teacher had uttered racist and antisemitic remarks, which caused the authorities to file charges against him under the national hate speech law. The Supreme Court upheld the conviction, reasoning that Canada's national values also guarantee social harmony and a multicultural environment. Citing American critical race theorists (including one of the present authors), the Supreme Court held that the guarantee of free speech must be understood in light of a broad range of social values, including diversity. Canada's hate speech law, which prohibits any statement that is "likely to expose a person or group of persons to hatred or contempt" on account of race, color, ancestry, place of origin, religion, sex, or sexual orientation, is one of the world's most stringent. Among other features, it lacks any requirement that prosecutors show proof of malicious intent or actual harm to win a conviction.[6]

Another section of Canada's federal statutes penalizes repeated communication by telephone of hate messages that expose a person or persons to hatred or contempt on the basis of race, sex, or national origin. Provincial legislation goes even further. For example, a June 1993 Human Rights Amendment in the province of British Columbia provides that no person shall publish or display any statement, notice, sign, or symbol that communicates discrimination, hatred, or contempt to a group on account of race, color, religion, sex, or sexual orientation.[7]

Tightly knit, densely populated, and with a history of ethnic warfare, Europe is understandably wary about organized hatred. Practically every European nation punishes hate speech and propaganda. Many also punish Holocaust denial. Some, such as Germany, prohibit Nazi or neo-Nazi groups from organizing or using the Internet.[8] The new European Commonwealth has also been developing procedures and tribunals for adjudicating interethnic hate and expression.[9]

Many of these national measures came about in response to U.N. conventions and agreements and were intended to provide enforcement at the local level. In the aftermath of World War II, the United Nations enacted the Universal Declaration of Human Rights, which protects freedom of speech in Article 19. The same right receives protection in Article 19 of the International Covenant on Civil and Political Rights, which guarantees that all citizens shall have the right to hold and express opinions without interference. Article 19 contains certain limits, however. The exercise of the rights of free speech and opinion carry with them "special duties and responsibilities," which member nations may, by law, spell out. These areas include "respect of the rights or reputations of others," and "protection of national security or public order . . . or of public health or morals." Article 20 goes on to spell out further limits on the right to speak. It provides that member nations may prohibit "any propaganda for war" and also "any advocacy of national, racial or religious hatred that constitutes incitement to discrimination, hostility or violence."[10]

Another document, the International Convention on the Elimination of All Forms of Racial Discrimination, requires member nations to punish "all dissemination of ideas based on racial superiority or hatred, incitement to racial discrimination, as well as all acts of violence or incitement to such acts against any race or group or persons of another color or ethnic origin." The Council of Europe has weighed in with a similar position. Article 9 of the European Convention on the Protection of Human Rights and Fundamental Freedoms provides for protection of freedom of speech, but goes on to say (in Article 10): "The exercise of these freedoms . . . may be subject to such formalities, conditions, restrictions or penalties as are prescribed by law and are necessary in a democratic society." The article then specifies the conditions under which speech may be limited for the common good, including protection of the reputation or rights of others.[11] Backed by legislation like this, the European Court of Human Rights and similar councils have found various forms of hate expression, including racist leaflets, Nazi propaganda, and Holocaust denial, to fall beyond the bounds of permissible expression.[12]

The European Union began with the principal purpose of promoting economic cooperation and peace through free trade. But following the Treaty of Amsterdam (1997), the EU has increasingly become committed to upholding human rights. Enactment of the Charter of Fundamental Rights at a council that met in Nice on December 7, 2000, gave further voice to this commitment, as did the establishment of the European Monitoring Centre on Racism and Xenophobia in 1997 during the European Year Against Racism. In June 2001, the Monitoring Centre launched its RAXEN Information Network aimed at increasing communication and cooperation among member states in combating intolerance and collecting data on hate groups.[13]

The Monitoring Centre in November 2001 put forward a Council Framework Decision on combating racism to propose model laws and regulations for offenses exhibiting fascism and xenophobia. The laws will deal with such matters as public incitement to racial violence or hatred; public insults or threats toward individuals or groups on the basis of race; public condoning of genocide or crimes against humanity; public dissemination of tracts or other material of a racist nature; and directing or participating in the activities of a racist group with the intention of contributing to criminal activities. It also encourages member states to enact enhancement statutes, like those in use in the United States (see Chapter 4), that increase punishment for offenses shown to have been committed with a racist motivation. If adopted, the proposal is likely to prove a key tool in EU action against racism and hate propaganda.[14]

Many non-European countries, such as India and South Africa, which share a history of ethnic strife, have enacted measures similar to those found in Europe. The South African Constitution, for example, provides for freedom of expression but specifically excludes hate speech. New Zealand prohibits publishing or broadcasting words likely to incite hostility or bring into contempt groups on the basis of color, race, or national origin and has enacted statutes against inciting racial disharmony. Many Caribbean nations have ratified the major European human rights treaties clarifying that freedom of expression does not extend to hate speech.[15]

How effective are hate-speech laws in discouraging racist incitement and abuse? And, have such laws in other countries proven *too* effective, leading to a cascading effect and loss of freedom of speech, opinion, and inquiry? Recent writing by international law scholars suggests that the laws do seem to have some beneficial effect. At a minimum, they enable monitoring commissions to compile statistics, issue progress reports, and coordinate the work of different nations. They also provide the basis for the occasional prosecution of notorious hatemongers, all of which presumably has some deterrent effect.[16]

Are the laws *too* effective? The press in Canada and Europe strikes most observers today as feistier and more independent than that in the United States, and less beholden to big-business interests and advertisers. The government-backed BBC and many English newspapers, for example, have provided a greater variety of views about the war in Afghanistan, the campaign against Iraq, and the various issues at stake in the war against terror than their U.S. counterparts have. No European or Canadian nation has proposed anything like the U.S. government's 2002 proposed total information awareness initiative, which would have permitted the government to monitor citizens' book purchases, E-mail, and credit card receipts. No European or Canadian organization posted on a Web site the names of professors and commentators who raised doubts about official U.S. policy, impugning their patriotism and fitness to teach. The climate of opinion in these areas seems at least as free as that in the United States.

While the press and media in these other countries seem no less free than their U.S. counterparts, they are more selective. For example, New Yorker Harold Mollin's TV spot featuring a huckster in an Indian headdress leading a group of senior citizens in a rain dance was rejected by the Canadian Broadcasting Corporation, which found it an affront to both First Nations and the elderly. Canadian radio and TV also seem to have survived without Don Imus, Howard Stern (who is heard only in Montreal), Jerry Springer, or Rush Limbaugh—all without a noticeable reduction in genuine social and political commentary.[17] The experience of other countries, then, does not bear out the fear some have expressed that placing limits on hate speech will weaken society's commitment to robust discussion of public issues.

QUESTIONS FOR DISCUSSION, CHAPTER 12

1. Compared to countries like Canada and Great Britain, the United States features a large minority population and a history of great cruelty toward Latinos, blacks, Asians, and Indians. Those other countries have enacted hate speech prohibitions, apparently without suffering a great diminution in freedom of thought and inquiry. Might the United States do the same? Should it?
2. What if you were behind a veil of ignorance and did not know whether your role in life was to be a white or nonwhite. You could live in Society A, which has adopted moderate hate speech controls, or Society B, which has adopted none. Both societies are equal in every other respect. Which would you choose?
3. Who is more inconvenienced—a white who is prohibited from uttering hate speech on the occasions when he might otherwise do so, or an African, Asian, Latino, or gay who must put up with it many times as he or she goes through life?
4. Why did the U.S. Supreme Court affirm a skinhead's right to burn a cross in the yard of a black family, when many other court systems would have sent him straight off to jail? Will this case one day be seen as an embarrassment similar to *Dred Scott v. Sandford* or *Plessy v. Ferguson*?

CLASS EXERCISE

Would you want to live in a country, otherwise comparable to the United States in quality of life, that punished hate speech and Holocaust denial?

What would you give up? What would you gain?

Recommended Reading, Chapter 12

Geoffrey Bindman, *How Can EC Law Confront Racism?*, New L.J., Mar. 11, 1994, at 352.

Kevin Boyle, *Hate Speech—The United States Versus the Rest of the World?*, 53 Maine L. Rev. 488 (2001).

Sandra Coliver, ed., *Striking a Balance: Hate Speech, Freedom of Expression, and Non-Discrimination* (1992).

Isaak I. Dore, *United Nations Measures to Combat Racial Discrimination*, 10 Denver J. Int'l L. & Pol'y 299 (1981).

Sionaidh Douglas-Scott, *The Hatefulness of Protected Speech: A Comparison of the American and European Approaches*, 7 Wm. & Mary Bill of Rts. J. 305 (1999).

European Parliament, Comm. of Inquiry on Racism & Xenophobia, *Report on the Findings of the Inquiry* (1991).

Stephanie Farrior, *Molding the Matrix: The Historical and Theoretical Foundations of International Law Concerning Hate Speech*, Berkeley J. Int'l L. 1 (1996).

J. Ingles, *Positive Measures Designed to Eradicate All Incitement to, Or Acts of Racial Discrimination: Implementation of Article 4 of the International Convention on the Elimination of All Forms of Racial Discrimination* (1986).

International Convention on the Elimination of All Forms of Racial Discrimination, opened for signature March 7, 1966, 660 U.N.T.S. 195.

Thomas David Jones, *Human Rights: Group Defamation, Freedom of Expression, and the Law of Nations* (1994).

Luke McNamara, *Criminalizing Racial Hatred: Learning from the Canadian Experience*, 1 Aus. J. Hum. Rts. 198 (1994).

Paul Meller, "Europe Moving Toward a Ban on Internet Hate Speech," *New York Times*, January 11, 2001 (Technology Section).

Notes

1. Dina Temple-Raston, "Radio Hate," *Legal Affairs*, September/October 2002, at 29.

2. Kevin Boyle, "Overview of a Dilemma," in *Striking a Balance*, 1–8 (Sandra Coliver, ed., 1992). See also Kevin Boyle, *Hate Speech—The United States Versus the Rest of the World?*, 53 Maine L. Rev. 485 (2001).

3. See generally *Striking a Balance*, supra.

4. Ibid.

5. (1991) 2WWWR1; (1990) 2 SCR 697; (1991) 1 CR (4th) 129.

6. Ibid. See also Jeff Brunner, *Canada's Use of Criminal and Human Rights Legislation to Control Hate Propaganda*, 26 Manitoba L.J. 82; Steven Pearlstein, "In Canada, Free Speech Has Its Restrictions," *Washington Post*, December 12, 1999, at A41.

7. See Luke McNamara, *Criminalizing Racial Hatred: Learning from the Canadian Experience*, 1 Aus. J. Hum. Rights 198 (1994).

8. See *Striking a Balance*, supra; Boyle, *Rest of the World?*, supra; Sionaidh Douglass-Scott, *The Hatefulness of Protected Speech: A Comparison of the American and European Approaches*, 7 Wm. & Mary Bill of Rights J. 305 (1999).

9. See Geoffrey Bindman, *European Community: How Can EC Law Confront Racism?*, New L.J., Mar. 11, 1994, at 352.

10. See, e.g., Tarloch McGonagle, *Wrestling (Racial) Equality from Tolerance of Hate Speech*, 23 Dublin U. L.J. 20, 29 (2001).

11. Ibid. at 31.

12. Ibid. at 32–37.

13. Ibid. at 37–38.

14. Ibid. at 37–39.

15. Petal Nevella Modeste, *Race Hate Speech: The Pervasive Badge of Slavery that Mocks the Thirteenth Amendment*, 44 How. L.J. 311, 326, 328 (2001).

16. Ibid. See also Frederich Kübler, *How Much Freedom for Racist Speech? Transnational Aspects of a Conflict of Human Rights*, 27 Hofstra L. Rev. 335 (1998).

17. See Steven Pearlstein, supra.

13

FIRST AMENDMENT ABSOLUTISM AND FALLBACK POSITIONS: SOCIAL POLICY OBJECTIONS TO HATE SPEECH REMEDIES

In earlier chapters, the reader encountered the ACLU (absolutist) position on hate speech regulation, which holds that our system of free speech should remain inviolate. Hate speech, no matter how abhorrent, is still speech, and, unless it accompanies an assault or other physical crime, must be tolerated in a society like ours. This position draws force from doctrines such as the prohibition on content regulation and maxims such as the cure for bad speech is more speech and we must protect even the speech we hate. It distrusts any governmental regulation of speech, believing that the first such step can easily lead us into the thickets of censorship. It points out that today's rejected idea is tomorrow's orthodoxy and warns of a slippery slope in which one form of state prohibition shades into another, then another, so that soon we have little freedom of speech left at all.[1]

In recent years, however, the absolutist position—itself a form of orthodoxy—has come in for increasing criticism. Women and minorities charge that it provides insufficient protection from hard-core pornography, sexual harassment, and racist hate speech and that the First Amendment must be balanced against other values. They point out that our system of free speech is not the seamless web its defenders like to imagine; indeed it contains dozens of exceptions (such as libel, defamation, false advertising, plagiarism, disrespectful words uttered to a judge or other authority figure, words of threat, and copyright) that seldom raise the absolutists' ire in the same way hate speech regulations do.[2]

More fundamentally, a new form of criticism, called First Amendment legal realism, described in the next chapter, argues that this noble amendment should be subjected to the same degree of legal skepticism and scrutiny as other legal norms. Faced with the prospect that their line in the sand will not stand much longer, many former absolutists are now shifting ground. Instead of arguing that the First Amendment forbids any regulation—a position increasingly difficult to maintain—they now argue that *even if* hate speech controls are legally permissible, courts, legislatures, and other bodies should not, as a matter of prudence, enact them. Like a hypothetical law against driving at night, laws against hate speech might be constitutional—there is no constitutional right to drive—they simply would be stupid, unwise, and unnecessary.

This new fallback approach, which has been appearing just as constitutional arguments seem to be losing ground, features two different types of argument. The first kind, associated with the moderate left, is paternalistic; it urges that hate speech controls would harm their intended beneficiaries. If women and minorities knew their own self-interest, they would not press for them. A second group of policy arguments is associated with libertarians and conservatives, who reason that hate speech controls are inconsistent with the very values minorities espouse. This chapter considers both forms of objection, and answers to each.

PATERNALISTIC ARGUMENTS AGAINST HATE SPEECH REGULATION

As faith in traditional free speech orthodoxy has weakened, hate speech's defenders have shifted ground. No longer able to take the high road of First Amendment absolutism—or even sure that it is the high road—many opponents of hate speech regulation are finding new arguments for their position. Even if controls on hate speech are not unconstitutional, they are unwise. Colleges might, perhaps, be able to enact carefully crafted hate speech codes that would withstand constitutional scrutiny. A trial court might find that a plaintiff victimized by racist invective has stated a cause of action, without fearing reversal by a higher court. A state bar committee might take action against a racist attorney, without fear that the state supreme court will reverse its ruling.

The new approach simply argues that all these actions are a bad idea. Even if a college or committee of bar examiners could get away with measures like the ones listed above, they still should not enact them. Like a ban on night driving, such measures would be foolish, unfair, or uneconomical. One set of arguments, associated with liberals, urges that anti–hate speech measures and rulings are poor policy because they harm the very women and minorities they are designed to protect. If these groups knew their own self-interest, they would desist from demanding such measures.

Just Letting Off Steam

One paternalistic argument against hate speech regulation is that it is better to allow hatemongers and racists to release their pent-up emotions harmlessly, in the form of speech, rather than through violent action. If they give vent to their feelings this way, they, and minorities, will be much safer—or so the argument goes.[3] The trouble with this argument lies with its empirical assumption.

Social science evidence indicates that permitting someone to say or do hurtful things to another person increases, rather than decreases, the chances that he or she will do so again.[4] Just as important, observers may do likewise, creating a climate in which the minority and others of his or her group are at even greater risk. Once the speaker forms the category of the victim who deserves what he gets—and suffers in silence—his behavior is apt to continue and even escalate to include material discrimination and physical bullying.[5]

If You Just Knew Your Own History

Another argument in the same vein holds that free speech has been minorities' best friend. If they realized what an important role it has played in historical reform movements, they would not call for limitations on such a vital right. Thus, spokespersons for the American

Ruffin v. Professional Services Industries, 2001 WL 128313, *2 (E.D.La.).

Not every verbal encounter may be converted into a tort; on the contrary, "some safety valve must be left through which irascible tempers may blow off relatively harmless steam." . . .

In contrast, however, in cases involving the use of harassing slurs and epithets over a period of time, courts have recognized that their cumulative effect may support an IIED [intentional infliction of emotional distress] claim. See, e.g., *Channey v. Home Depot, USA*, 1999 WL 649633 (E.D.LA. Aug. 24, 1999)("a pattern of emotionally abusive behavior, including repeated name calling (including "boy" and "nigger" in front of other employees)" may support an IIED claim; *Walters v. Rubicon*, 706 So.2d 503 (La.Ct.App. 1st Cir.1997)(continuous cursing, screaming, and threats of supervisor may support an IIED claim). The instant case is more similar to this latter group, in that the name-calling and use of epithets occurred over a period of many months. And, while the Court does not condone the use of any racial epithets, the Court is also impressed by the fact that the comments attributed to Adams (especially his pro-lynching remark) rank quite a bit higher on the outrageousness scale than the garden-variety epithets found not to amount to IIED in the cited caselaw.

Civil Liberties Union have repeatedly pointed out how important free speech and assembly were for Martin Luther King Jr., Cesar Chavez, Corky Gonzalez, and other minority leaders.[6]

This argument, too, is paternalistic; it invokes the best interest of minorities in arguing against a measure that many believe would protect them and their children. It, too, stands on empirically weak ground. *Speech* may have been a vital weapon in the arsenal of these and other minority leaders. But our *system* of free speech was not. In the 1960s, minorities sat in, were arrested and convicted; marched, spoke, chanted—and were arrested and convicted; demonstrated, sang "We Shall Overcome," and were arrested and convicted. True, in some cases, years later and after the expenditure of thousands of dollars and hundreds of hours of gallant lawyering, their convictions might be reversed on appeal. But, the First Amendment, at least as then understood, did little to protect them. Throughout history, minorities have registered their greatest advances when they acted in defiance of the First Amendment, rather than in accord with it.[7]

History shows that minorities' protest rights are respected only when their behavior is meek, mild, decorous, and mannerly. As soon as their protest becomes strident, noisy, or obstructionist, it ceases to qualify for protection. Free speech is helpful only when minorities need it least.[8]

TALKING BACK TO THE AGGRESSOR

Other liberal figures, such as Nat Hentoff, allied with the ACLU urge that minorities learn to talk back to their aggressors. The cure for bad speech is more speech. Instead of silently internalizing the insult or filing a complaint, the minority targeted by a racist epithet or slur should speak back to his tormentor.[9] The victim might point out, for example, that the speaker is wrong on the facts—minorities have made many contributions to America. Many succeed at college, fight in the Army, help find cures for diseases. He or she can point out that the speaker's behavior is out of keeping with this nation's commitment to freedom and equality, that the victim has a right to be where he or she is, and that hate speech is a sign of a weak intellect and poor vocabulary.

The difficulty with this position is that hate speech is rarely an invitation to a dialogue; it is like a slap in the face. The speaker is not inviting an intellectual discussion of, for example, the merits of affirmative action or the black studies curriculum. He or she is uttering a performative—a word that enacts its own message without the need of decoding. The idea that talking back to the aggressor is wise, sensible, or even safe lacks a sense of reality. In fact, many incidents of racial violence and murder began this way. The victim spoke back to the hate speaker and his friends; a minute later, he paid with his life (see Chapter 4).

THE BACKFIRE THAT WAS NEVER HEARD

A final argument associated with the moderate-left position is that measures to control hate speech merely backfire against minorities themselves. The white who hurls a vicious epithet will go unpunished or receive a slap on the wrist. The black or Latino who mutters something about "typical honky behavior" will come in for harsh punishment.[10] The empirical evidence offers scant support for this proposition. FBI statistics on hate crime, and less systematic compilations on the incidence of hate speech, show that it is mainly minorities who are victimized, not whites.[11] And the frequency of prosecution mirrors that of the crimes themselves—the main class against whom charges are brought is whites, especially white males.[12] Racism is, of course, a two-way street. Minorities who gang up on or belittle whites deserve to be charged with hate offenses. But these cases are the exception. Because whites in this society enjoy more power and influence than blacks, Latinos, Asians, and Indians, they are more apt to use hate speech to enforce the status quo and protect the privileges of whiteness.

THE TOUGH LOVE OR CONSERVATIVE SCHOOL

A second set of arguments focuses on the role of victimization, and is the stock-in-trade of a certain type of conservative we might call the "tough love" school. What these arguments have in common is a certain let-it-roll-off-your-back toughness and a refusal to credit the hateful words with any efficacy.

SELF-VICTIMIZATION ("DON'T DWELL ON IT")

One variation of the tough love position holds that hateful words have no more efficacy than that which victims choose to give them. The best response to a hateful racist slur is to look the other way or laugh at it. Enacting laws or legal doctrines against hate speech simply encourages minorities to think of themselves as victims. Instead of rushing to the authorities whenever they hear something that offends them, people should learn to talk back or ignore the offensive words. Complaints and lawsuits simply reinforce in the minds of victims that they are weak and helpless; with such a self–image it is easy to overlook the opportunities that are, in fact, open to one.[13] Writer Dinesh D'Souza, for example, argued that hate speech controls reinforce a "cry-baby" attitude;[14] Henry Louis Gates, that they encourage a "therapeutic" mindset that sees everything in terms of emotional and mental well-being.[15]

Like some of the other positions we have considered, the don't-dwell-on-it argument rests on questionable premises. Does filing a hate speech complaint or challenging a teacher who tolerates a racially discriminatory classroom environment encourage passivity among minorities? In one way of looking at it, it does not; indeed, it fosters the opposite attitude. Those who charge their harassers are taking forthright action instead of passively "lumping it" when verbal abuse strikes. They takes charge of their destiny, instead of pretending that the incident did not happen.

Further, providing judicial or administrative remedies for hate speech does not at all foreclose other remedies. An individual targeted with hate speech can still deck the speaker with a good right hook; can draw himself up and regale the other with a few choice words of his own; or can choose to put the incident out of mind and get on with his or her life. It is interesting that society does not encourage members of the ruling class to "look the other way" or "rise above it" when they are victimized by their stock broker, for example, have their hubcaps stolen, or suffer some other form of mistreatment characteristic of their class.

The Deflection (From Important Matters) or Waste-of-Time Argument

A related argument posits that providing remedies for hate speech is a distraction from more important matters that minorities should be attending to.[16] Those other matters might include getting a good education, learning English (in the case of Latino or Asian immigrants), or striving to save money and get ahead at work.

Of course, nothing is wrong with doing those things and working for a racism-free environment, too. The proponents of this argument seem to believe they are mutually exclusive, when, as previous chapters

have shown, racism in the environment can significantly impair a minority person's well-being and ability to take advantage of the very opportunities the conservative touts. D'Souza, for example, accused
minority students on campus of wasting time dwelling on minor griev-
ances and signs of racism, when they would do better to enroll in
tough courses like calculus and physics.[17] It may be that a few students
of color dwell excessively on verbal slights and insults. But the thousands of cases of hate speech social scientists have documented, on
campus and elsewhere, surely require some attention. The many Western industrialized countries that have enacted laws and measures designed to control hate speech suggest that the effort is not a waste of
time, but an essential safeguard for a decent society (see Chapter 12).

"Get It Out in the Open"

A third argument in the tough love arsenal holds that hate speech
should not be driven underground but allowed to remain out in the
open. The racist who is known is safer than the one you do not know.
Better to know who your enemies are than drive them underground.
Once they state their position, you can organize against or simply
avoid them. On a college campus, a further advantage accrues: Incidents of racism and racist speech can serve as the occasion for useful
discussions and institutional self-examination. The campus may
emerge a stronger, more tolerant place as a result.[18]

The argument—that racist speech can serve as a useful bellwether—
does make one valid point: The racist who is known is, all things
being equal, less dangerous than one who is not. But the argument
overlooks an important point: The racist who is deterred—by rules,
official policies, and firm penalties—from engaging in racism is the
safest one of all. Since most conservatives believe in law and punishment as means of shaping social behavior, they ought to find this
counterargument persuasive. And, what of the "town hall" argument
that incidents of racism should not be driven underground, but used
as the occasion for public discussion?[19] They of course should—but
those discussions could take place in any event. Rules and official
policies discouraging hate speech are not apt to work perfectly; some
hate speech will occur, anyway. It can then serve as the occasion for
the types of discussion the argument values—and without leaving

racial and sexual minorities constantly exposed and unprotected in the meantime.

A WHIFF OF CLASSISM?

A further argument from the neoconservative, or tough love, camp is that rules against hate speech are classist. They leave untouched the genteel bigotry of the educated class, who will be free to write and teach demeaning notions such as the "culture of poverty" that supposedly holds minority people down, or write books like *The Bell Curve* implying that minorities are genetically inferior to whites. The rules will end up punishing only naïve speakers from small towns who have never learned that certain words should not be spoken, or else blue-collar workers and children of working-class families who are raised to expect a certain type of rough, give-and-take talk.[20] D'Souza, for example, argued that hate-speech rules, on campuses at least, aim to impose a type of "social etiquette," while overlooking the more refined glances, rolling eyes, and polysyllabic phrases of university professors and writers at think tanks.

Henry Louis Gates offered the following example to illustrate classism lurking in hate speech rules:

> A. LaVon, if you find yourself struggling here, you should realize it isn't your fault. It's simply that you're the beneficiary of a disruptive policy of affirmative action that places underqualified, underprepared and often undertalented black students in demanding educational environments like this one. The policy's egalitarian aims may be well-intentioned, but given . . . that aptitude tests place African Americans almost a full standard deviation below the mean, even controlling for socioeconomic disparities, they are also profoundly misguided. The truth is, you probably don't belong here, and your college experience will be a long downhill slide.
>
> B. Out of My Face, Jungle Bunny[21]

But this argument of classism is in one sense off target. Most campus codes do prohibit only the direct, one-on-one expressions of contempt and hatred. Gates's example A is, arguably, an invitation to a dialogue. The speaker gives reasons, even if plainly invalid ones, for his racist conclusions. A black or brown university undergraduate should be able to marshal arguments in return. (For example, yes, professor, standardized tests do indicate a disparity between the scores of whites and blacks, but what about the racist history of those tests? Are not many of the items culturally biased? Do not white students often benefit from test-prepping and coaching? Do the tests not predict only a small amount of the variation in first-year grades—about 16 percent, in fact?) By contrast, what sort of reply might one make to the jungle-bunny accusation? Unlike example A, it is not open to counterargument, and has overtones of a direct, physical threat. Whether uttered by the millionaire's or the factory worker's son, it deserves discouragement and firm sanctions. The first example, whomever utters it, is plainly less damaging and less calculated to wound.

What lies behind the many varieties of tough love argument is a common conservative mistake—believing that the playing field is equal. The mistake is in a way natural, for First Amendment ideology seems to presuppose this in the notion of a marketplace of ideas. The core problem for the conservative, in light of the advent (see next chapter) of First Amendment legal realism, is that there is no correlate for hate speech against whites. No canceling message exists for "Nigger, go back to Africa." Vituperation aimed against blacks, Latinos, Asians, gays, and lesbians wounds; yet there is nothing comparably damaging for whites. *Honky* seems more a badge of respect than a sharp put-down. *Cracker*, although disparaging, also has overtones of grudging admiration (see Chapter 11). The fact is that terms like *nigger*, *kike*, *spic*, *chink*, and *fag* call up and reinforce histories of subordination. Slang terms for whites carry nothing comparable behind them. Ideological arguments based on a priori assumptions of a free, equal marketplace of ideas in which everyone participates equally end up reinforcing the very inequality that hate speech controls and international conventions are aimed at redressing.

QUESTIONS FOR DISCUSSION, CHAPTER 13

1. Can you think of any additional paternalistic (for their own good) or tough love (they should get over it) arguments against hate speech regulation, other than the ones reviewed in this chapter?

2. Have you heard arguments like the ones considered (and re-butted) in this chapter before? Had you ever heard them answered as you did in this chapter?

3. Reverse the process for a moment. If the main policy arguments against hate speech regulation are all seriously flawed, can you make a good policy argument in *favor* of hate speech controls or remedies, and what would that argument be?

4. What about the slippery slope argument that if we allow one rent in our fabric of First Amendment liberties, say for hate speech controls, we'll be tempted to enact another, then another, and pretty soon we can't have any free speech left at all?

5. What about the related drawing-the-line argument? It's hard to define hate speech precisely. Therefore, we shouldn't have the category at all.

6. What about the Big Brother argument? If you give the government the power to decide what hate speech is, they'll demand a second power, then a third, and pretty soon we won't be able to say anything at all.

Class Exercise

You attend a purely private university, where the First Amendment does not apply. So, the only issue before the community is whether taking measures to discourage hate speech is a good idea on policy grounds.

Is it? One half of the class takes the pro position; the other, the anti side.

Recommended Reading, Chapter 13

Jean Nash Johnson, "New Study Says Venting Anger Increases Hostility: Study Prompts Debate about Best Theory to Deal with Strong Emotion," Boulder (Colorado) *Daily Camera*, March 10, 1999, at 7A.

Charles R. Lawrence, *If He Hollers, Let Him Go: Regulating Racist Speech on Campus*, Duke L.J. 431 (1990).

Nadine Strossen, *Regulating Hate Speech on Campus: A Modest Proposal?*, 1990 Duke L.J. 484 (1990).

NOTES

1. For a collection of essays positing all of these views, see Henry Louis Gates et al., *Speaking of Race, Speaking of Sex: Hate Speech, Civil Rights, and Civil Liberties* (1998).

2. For a collection of writings putting forward all of these views, see Laura Lederer and Richard Delgado, eds., *The Price We Pay: The Case Against Racist Speech, Hate Propaganda, and Pornography* (1995).

3. See Nat Hentoff, *Free Speech for Me—But Not for Thee: How the American Left and Right Relentlessly Censor Each Other,* 134 (1992).

4. See Gordon Allport, *The Nature of Prejudice,* 467–473 (1954); Leonard Berkowitz, "The Case for Bottling Up Rage," *Psychology Today,* July 1973, at 24.

5. E.g., William Peters, *A Class Divided: Then and Now* (1971); Craig Haney et al., *Interpersonal Dynamics in a Simulated Prison,* 1 Int'l J. Criminal. & Penal. 69, 80–81 (1973).

6. See Nadine Strossen, *Regulating Hate Speech on Campus: A Modest Proposal?*, 1990 Duke L.J. 484, 567 (1990).

7. See Juan Perea et al., *Race & Races: Cases and Resources for a Diverse America,* 758–782 (2000).

8. Ibid.

9. *Not for Thee,* supra, at 167.

10. See *Not for Thee,* supra, at 169; Strossen, *Modest Proposal,* supra, at 512.

11. See "Race Bias Prompted Most Hate Crimes: FBI's First National Statistics Show Blacks as Main Targets," *San Francisco Chronicle,* January 5, 1993, at A2.

12. See Deb Riechmann, "Colleges Tackle Increase in Racism on Campuses," *Los Angeles Times,* April 30, 1989, pt. 1, at 36 (reporting statistics compiled by National Institute Against Prejudice and Violence).

13. E.g., Stephen Carter, *Reflections of an Affirmative Action Baby,* 177 (1992); Donald Lively, *Reformist Myopia and the Imperative of Progress,* 46 Vand. L. Rev. 465, 888 (1994); Dinesh D'Souza, *Illiberal Education,* 153 (1991); Henry Louis Gates Jr., "Let Them Talk," *New Republic,* September 20, 1993, at 46–48.

14. *Illiberal Education,* supra, at 128, 279.

15. "Let Them Talk," supra, at 46–48.

16. See Lively, *Myopia,* supra, at 875, 880, 892.

17. See D'Souza, *Illiberal Education,* supra, at 140–155, 230–242.

18. See, e.g., V. Herron, Note, *Increasing the Speech*, 67 S. Cal. L. Rev. 407, 424 (1994); Carter, *Affirmative Action Baby*, supra, at 179; D'Souza, *Illiberal Education*, supra, at 231–242.

19. E.g., D'Souza, *Illiberal Education*, supra, at 153; Carter, *Affirmative Action Baby*, supra, at 175.

20. See Gates, "Let Them Talk," supra, at 45; Lively, *Myopia*, supra, at 893–894; D'Souza, *Illiberal Education*, supra, at 241.

21. Gates, supra, at 45.

14

THE FUTURE: FIRST AMENDMENT LEGAL REALISM

Americans are, for the most part, down-to-earth people with no great love of grand theory.[1] Lawyers, too, as a group are committed to practical, balanced decisionmaking.[2] Nevertheless, our legal system has one area, and only one, in which the rules at play embody just the opposite qualities—in which mechanical tests, holy-sounding trump cards, and ancient shibboleths foreclose argument and sensible debate.

That area is the First Amendment. Recently a small group of reformers has set out to free speech and expression from their current straitjacket. Over the last century, practically every area of American law has matured from the "mechanical jurisprudence" approach, which held that cases could be solved through logic and appeals to precedent alone, to "legal realism," which maintains that legal reasoning must also take into account social policy, common sense, and experience.[3] But in the area of free speech, archaic formulas such as the prohibition against content regulation, the maxim that the cure for bad speech is more speech, and the speech/act distinction continue to hold sway, creating a system of law that operates in robotic fashion, failing to take account of context, nuance, history, and the harms that speech can cause to disempowered people.[4]

The new approach endeavors to oblige society to take account of such harms. It points out how speech and equality stand in reciprocal relation; neither can thrive without the other. Speech without

> ## Judge Nancy Gertner in United States of America v. Leviner, 31 F. Supp. 2d 23 (D. Mass. 1998).
>
> The scholarly and popular literature strongly suggest . . . racial disparity in the rates at which African Americans are stopped and prosecuted for traffic offenses. That literature, together with the specific facts about Leviner's record and background, compel me to depart from the Guidelines range. . . .
>
> While the Sentencing Guidelines were designed to eliminate unwarranted disparities in sentencing, and constrain a judge's discretion, they are not to be applied mechanistically, wholly ignoring fairness, logic, and the underlying statutory scheme. . . .
>
> Motor Vehicle offenses, in particular, raise deep concerns about racial disparity. Studies from a number of scholars, and articles in the popular literature have focused on the fact that African American motorists are stopped and prosecuted for traffic stops, more than any other citizens. And if that is so, then it is not unreasonable to believe that African Americans would also be imprisoned at a higher rate for these offenses as well.

equality is a lecture, a sermon, a rant. Speech, in other words, presumes equality, or something like it, among the participants in a dialogue. But equality presupposes speech, too, for without it, inequalities might aggregate without the possibility of collective action and reform.[5]

Advocates of the new approach point out how backers of the traditional absolutist view of the First Amendment are caught up in "ideological drift"—the failure to observe how an instrument, speech, that formerly served progressive causes has been captured by the libertarian right (as well as by white supremacists, pornographers, and other dubious allies).[6] They are also enmeshed in a romantic view of the First Amendment that obliges them to defend even "the speech we hate" in order to assure protection for that which we hold dear.[7]

Under the combined force of the above critiques, the old absolutist First Amendment paradigm is beginning to weaken, replaced by First Amendment legal realism and a healthier, more pluralistic view of the role of speech in guaranteeing democracy. The new view considers speech as one value among many. It looks to what is at stake in a particular speech controversy. It marshals linguistic science, history, sociology, politics, and the other tools of the realist approach in an effort to understand how speech works in our system of governance—as well as in particular disputes.[8]

The transition is far from complete. Defenders of the old speech-over-all approach still raise all the old arguments, still maintain that opening a single crack in the (already cracked) edifice of free speech protection will cause the entire structure to come tumbling down. They still maintain (see Chapter 13) that if minorities knew their own self-interest—and their own history—they would not be clamoring for controls on hate speech. They warn that controls can enfeeble minorities and mire them in an orgy of victimization, or that the search for legal remedies is itself classist, as it is calculated to fall heavily on the crude racism of the factory worker while leaving untouched the more genteel (and more damaging) versions favored by the intellectual class.

COMPONENTS OF THE NEW FIRST AMENDMENT LEGAL REALISM

Skepticism

One component of the new paradigm is skepticism. In the early years of First Amendment theorizing, we made grand claims for what the system of free expression could do.[9] Today, we realize that the marketplace of ideas works best in connection with small, bounded disputes: Is this parking space better than that one? Will an object fall faster in air or in a vacuum? Will school vouchers help or hurt inner-city schools? With such narrow, clearly defined problems, speech can often help us avoid error and arrive at consensus.[10] But with ills like racism or sexism that are deeply embedded in culture and language, speech is much less helpful. These broad-scale ills shape the very systems of thought and communication that we rely on to understand and cope with our world. Engrained in our vocabulary, narratives, and pre-understandings, they are the stuff out of which we make sense of the world around us. One cannot easily speak out against one of these pre-understandings without seeming inconsistent or incoherent.[11]

COMPARATIVE AND EMPIRICAL EXAMINATION OF FREE SPEECH CLAIMS

A second component of the new approach is willingness to subject claims about the necessity of preserving speech inviolate to comparative and empirical examination. For example, some free speech defenders maintain that tolerating any new exception to the protection we afford speech will endanger the spirit of free inquiry. The first compromise will lead to another, then another, and pretty soon we will not have any freedom of speech at all.[12] Toleration of a few wounded feelings on the part of minorities and gays is the "price we pay" for living in a free society.[13]

But international and comparative analysis is increasingly showing that this need not be so—that Western industrialized societies, like Canada and Germany, that control hate speech and antisemitism have not suffered an erosion of the spirit of free inquiry. If anything, the press is more independent and feistier in those countries than here (see Chapter 12). Hate speech silences its victims, causing them to withdraw from forthright engagement with their fellow citizens (see Chapter 1). It results in less, not more, speech; less, not more, dialogue. Scholars have likened our society's hands-off approach regarding hate speech to a "contract of indifference," like the conditions that prevailed just before the German Holocaust and Southern slavery.[14] In enacting the Fourteenth Amendment, Andrew Taslitz argued, society changed the First Amendment from a cold, indifferent provision to a more empathic instrument.[15]

LEGITIMATION

A further component of the new First Amendment legal realism is willingness to examine the way in which the very system of free speech can legitimize an unfair social order.[16] If we could say we have a perfect marketplace of ideas, it must follow that the current set of ideas is the best. Our (European, Western) ideas competed against their (primitive, lazy, backward) ones, and won. It was a fair fight. Our ways of thinking, speaking, and living must be superior, since they were tested in competition.[17]

But suppose that the fight was not fair. Certain speakers may have been silenced or marginalized. Because of stereotypes, we may have given their ideas little credence. Perhaps they lacked the money to get their ideas into print or on television. Perhaps the dominant narrative renders their ideas and narratives unsayable, absurd, inconceivable, or ridiculous. Then, we would be, without knowing it, subscribing to a system of thought that, in effect, validated itself while excluding other speakers and forms of knowledge that might be equally worthy.[18]

SPEECH AS AN INSTRUMENT OF POSITIVE HARM

This leads to a fourth component of the new approach, namely that language can sometimes serve as a means by which dominant groups maintain control over others. Repeated depiction of a minority group as stupid, immoral, or base can construct social reality so that members of that group experience great difficulty in daily life. They fall behind so that they actually appear to be stupid, dirty, or lacking in pride. No one will befriend them. Merchants will prefer to deal with others. The police will suspect them of crimes. Society will not know how this happens, since the members of the out-group will appear not to be constructed, but actually "that way."[19]

By the same token, speech that interferes with the preferred activities of the empowered group will be curtailed. We will find a First Amendment "exception" for it. Over time, these exceptions will seem natural and commonsensical. Of course, there would be an exception for state secrets, we will say, or for false advertising, plagiarism, or words of threat. But when someone suggests a further exception for some of the most vulnerable members of society, eighteen-year-old undergraduates of color on white campuses or women depicted in hard-core pornography, we recoil in dismay: The First Amendment must be a seamless web (see Chapter 4).

Burdens of Proof

First Amendment realism is encouraging us to realize that even labeling a problem a First Amendment one is to select a paradigm without
noticing it. Why should we be a "problem," an anomaly in your preferred way of looking at things, feminists and minorities are beginning
to ask. Or, to put it another way, why should we (minorities and
women) be mere compelling state interests in your jurisprudence,
rather than the other way around? Perhaps it makes just as good sense
to place equality at the center. Then, the desire of a hate speaker to receive an "exception" (to the rule of equality) would require unusual
justification. Treating hate speech as a First Amendment problem is
not an inevitable consequence of some unseen structure of ultimate reality. Perhaps it is, instead, a problem of equality. Then, the burden of
persuasion would lie with the one seeking to defeat that value,
through an exception for a type of speech.[20]

The Content of Our System of
Free Speech, and Who Benefits?

The new-realist approach also allows us to focus on just what it is
that is coming under the mantle of the First Amendment and who
benefits from that mantle. Many defenders of hate speech depict the
First Amendment in highly romanticized terms, neglecting to mention
that the most avid defenders of it (as well as the most lavish contribu-
tors to free speech organizations and the ACLU) are pornographers,
publishers of porn and soft-porn magazines, and the cigarette lobby,
ever anxious to have cigarette smoking and advertising considered
constitutional rights.[21] Our system of free speech produces a great
deal of trash. Much TV programming is inane. A handful of mystery
writers account for two-thirds of all books sold, with self-help books
making up much of the rest. Nearly one-half of all E-mail messages
are spam.[22]

Many aspects of the current situation remind one of the strains and
stresses associated with a paradigm shift. One sees an increase in ad
hominem arguments ("You can't seriously be advocating modifying
our proud system of free speech!") and of righteous beleaguerment.

One sees an increase in the decibel level, an effort to have it both ways ("How about the narrowest possible hate speech code?").

The principal anxiety of the defenders of the First Amendment faith seems to be that the new paradigm will not provide the same sturdy tool for protecting human rights and freedoms. But the answer is the same as it would have been had we put a similar question to Oliver Wendell Holmes, Roscoe Pound, or Felix Cohen seventy years ago when legal realism was replacing mechanical jurisprudence. They might have replied that faith in law as a type of algebra, a perfect machine yielding precise, determinate answers to every legal question, could not possibly benefit minorities and the poor, and that learning how law really works is an important step toward social reform. They might have pointed out that safety does not lie in pleasant myths or reassuring bromides, but in constant vigilance and struggle. Similarly, those championing equality and human dignity have nothing to fear from the emerging First Amendment realist paradigm.

In any event, it is too late to turn back. The case against hate speech and mechanical application of absolutist First Amendment principles is beginning to appear irresistible. This book has explicated much of that case, by showing how speech can harm, how it frequently does, how other societies have shaped legal rules to take account of and avoid that harm, and how the skies will not fall if the United States follows their lead. America will still be the same country; indeed, we will have a legal and social system that is fairer, more inclusive, and in which outsiders are not regularly demonized, marginalized, stereotyped, reviled, and excluded. That will be a good first step toward preparing the way for the multiracial America that demographers tell us lies only a few decades ahead.

QUESTIONS FOR DISCUSSION, CHAPTER 14

1. We are all taught to think of free speech in the most exalted terms. But much speech (writing, TV plots, and so forth) is banal or sordid. Why do we persist in ascribing such a high value to speech and resist any new restrictions on it?

2. You have probably heard that the best cure for bad speech is more speech—that more speech will correct the error inherent

in bad speech. Speech, in other words, functions like a market, in which the producer of a good product should drive the producer of a bad one out of business. Does speech, in fact, work that way?

3. Suppose a snarling bigot approaches a black undergraduate and tells him he bugs the heck out of him and that he has no place on this campus. The African American draws himself up and says, "Sir, I beg to differ. Our institutions, not to mention the equality principle itself, hold that I, an African American, am entitled to participate in higher education on equal terms with you or anyone else. Now that I have informed you of your error, I am sure you will retract your statement and welcome me as an equal citizen, if not a brother in spirit."

Such a response would be preposterous, and to assume that it (or something like it) is the preferred remedy is perverse. Yet, many solemnly repeat that the best cure for bad speech is more speech. Why?

CLASS EXERCISE

Is opposition to hate speech a conservative or a liberal position? And conversely, is defending the right of a hate speaker to spew vitriol liberal or conservative? Argue both views to another person: Which one is more convincing?

RECOMMENDED READING, CHAPTER 14

Jody Armour, *Negrophobia and Reasonable Racism* (1997).

Lee Bollinger, *The Tolerant Society: Free Speech and Extremist Speech in America* (1986).

Felix Cohen, *Transcendental Nonsense and the Functional Approach*, 35 Colum. L. Rev. 809 (1935).

Karl Llewellyn, *Some Realism about Realism . . . Responding to Dean Pound*, 44 Harv. L. Rev. 1222 (1931).

Steve Shiffrin, *The First Amendment, Democracy, and Romance* (1990).

Nadine Strossen, *In the Defense of Freedom and Equality: The American Civil Liberties Union Past, Present, and Future*, 29 Harv. C.R.–C.L. L. Rev. 143 (1994).

Nadine Strossen, *Defending Pornography: Free Speech, Sex, and the Fight for Women's Rights* (1995).

Mark Tushnet, *New Meaning for the First Amendment: Free Speech May Be Seen as a Tool for Protecting Those in Power*, ABAJ, Nov. 1995, at 56.

Samuel Walker, *Hate Speech: The History of an American Controversy* (1994).

NOTES

1. See, e.g., John Dewey and James H. Tufts, *Ethics* (1908).

2. See, e.g., Richard A. Posner, *The Jurisprudence of Skepticism*, 86 Mich. L. Rev. 827 (1988); Margaret J. Radin, *Reconsidering the Rule of Law*, 69 B.U. L. Rev. 781 (1989).

3. See Karl N. Llewellyn, *A Realistic Jurisprudence*, 30 Colum. L. Rev. 431 (1930).

4. See Richard Delgado, *Toward a Legal Realist View of the First Amendment*, 113 Harv. L. Rev. 778 (2000).

5. Ibid.; Richard Delgado and Jean Stefancic, *Hateful Speech, Loving Communities: Why Our Notion of "A Just Balance" Changes So Slowly*, 82 Calif. L. Rev. 851 (1994); Richard Delgado, *Campus Antiracism Rules: Constitutional Narratives in Collision*, 85 Nw. U. L. Rev. 343 (1991).

6. See Jack Balkin, *Ideological Drift and the Struggle over Meaning*, 25 Conn. L. Rev. 889 (1993).

7. Richard Delgado and David Yun, *The Speech We Hate*, 27 Ariz. St. L.J. 1281 (1995).

8. See Richard Delgado, *First Amendment Formalism Is Giving Way to First Amendment Legal Realism*, 29 Harv. C.R.–C.L. L. Rev. 69 (1994).

9. See *Giving Way*, supra; Steven Shiffrin, *The First Amendment, Democracy, and Romance*, 86–105, 140–169 (1990).

10. See Richard Delgado and Jean Stefancic, *Images of the Outsider in American Law and Culture: Can Free Expression Remedy Systemic Social Ills?*, 77 Cornell L. Rev. 1258, 1258–1262 (1992).

11. Ibid. at 1258–1261, 1270–1286.

12. See Frederick Schauer, *Slippery Slopes*, 99 Harv. L. Rev. 361 (1989).

13. See Laura Lederer and Richard Delgado, eds., *The Price We Pay: The Case Against Racist Speech, Hate Propaganda, and Pornography* (1995).

14. See Andrew Taslitz, *Hate Crimes, Free Speech, and the Contract of Mutual Indifference*, 80 B.U. L. Rev. 1283 (2000).

15. Ibid.

16. E.g., Stanley Ingber, *The Marketplace of Ideas: A Legitimating Myth?*, Duke L.J. 1 (1984); Cass R. Sunstein, *Free Speech Now*, 59 U. Chi. L. Rev. 255 (1992); Delgado, *Giving Way*, supra.

17. See Ingber, supra.

18. *Giving Way*, supra; *Images of the Outsider*, supra.

19. *Images*, supra.

20. See *Giving Way*, supra.

21. Ibid. *Toward a Legal Realist View*, supra.

22. *Legal Realist View*, supra.

APPENDIX:
INTERNATIONAL TREATIES
AND DOCUMENTS

INSTRUMENTS

Convention on the Elimination of All Forms of Racial Discrimination

European Convention for the Protection of Human Rights and Fundamental Freedoms

International Covenant for Civil and Political Rights

UNESCO Convention Against Discrimination in Education

SECONDARY SOURCES

Kevin Boyle, *Hate Speech—The United States Versus the Rest of the World?* 53 Maine L. Rev. 488 (2001).

Sandra Coliver, ed., *Striking a Balance: Hate Speech, Freedom of Expression, and Non-Discrimination* (1992).

Commission of European Communities, *Legal Instruments to Combat Racism and Xenophobia* (1992).

Isaak I. Dore, *United Nations Measures to Combat Racial Discrimination*, 10 Denver J. Int'l. L. & Pol'y 290 (1981).

Sionaidh Douglas-Scott, *The Hatefulness of Protected Speech: A Comparison of the American and European Approaches*, 7 Wm. & Mary Bill of Rts. J. 305 (1999).

European Parliament, Committee of Inquiry on Racism and Xenophobia (1991).

Fredrick Kubler, *How Much Freedom for Racist Speech? Transnational Aspects of a Conflict of Human Rights*, 27 Hofstra L. Rev. 335 (1998).

Dominic McGoldrick, *Human Rights Committee: Its Role in the Development of the International Convenant on Civil and Political Rights*, 13 Aust. Y.B. Int'l. L. 177 (1992).

CASES

Regina v. Butler, 89 D.L.R. 4th 449 (1992) (Can.).

Regina v. Keegstra [1990] 3 S.C.R. 697 (Can.).

GLOSSARY

ACLU (American Civil Liberties Union). Prominent national organization dedicated to advancing cause of civil liberties, including speech.

Antisemitism. Prejudice against or dislike of Jews and Jewish culture.

Aryan supremacy. Belief that Euro-American (Aryan) genes and culture are superior to those of other races, especially black and brown ones.

Bellwether argument. Argument against hate speech controls, such as campus speech codes, that holds that it is better to let expressions of hate be out in the open, as opposed to repressed. Once out in the open, they serve as markers so that one can see who is harboring prejudice and ill will toward minorities and take action accordingly.

Best friend argument. Argument against hate speech controls that holds that minorities have benefited greatly from our system of free expression and should be reluctant to place strictures on it.

Brown v. Board of Education. Celebrated 1954 U.S. Supreme Court decision found in volume 347 of Supreme Court Reports, beginning at page 483, that repudiates the former separate-but-equal doctrine and orders desegregation in public schools.

Campus speech codes (antiracism rules). College and university guidelines that prohibit various forms of disrespectful speech aimed at minority groups.

Censorship. Governmental interference with freedom of expression, generally based on its content.

Chink. Pejorative term for Asian.

Classist argument. Argument against anti-hate speech rules and laws that holds that they will fall heavily on the uneducated and blue-collar speakers, while exempting the refined and equally harmful speech of elites.

Color blindness. The position that the law should take no note of race or color and that official action should affect all groups equally, without exceptions.

Confrontation theory. Theory that holds that the best way to minimize racism and prejudice is to arrange social settings and laws so that every undesired appearance of either is immediately noticed and checked.

Content discrimination. First Amendment doctrine that forbids limitations on speech based on content, that is, on what is said.

Critical race theory. Radical legal movement that aims to transform the relationship among race, law, and power.

Cyberspace. Integrated network of Web sites and computers enabling rapid transmission of messages and data.

Dred Scott v. Sandford. 1856 U.S. Supreme Court decision, found in volume 60 of Supreme Court Reports at page 393, that holds that African American slaves do not enjoy the rights of citizens.

Empathic fallacy. The mistaken belief that consciousness, which consists in large part of a set of preexisting narratives and scripts, will readily accept a new one that contradicts the old stock of narratives.

Epithet. A derogatory word used to demean another person or group.

Fighting words. Legal doctrine that holds that words that are calculated to evoke an immediate strong reaction fall outside First Amendment protection.

First Amendment. Amendment to the United States Constitution that provides for free speech, religion, press, and assembly.

Formalism. Legal doctrine that holds that decisions should be arrived at by considering only formal matters such as precedents and statutes.

Greaser. Derogatory term for Mexican or Mexican American.

Hate radio. Radio programs, usually hosted by a single individual, devoted to spreading negative information and attitudes about outsider groups, such as women, Jews, welfare recipients, people of color, and liberals.

Holocaust denial. Denial that the Holocaust ever happened or that it was as large as most believe it was. Deemed a criminal offense in some European countries.

Intentional infliction of emotional distress. A tort action that provides redress against one who has performed an outrageous act at another's expense.

International law. Treaties, conventions, and customary norms that govern the relationship of nations to one another, or by which they bind themselves to enforce certain values, such as nondiscrimination.

Legal realism. School of legal thought that disavows mechanical jurisprudence in favor of social science, policy judgments, and pragmatism.

Libertarianism. Social and political position that seeks to maximize individual liberty and reduce state regulation. Generally adverse to controls on hate speech.

Marketplace of ideas. Notion that a free exchange of ideas is the best guarantor of truth and good government.

Mascot. Sports figure or logo, such as an Indian warrior or animal, that symbolizes a team.

Microaggression. Stunning, small encounter with racism, which usually goes unnoticed by members of the majority race.

Plessy v. Ferguson. 1896 U.S. Supreme Court decision, found in volume 163 of United States Reports at page 537, that approved a legal regime of separate-but-equal treatment for blacks.

Prejudice. Belief or attitude, generally unfavorable, about a person or group before the facts are known.

Pressure valve argument. Argument against hate speech controls that reasons that a bigoted person who is forced to bottle up his hatred of minorities will sooner or later explode and do something even more harmful.

Race. Notion of a biologically distinct type of human being usually based on skin color and similar characteristics.

Racism. A program or practice that disadvantages on the basis of race or ethnicity.

Reverse enforcement argument. Argument against hate speech rules that warns that they will simply end up being applied against minorities themselves, when, for example, they complain of unfair conditions.

Rules of professional responsibility. Official rules that govern lawyers in their practice of law and entry into the profession.

Silencing. Argument for limitations on hate speech that reasons that this form of utterance will cause its victims to fall silent, so that net discourse is reduced.

Skinheads. Self-conscious collection of countercultural youth who sport distinctive haircuts, clothing, and attitudes, often including dislike of minorities.

Slippery slope argument. Argument that holds that a new legal measure may inevitably lead to another, then another, with the result that an entire area will be governed by excessive regulation.

Slur. *See* epithet.

Socioeconomic theory of racism. Theory that prejudice and discrimination increase as social groups compete for limited resources, such as jobs.

Stereotype. Fixed, negative image of members of a group.

Stigma. A mark of shame or disgrace.

Tort action. A civil suit to recover damages for a legal wrong.

Tough love school. Group of scholars and others who believe that minorities incensed over racism and hate speech should toughen up.

Viewpoint discrimination. Legal doctrine that holds that the First Amendment forbids regulation of speech based on the speaker's viewpoint or position.

Whiteness. Quality pertaining to Euro-Americans or Caucasian people or their culture and traditions.

Wop. Derogatory term for Italians and Italian Americans.

Xenophobia. Fear of outsiders, frequently expressed by intense nationalism.

INDEX

abuse, racial. *See* racial insult(s)
ACLU, and free speech absolutist
    position, 34–36, 203–214. *See*
    also First Amendment
African Americans: hate speech
    incidents against, 33, 67, 71,
    73, 94–95, 96–102, 105, 112,
    113, 118, 141, 145–147, 153,
    162, 165, 206
Aguilar v. Avis Rent a Car System,
    Inc., 64–65, 74
Alcorn v. Anbro Engineering, Inc., 47
American Bar Association, and
    position on hate speech, 153
American Civil Liberties Union. *See*
    ACLU
angry white male, 178
anti-racism rules, campus. *See* hate
    speech codes
anti-Semitism. *See* Jews: hate speech
    incidents against
Arabs. *See* Muslims
Asians: effect of hate speech on,
    13–14
    hate speech incidents against,
    51–53, 59, 64, 66, 68, 69–70,
    72, 73, 125–126
Avis. See *Aguilar v. Avis Rent a Car*
    System, Inc.

Beauharnais v. Illinois, 17
bellwether argument, 36, 210–211

best friend argument, 35, 36
bigotry. *See* racism
black church burnings, 189
black nationalists, 181–182
blacks. *See* African Americans
book banning, 100–101
Brawley, Tawanna, case of, 188
Briggs v. Sylvestri, 72
Brown v. Board of Education, 95
Bullard v. Florida, 66–67
burdens of proof: placement of, and
    First Amendment legal realism,
    222

campus anti-racism rules. *See* hate
    speech codes
Canada, hate speech regulation in,
    196–197, 199–200
Caribbean nations, hate speech
    regulation in, 199
Castorina v. Madison County School
    Board, 97
Charter of Fundamental Rights
    (European Union), and human
    rights, 198
Child Pornography Prevention Act of
    1996, 128
children: and broadcasting, 102
    definition of, 94–95
    effect of racial labeling on, 14–15,
    33
    and hate music, 103–105